*Hard, Hard Religion*

JOHN HAYES

# Hard, Hard Religion

## Interracial Faith in the Poor South

The University of North Carolina Press  *Chapel Hill*

*This book was published with the assistance of the Fred W. Morrison Fund of the University of North Carolina Press.*

© 2017 The University of North Carolina Press
All rights reserved
Set in Arno Pro by Westchester Publishing Services
Manufactured in the United States of America

The University of North Carolina Press has been a member of the
Green Press Initiative since 2003.

Library of Congress Cataloging-in-Publication Data
Names: Hayes, John, 1972– author.
Title: Hard, hard religion : interracial faith in the poor South / John Hayes.
Other titles: New directions in southern studies.
Description: Chapel Hill : University of North Carolina Press, [2017] | Series: New directions in southern studies | Includes bibliographical references and index.
Identifiers: LCCN 2017009455| ISBN 9781469635316 (cloth : alk. paper) | ISBN 9781469635323 (pbk : alk. paper) | ISBN 9781469635330 (ebook)
Subjects: LCSH: Christianity—Southern States—20th century. | Working class—Religious life—Southern States. | Folklore—Southern States.
Classification: LCC BR535 .H387 2017 | DDC 270.0975—dc23
LC record available at https://lccn.loc.gov/2017009455

Cover illustration: Baptist church at Irwinville Farms, Georgia, 1935, photographed by Arthur Rothstein (courtesy of the Library of Congress, Prints & Photographs Division, FSA/OWI Collection, LC-USF34-T01-000348-D).

An early version of chapter 2 previously appeared as "Pleading with Death: Folk Visions of Death (and Life) in the New South," *Southern Quarterly* 53, no. 1 (Fall 2015): 105–20.

# Contents

# Figures

## Acknowledgments

Writing can seem like such a solitary undertaking, but a community—distant and near, historical and contemporary, academic and personal—is never far from the craft. Many people have helped me in a variety of ways in the years that I've been working on this project. To everyone who has offered support, in ways both large and small, a hearty thank-you.

The strange literary vision of Flannery O'Connor lit a spark in my imagination and opened my mind to the possibility of a religious South beyond what I was encountering in the historiography. O'Connor has been a guiding voice throughout the project, and I wish I could have met her to personally convey a gratitude that goes beyond the academic. I'm sure such a meeting would have been (appropriately) awkward and weird. Ralph Wood introduced me to O'Connor many years ago, and more recently, he was the first generous, helpfully critical reader of an early draft. I owe him a special debt for intellectual fire-kindling and a friendship that stretches over the years . . . and for that unforgettable role in *Down the Broken Backroads*.

Professors and fellow graduate students at the University of Georgia and colleagues at Wake Forest and Augusta University have been vital in refining my historical discernment, sharpening my writing skills, and pushing me to develop my own voice in dialogue with the scholarship. A special thank-you to James Cobb, Kathleen Clark, Michael Winship, Robby Luckett, Chris Huff, Ichiro Miyata, Chris Manganiello, Ivy Holliman Way, Eric Millin, Darren Grem, Keira Williams, Tammy Ingram, Nate Plageman, and my ever-supportive colleagues in Allgood Hall.

Exchanging ideas and trying out new thoughts at conferences and in the back-and-forth of writing has been critical to the solitary work of research and writing. There have been a host of dialogue partners, but I am especially indebted to Paul Harvey, Charles Wilson, Ted Ownby, and Beth Schweiger. Michael Pasquier has been an especially encouraging voice, and Alison Greene gave a wonderfully generous critical reading of the final draft. At UNC Press, Mark Simpson-Vos has been a wise, considerate guide through the manuscript process.

Specially funded programs have not only been a treat but provided time, peer sanction, and rich dialogue. The two months funded by a 2015 NEH

Summer Stipend were essential, allowing me to do nothing but write, propelling me from one-third of the way through to four-fifths. A 2012 Cree-Walker Summer Stipend from Augusta University likewise gave me open time to write the first draft of the early chapters. The 2010–12 Lilly-funded Young Scholars in American Religion program was wonderful, giving me rich intellectual camaraderie and opening me to new lines of inquiry. Thank you to the other "young" scholars, and to our fearless leaders Ann Braude and Mark Valeri, from the tortoise of the group.

The research for this book took me to a variety of places, from archives in well-known institutions to dirt roads in Sumter County, Alabama, and a hilltop cemetery in Sodom, North Carolina. I owe a particular debt to the American Folklife Center at the Library of Congress for steering me in the right direction early on and for the vivid panoply of old field recordings. Baylor's Institute for Oral History gave me a generous fellowship and a succinct glimpse into the poor South of Willie Johnson's central Texas milieu. Throughout the project, I've relied heavily on the fieldwork of numerous folklorists, but I am especially indebted to Carl Lindahl and Alan Lomax. Without their work, the expansive inner lives of Lloyd Chandler and Vera Hall would surely be lost to posterity. Similarly, the wonderful fieldwork of Robert Coles not only documented the rich interiority of the poor and provided the book's title, but—crucially—it was the first thing to reveal connections between O'Connor's fictional characters and the real-world poor of the South. More recently, Sue and Vince Vilcinskas showed a total stranger warm hospitality and provided tangible connections to the world of Lloyd Chandler.

Family and friends have been an encouraging, enlivening community of support as this project has moved from raw idea to final form. They have simultaneously kept my ideas grounded in real-world complexities and inspired me to think beyond what is simply at hand. Thank you to my caring, generous parents; to Bob, Tooks, and their families; to Ranie Neislar, Wanda and Ron Neislar, Robert Scott and Elizabeth Dubberly, Josh and Claire Dixon, Pete and Meredith Candler, Jim Dodge, Tony Chackal, Jon-Michael Sullivan and Kristen Smith, Allison Lowe Huff, Vivian Mobley, Lynn Carr McIntosh, Charles Lewis, Lisa Parrish, the radical Jesus man Nathan Parrish, the inclusive communities of Peace Haven and St. Augustine's, crazy Willie and bossy Veda, my inspiring students at Augusta, and others who have been vital in helping me along the way.

*Hard, Hard Religion*

# Beneath the Bible Belt

When the American painter Thomas Hart Benton turned his attention to the South as he was crafting his monumental *The Arts of Life in America* mural series in 1932, his imagination was drawn to religion. His finished product, *Arts of the South*, vividly evokes scenes that Benton had witnessed on travels through the region in the late twenties and early thirties. Religious phenomena dominate the painting: a simple wooden church pierces the horizon on the painting's left side, a preacher thunders as a small crowd prays and sings on the painting's right side, and in the middle, a man clutches his hands together and cries out in a gesture of passionate prayer (see fig. 1). Benton was interested in the indigenous cultures of American regions, in grassroots creativity. As the clothing, settings, and muscular bodies of the characters of *Arts of the South* suggest, Benton found such creativity among the region's poor, among working people engaged in hard manual labor.[1]

In the late thirties and early forties, photographers working for the New Deal's Farm Security Administration (FSA) traveled throughout the country, compiling an extensive documentary record of some 175,000 images. The photographs capture a variety of subjects: the hard labor and harsh living conditions of sharecroppers, the liberal idealism of agricultural resettlement communities, the massive national mobilization for World War II. They also capture religion (see figs. 2 and 3). Analyzing the FSA's significant visual documentation of religion in the South, Colleen McDannell argues that though they weren't looking for it, the photographers stumbled upon nothing less than "another South"—a religious milieu very different from the hostile, dismissive representations prevalent in American culture. Among impoverished rural people, they encountered a complex faith, "a religious world not bound up in Biblicism and moralism," a "sensual religion" that "brought beauty into" the lives of the poor.[2]

In the violent, enigmatic fiction that she crafted from the late forties through the early sixties, Flannery O'Connor explored the interiority, the inner struggle and strife, of a very distinct Southern religious milieu. Her first novel, 1952's *Wise Blood*, introduced the jarring figure of Hazel Motes, an ex–farm boy from a vanished rural hamlet, fresh from four years in the U.S. military and eager to repudiate the Christianity of his upbringing. Haunted by

FIGURE 1 Thomas Hart Benton, *Arts of the South* (American, 1889–1975; *The Arts of Life in America: Arts of the South*, 1932; egg tempera and oil glaze on linen; 93 ¾ × 157 ¼ in.; courtesy of the New Britain Museum of American Art; Harriet Russell Stanley Fund 1953.2_2).

FIGURE 2 "Preacher and his wife sitting under photos taken of them twenty years ago. They live in an old converted schoolhouse with two grandchildren. The rest of their children have moved out of the county. Heard County, Georgia" (photograph by Jack Delano; Library of Congress, Prints & Photographs Division, FSA/OWI Collection, LC-USF34-043918-D).

FIGURE 3 "Members of the Primitive Baptist Church in Morehead, Kentucky, attending a creek baptizing by submersion" (photograph by Marion Post Wolcott; Library of Congress, Prints & Photographs Division, FSA/OWI Collection, LC-USF34-055314-D).

the "wild ragged figure" of Jesus, who moved "from tree to tree in the back of his mind," Hazel becomes a fervent street preacher of nihilism, of the "Church without Christ." Yet his ascetic zeal for anti-Christianity leads him, after a shattering crisis moment, back to violent appropriation of the faith he has tried to reject: he wraps his chest with barbed wire and wanders the streets daily in his own grassroots version of penance.[3]

O'Connor's fiction explores various types of people within the Southern social hierarchy, and yet much of it—both of her novels and about half of her stories—dwells on people that a man in her home of Milledgeville, Georgia, dismissed as "poor folks," that a *Time* reviewer dismissed as "God-intoxicated hillbillies" and "God-drunk backwoodsmen."[4] Like Benton in *Arts of the South* and the FSA photographers in their documentation of Southern religious life, but more profoundly and over an entire career, O'Connor found herself gravitating to the region's poor. Reflecting on this later in her writing life, O'Connor, the Catholic intellectual, became explicit and self-conscious:

she felt "kinship with backwoods prophets," she said; her "underground religious affinities" drew her "directly to those aspects of Southern life where the religious feeling is most intense and where its outward forms are farthest from the Catholic."[5]

It's a well-established trope, perhaps even a cliché, that the American South of the early to mid-twentieth century was an especially religious society. Few people are unfamiliar with the phrase that prominent journalist H. L. Mencken coined in the mid-1920s to express this: the "Bible Belt."[6] The imaginations of a prominent American painter, of FSA photographers like Marion Post Wolcott and Jack Delano, and of an enduring Southern writer were certainly fired by this regional religiosity. Yet what attracted them were not the most obvious manifestations of religion—the innumerable lofty spires of "First" churches on main streets, prominent and widely respected ministers, social extensions of religion like women's clubs and children's homes—but rather grassroots religious creativity, religious phenomena emerging from the social periphery, what scholars of religion have variously called "folk religion," "popular religion," "vernacular religion," "lived religion."[7]

Assessing historical scholarship on religion in the South in a 1997 essay, which notes creative work on religious contexts like Puritan New England and the North in the era of the market revolution, Donald Mathews lamented that "popular religion in the South remains unstudied."[8] In the two decades since Mathews's critique, the collective work of historians and religious studies scholars has offered a complicated, contentious portrait of the changing fortunes of religious groups in the region. It has historicized the Bible Belt as a distinct era in regional history, and it has explored regional religious activity that does not at all fit into evangelical or Bible Belt categories. And yet Mathews's lament largely holds: though scattered articles and sections of a few books have touched on it, no book-length study has offered a focused exploration of the regional religious milieu documented by O'Connor, Benton, and FSA photographers.[9] The grassroots religious creativity beneath the well-known, well-documented Bible Belt has remained shadowy. This book attempts to end that obscurity.

*Hard, Hard Religion: Interracial Faith in the Poor South* is a historical excavation of a hidden layer of religious activity, a vibrant world of grassroots ferment and folk creativity. It weaves together the findings of folklorists, sociological field studies, oral historians, early recorded music, and elements of material culture to trace the characteristic themes of this hidden religious culture. The book shows that the artistic sense of O'Connor, Benton, and the FSA photographers as to the social location of this religious world—that it existed among the region's poor—was no projection but rather an uncommon insight into regional religious dynamics. *Hard, Hard Religion* is thus a study of poor people's religious creativity, of how impoverished people crafted a distinct religious culture—of vivid verbal expression, of complexity and beauty, of intense inner struggle about questions of ultimate meaning.

The book fuses two enduring images of the early twentieth-century South: that of an especially religious region—the nation's "Bible Belt"—and that of a poor region in a prosperous country—or, "the Nation's No. 1 economic problem," in Franklin D. Roosevelt's famous phrase.[10] Both images are familiar in popular representation and in historical scholarship. And yet the two have rarely been thought of together in any sustained way. The work of historians of religion and religious studies scholars—a nuanced, steadily growing body of work—far too often remains unread by historians who study other aspects of the South. Likewise, historians of the early twentieth-century South have largely continued to work within the basic parameters established by C. Vann Woodward in *Origins of the New South* (1951) and *The Strange Career of Jim Crow* (1955): themes of politics and race predominate. Religion may appear in the backdrop in the work of Southern historians—"it's just there," in William Faulkner's oft-quoted phrase—and yet it rarely plays any functional role in the historical analysis.[11] This book seeks to bridge this divide, to weave careful religious analysis into a clear social context. It explores, simultaneously, how the regional experience of poverty informed religious life, and how grassroots religious creativity flourished among the region's poor.

The "poor" here are the poor pictured in *Arts of the South* and the FSA photographs: poor blacks *and* poor whites. Yet long-established scholarly paradigms have worked to obscure and even deny any common ground that poor blacks and poor whites may have shared. Codified in scholarship on religion are two very different strands of regional religious life, distinct in both trajectory and characteristic themes. These strands are separated by the color line—(white) Southern religion, or evangelical Protestantism; and "the black church," or African American Christianity. So distinct are these strands that, with the exception of a few books, they are divided into entirely separate bodies of scholarship, books that analyze one or the other but not both. Religion scholar Albert Raboteau speaks for this lengthy historiography when he writes, "The segregation of black and white churches signified the existence of two Christianitys in this nation, and the deep chasm that divided them demonstrated the failure of the nation's predominant religious institution ... to achieve meaningful, sustained community across racial lines."[12]

*really?*

This categorical separation has a strong compliment in historiography of the early twentieth-century South. After Populism's brief moment of interracial politics in the 1890s, the dominant scholarship argues, white supremacy became ascendant. The culture of segregation blurred substantive class divisions, imagined race as the marker of identity, and rendered interracial activity unimaginable. Segregation buttressed a rampantly unequal social order that continued into the mid-twentieth century. Poor whites sustained this unequal social order rather than trying to challenge it because white solidarity carried a sanction and emotional appeal that attempts to overcome their own poverty did not. Propertied whites exploited the labor of poor blacks (even as some blacks carved out propertied lives within the structures of Jim Crow), and poor whites fortified the system by eagerly participating in the rituals of segregation, enjoying the symbolic compensations of white supremacy while remaining stuck in poverty. Race was *the* principle of social organization in the early twentieth-century South—"the central metaphor of the new regional culture," in historian Grace Hale's phrase.[13]

Certainly there were, and are, substantive differences between white evangelical Protestantism and African American Christianity. These "two Christianitys" have been (and continue to be) distinct in a number of meaningful ways. This book argues for the presence of something outside these parameters: a folk Christianity that has been evoked in literature and art, suggested by a few historians, but never explored with the sustained analysis of a monograph. This folk Christianity was much more than a variation on a theme—more than white evangelical Protestantism or African American Christianity with some grassroots shading or localized inflection. It was differentiated by a number of characteristic themes, but undergirding all of these was its most striking difference: it was the fruit of a delicate but real interracial exchange among the poor.

In the interstices of inequality in the early twentieth-century South, in a circumscribed world marked by intense poverty, poor blacks and poor whites listened to each other, borrowed from each other, and learned from each other about what it meant to be Christian in a hard world of toil and limit. In this exchange, they crafted a distinct Christianity that articulated the sufferings and longings, the hopes and frustrations, of impoverished people. This was not a direct challenge to the structures of power in the South, nor was it a politicized movement like Populism. The interracial exchange of poor blacks and poor whites did not fuel an activism that sought to unmake the structure of white supremacy, like the later civil rights movement. The interracial religious exchange that this book explores happened underneath the umbrella of

*how so??.*

Jim Crow, within a society shaped by a powerful white supremacy. And yet in listening to each other, borrowing from each other, and learning from each other, poor blacks and poor whites participated in a cultural space where race was not the decisive element or central metaphor—where being poor and being Christian became the paramount concerns.

Without denying the visceral and violent power of white supremacy, this book challenges the insistence of many Southern historians that race was the defining element in the early twentieth-century South, *the* marker of identity. It simultaneously challenges the long-established frame of scholars of Southern religion that race was *the* boundary of difference. It seeks to show the real presence of a cultural space of interracial exchange, of a folk Christianity crafted in a common poverty. A few glimpses of this possibility are apropos.

In his 1903 masterpiece *The Souls of Black Folk*, in the midst of dark meditations on the expanding power of racism, W. E. B. Du Bois argued that "the religion of the poor whites is a plain copy of Negro thought and methods."[14] Du Bois's claim has had no afterlife in the scholarship, but clearly he saw something real in his Georgia and Tennessee fieldwork that led him to this unusual claim. Richard Wright, whose *Black Boy* and *Native Son* presented profound fictional explorations of race, sought to articulate the unheard thoughts of poor blacks in his 1941 "folk history." He found curious reflections on a social order maintained by racially dividing the poor despite their real commonalities: "Sometimes, fleetingly, like a rainbow that comes and vanishes in its coming, the wan faces of the poor whites make us think that perhaps we can join our hands with them and lift the weight of the Lords of the Land off our backs. But, before new meanings can bridge the chasm that has long been created between us, the poor whites are warned by the Lords of the Land that they must cast their destiny with their own color, that to make common cause with us is to threaten the foundations of civilization."[15]

Lillian Smith, one of the foremost native white Southern critics of Jim Crow, hardly one to sugarcoat racial realties, described a strange dynamic in a 1955 letter to Fisk sociologist Charles Johnson. Of a church of white mountaineers in Rabun County, Georgia, near the camp that she owned and operated, she wrote, "It is officially a white church. But they invite the Negro Baptists—over in the valley—to come very often to their church; and they go to the Negro Baptist church. I mean by 'they': the entire congregation. Both Baptist rural groups (white and Negro) use my swimming pool for their baptisms. Last summer, the white group invited the Negro group to witness the baptism service. There were white and colored rural Baptists roaming all around my place."[16] Child psychiatrist Robert Coles, whose *Children of Crisis* highlighted racial dynamics through its analysis of black and white children's attitudes to school desegregation, went on to conduct extensive fieldwork with poor southerners—black and white—throughout the 1960s. As Coles talked and listened to the poor, in shacks and cabins, from remote Kentucky hollows to the open Alabama Black Belt, he was led time and again to think of the fiction that had left such an impression on him, that of Flannery O'Connor. He came to see that in his fieldwork, he was in the company of nothing less than "her chosen ones—the South's impoverished, hard-praying, stubbornly enduring rural folk, of both races."[17]

These glimpses hint at obscured dynamics, at strange patterns beneath the surface of a Jim Crow society. They offer suggestive evidence that the artistic imaginations of O'Connor, Benton, and the FSA photographers were not dreaming up religious phenomena out of thin air; rather, they were discerning something actual but concealed, something real but hidden. Collectively, all this observation and evocation suggests that the folk Christianity born of interracial exchange was of a distinct, specific era of regional life.

That era was the New South—the social order that emerged after the intense drama, expansive possibilities, and crushed hopes of Reconstruction. By the 1880s, this new society was clearly taking shape. It was a world of labor-intensive agriculture, of new forms of resource extraction and industrial manufacturing, of expanded commerce and market activity, of an ascendant white supremacy. It was a world of cotton and tobacco farms; of coal mines, timber camps, and textile mills; of bustling new towns and extensive railroad lines; of a sharply drawn color line. The Populist movement of the 1890s sought to shape the inner mechanisms of this new order—its finance and marketing—and contained an implicit challenge to white supremacy, but the movement's demise after 1900 meant that the society continued to develop along its post-Reconstruction trajectory. Though notable changes came to the New South after World War I—new roads, automobiles, chain stores, textile industry dominance, and significant out-migration of African Americans—the basic structures of the society remained intact until the eve of World War II. Then, in three transformative decades, the cumulative effects of New Deal agricultural policy, national industrial recruitment, federal spending on infrastructure and the military, and the civil rights movement unmade the structures of the New South and birthed a very different order, a "Sun Belt." The folk Christianity that this book explores was a New South development, neither perennial nor historically vague. Though it was informed by pre–Civil War traditions—subversive aspects of the early evangelical groups, syncretistic features of slave Christianity—it emerged after the legalized racial hierarchy of free/slave had been abolished. It emerged in the context of a modernizing society, a society of an unfolding market capitalism and an ascendant culture of segregation. It emerged, this book argues, as millions of blacks and whites came to see that while some people clearly realized "the promise of the New South," they did not.[18] They came instead to participate in a modern poverty: a poverty of debt, propertylessness, commodity production, frequent mobility, and distant consumerism. The lives of poor blacks and poor whites were not the same—the culture of white supremacy was always there, sending powerful messages and spreading its sharply circumscribed vision. Indeed, for the dominant historiography, these messages were so powerful that the potential commonalities of poverty, commonalities that might have nurtured a shared identity, were effectively erased and annulled. This book argues, in contrast, that the modern poverty of the New South became a space in which poor blacks and poor whites spoke to each other and borrowed from each other religiously, learning in the commonality of their poverty what it meant to live as Christians in the confined horizons of a modernizing society.

The book thus emphasizes the power of class in Southern religious life. In pre–World War II American religious history and pre–civil rights Southern history, class was a central category of analysis: some of the most basic questions in both disciplines were articulated in class terminology.[19] For differing reasons in the two disciplines, class receded to the background. For the New South era more specifically, the argument of the dominant contemporary historiography is that whatever real and substantive differences there were in the social structure (wide differences of wealth and poverty being the most obvious), the ideology of white supremacy was so powerful that class formation was inhibited and prevented by an aggressive process of race formation. "White" and "black" became the dominant way in which the region's people imagined their identity; identities that might have been based on social structure were overshadowed by a Jim Crow culture that imagined binary divisions of the color line.

*Hard, Hard Religion* argues that a distinct folk Christianity was a critical factor in opening up a sense of commonality among poor blacks and poor whites in the New South. Put differently, poverty in itself was not the source of this sense of commonality; rather, poverty in symbiotic relationship with a grassroots religious culture became the basis of a sense of class commonality. The grassroots religious culture brought a different imaginative vision than the ideology of white supremacy, fostering identification outside the categories of white and black. In giving voice to struggles and longings born in poverty, folk Christianity was critical to a process of New South class formation: in its vision, whites and blacks could see themselves as "the poor." The book thus follows newer scholarship on the importance of culture for class formation, seeking to avoid the often-reductionist older scholarship for which " 'social being' determines 'social consciousness' " and for which the "economic base invariably precedes its cultural superstructure."[20] New South poverty did not automatically generate a class of "the poor," nor was folk Christianity merely the cultural articulation of New South poverty. Rather, religious culture informed the social experience of poverty, and the social experience of poverty informed religious culture—yielding a distinct folk religion of the poor.

Few religious tropes are more established than the characterization of poor people's Christianity as intensely otherworldly. In the 1840s, Karl Marx argued that religion was "the opium of the people," a distracting illusion that kept the working class from focusing on their material, this-worldly struggles. American labor songster Joe Hill's 1910s satire of a popular gospel song echoed Marx and has left an enduring image in its depiction of the Christianity preached to the working class as mere "pie in the sky." In his influential 1911 *Social Teaching of the Christian Churches*, German church historian Ernst Troeltsch characterized "sects"—religious movements of the "lower classes"— as intensely ascetic and eschatological, practicing "renunciation of or hostility to the world." Echoing Troeltsch, American church historian H. Richard Niebuhr argued in his 1929 *Social Sources of Denominationalism* that "churches of the disinherited" were marked by a strong "propensity toward millenarianism," that "from the first century onward, apocalypticism has always been most at home among the disinherited." The two leading historians of Southern religious life who have focused on the poor (though exclusively on poor *whites*) have largely followed this tradition in characterizing the religion of the Southern poor. A "message combining rejection of this world and centering of man's hopes in the next" was "escapist and narcotic," David Harrell wrote, but such a message "made sense to destitute southerners." Similarly (though finding heightened politicization in the 1930s), Wayne Flynt argued that the religion of poor whites largely "rejected the secular world and awaited transportation to a heavenly kingdom," that this otherworldly religion was a coping mechanism for "the abuse, defeat, and powerlessness of a life full of pain."[21]

*Hard, Hard Religion* directly challenges such characterizations. As McDannell suggested in her analysis of FSA photographs, the religious culture of the poor was "sensual"; it "brought beauty *into*" (my emphasis) the everyday lives of the poor. Likewise, in her theorizing on the real-world poor who inspired much of her fiction, Flannery O'Connor argued that the narrative world of the Bible infused the everyday and the mundane: "When the poor hold sacred history in common, they have ties to the universal and the holy, which allows the meaning of their every action to be heightened and seen under the aspect of eternity."[22] What O'Connor saw was the exact opposite of an otherworldly orientation: the sacred and holy were woven into the fabric of everyday, this-worldly life, imbuing it with mysterious, transcendent significance.

Two vivid anecdotes give concrete meaning to such claims. The first involves Lloyd Chandler, a poor white man in the tobacco-producing hollows of ruggedly mountainous Madison County, North Carolina. When he was in his mid-fifties, he experienced a startling, disruptive, life-altering vision. He fell into a deep sleep one night and woke up to find himself in a strange kingdom, a kingdom of moles—the tiny, blind pests that he regularly stomped to death after catching them in his vegetable garden. In this molehill monarchy, the tables were now turned: the moles had captured him, and they had him locked up in a cell. Different moles would come by the cell, and they would point at him, telling their children, "Look. This is the man that killed your father," or "This is the man that killed your mother." They were "very, very *ill* with him," and they held him captive for quite some time.

Finally, a dreadful day came. He was taken to a large room, where a queen mole sat on a throne. Chandler's accusers came forward one after another to recount the many murders he had committed. The evidence mounted, and it was clear that they were seeking his death as a just punishment. Then something unexpected happened. The queen called him to the throne and asked him a question of mercy: "If we would let you go, would you promise that you would never kill another mole?" Chandler made a solemn promise that he never would.

He woke up from the vision, and for the rest of his life, some twenty-five years, he kept his promise. Moles continued to burrow into his vegetable garden, gnawing the roots of the food he subsisted on, so he would capture them. But then he would do something dramatic: he would carry them two miles into the woods, on a rough path that he had blazed, to his "praying ground" beside a small dogwood tree. There, where he regularly knelt and prayed while clutching the dogwood tree, he would release them.

He did this many, many times in the long years from his vision until his death at age eighty-one. One time, after catching a mole in the exact same garden spot where he had caught three previous moles, he became convinced that it was in fact the same mole, somehow finding its way back from the release spot deep in the woods. So he took the mole and cut a clear line in the hair of its back. He then resumed his regular practice and carried the mole two miles into the woods. About a week later, when he was working in his garden, he noticed movement in the same spot. He dug into the ground, caught the mole, and lifted it up to see a clear line in the hair of its back: it was the same mole, determined to return! Chandler marveled at the little creature's plucky navigation.[23]

Chandler's practice of capturing, carrying, and releasing moles was a symbolically rich Christian ritual, a prophetic prefiguring of a world in which all of God's creatures could live in charity and fellowship, not violence and competition. The ritual was also physically painful for Chandler, and this deepened its meaning. As a young man, he had been unusually violent and destructive. He performed wild, dramatic actions that scared his neighbors while enacting a darkly nihilistic repudiation of life. One time in a wrestling match, however, Chandler was defeated and badly disabled: his opponent forced his right leg out of its socket. Chandler lived with the disability the rest of his life, one leg effectively six inches longer than the other, pivoting on his right foot's toes to walk and often swelling his right thigh with fluid. Any walking—but especially his ritualized two-mile forest trek, "around under rock cliffs up over ridges and down through the hollers," with captured mole in hand—hurt him.[24] Like O'Connor's fictional Hazel Motes, Chandler was enacting a strange penance, a prophetic act in very tangible, earthy, *this-worldly* ways.

The second anecdote comes from Vera Hall, a poor black woman in the fertile, cotton-producing Black Belt of central Alabama. Hall was an unusually gifted singer, and she carried in her memory an extensive body of songs. Behind one of her favorite songs, "No Room at the Inn," was a story that she often told and ruminated on. It was her account of Christmas:

> The steers was looking out, through the cracks, as Mary and Joseph was going from door to door, asking people to let her come in, and nobody would let her come in. They turned her away everywhere she went. That mean old manager at that hotel, oh, he just looked at her with that harsh look in his eyes and just drove her away. Those steers and oxens was down there in the barn, they was looking out through the cracks, great big old cracks, just with great big watery eyes, just beckoning, it looks like to me, beckoning for her to come in, that they would get back and give her room for the little baby Jesus to be born. . . . They had to go in that stable for Jesus to be born on that old, nasty, dirty hay—trotted all down and dirty. . . . But those steers, oxens, got all back off in a corner, and give Jesus the whole place, made room in there for Mary to lay down and Jesus be

*(handwritten margin note: from a ? Did Chandler describe it as such?)*

FIGURE 4 *Lloyd Chandler on the Porch of His Cabin, Sodom, North Carolina* (John Cohen/ Getty Images).

born. . . . And they breathed their warm breath there to keep him warm. He was naked, he didn't have on a thread, he didn't have on a string, laying in the grass, laying in the hay.[25]

In Hall's telling, mute work animals become the main characters. Trying to find a room on a cold night, Mary and Joseph are rejected repeatedly, with the hotel manager being especially prominent in his coldness. The setting seems less first-century Palestine and more twentieth-century Livingston, Alabama—the seat of her rural county. Who shows hospitality to the shunned couple, to Mary on the verge of giving birth? The steers and oxen: they weep at humanity's coldness, they invite Mary and Joseph into the barn, they make a place for Mary to lie down, and they breathe on the naked Jesus to keep him warm.

Hall takes a birth narrative that can rather easily be softened and sentimentalized and pushes it in harsh, oppositional directions. The stable is a rough, dirty scene, where work animals live and dwell. In the town, Mary and Joseph are not just unable to find a room but actively shunned and rejected, turned away from door after door and back out onto the street. Jesus's parents are so poor, in Hall's telling, that he lies in the hay as an infant, utterly naked. Human beings offer no welcome, no celebration, not even patronizing charity. In striking contrast, the steers and oxen display idealized Christian behaviors that the human beings do not: sympathetic care and warm hospitality. They do all that they are able, blowing warm breath on the infant even as he lies unclothed in the "old, nasty, dirty hay."

Hall's Christmas story led her to reflect on the hospitality she herself had experienced from her family's milk cow: "When I was a child we had a very, very gentle cow, her name was Mary. And my oldest sister used to go out and milk her, she'd sit on the box and be milking her. I'd stand in front—cold, frosty morning—and I'd be wringing my hands like this, and her warm breath would keep my hands warm. I'd walk up and let her breathe down in my bosom, so she could keep me warm down there—it was chilly! That's the way they did to baby Jesus, they kept him warm with their breath, sure did, they kept him warm. But there was no room, no room for him to be born."[26]

Animals displaying or revealing Christian reality—Hall's Christmas story, though very much her own, is a kindred spirit to Lloyd Chandler's vision of the moles. In both cases, there is an element of mystery. Animals are doing things that animals can't actually do—human things, like offering forgiveness or hospitality—and yet the animals' actions function as an admonition, a judgment, on what human beings are not doing. Naked Jesus in the dirty hay, kept warm by heavy cattle-breathing; Chandler ritually carrying moles to his secluded praying spot in the woods—in both cases, Christianity is rough and dirty. Sacred realities are not spiritualized but quite tangible, earthy. And yet in both cases, Christian sacred reality is not at home in the world. It's tangibly close yet foreign and strange too. Hall's Christmas story looks back to Jesus's unwelcome, even shunned birth, while Chandler's strange ritualized mole-carrying prophetically points to the way the world could be but is not. In both cases, though very material, this-worldly realities display the Christian sacred, something remains quite elusive and "other," finding "no room" in the world of ordinary experience. The earthy and the mystical are held in a striking tension.

In his 1949 *Jesus and the Disinherited*, theologian Howard Thurman argued that Christianity held special meaning for the poor, for "the cast-down people in every generation and in every age."[27] It was not about otherworldly compensation for people experiencing a this-worldly lack. Rather, Thurman argued, it was about liberation out of the cycles of fear, deception, and hatred that threatened to engulf the inner lives of the poor—liberation into a full

FIGURE 5 *Vera Hall on the Porch of Her House, Livingston, Alabama* (photograph by Alan Lomax; used with permission from the Alan Lomax Archive, Association for Cultural Equity).

humanity in this world. This book is about one instance of this phenomenon: the power that Christianity held for the poor of the New South. It is a study of a grassroots religious culture that impoverished southerners crafted, a culture embodied in such forms as haunting songs of death, mystical tales of conversion, and sacramental decoration of graves. As the examples of Chandler and Hall suggest, the Christian vision of this culture was tangibly this-worldly, with intimate meaning in the everyday lives of the poor.

This book employs the category of "folk religion" to interpret this grass-roots culture.[28] The category seeks to express two things: the largely hidden processes by which this culture was sustained and disseminated, and the socially marginalized position of its practitioners. In religious studies scholarship, the older category of folk religion has been supplanted by the categories of popular religion, vernacular religion, and lived religion. These three categories seek to capture religious life that spills out of, or exists independently of, religious institutions; religious activity that "ordinary" people, people who are not religious officials, engage in; and religious beliefs and practices that in everyday performance differ substantively from formal prescriptions of normative orthodoxy. Certainly all these phenomena are at play in the religious milieu explored in this book. But such phenomena were also very much at play in the familiar milieu of the Bible Belt. Small-town merchants composed gospel songs that became widely disseminated through inexpensive shape-note songbooks. Funeral homes advertised their services on handheld fans manufactured for use in churches. Pious women turned their parlors into spaces celebrating the virtues of respectable domesticity. Fraternal organizations as diverse as the black Odd Fellows and the second Ku Klux Klan drew heavily on evangelical beliefs and rituals to mobilize men. Independent evangelists crisscrossed the region, setting up camp in vacant lots and clearings on the edge of towns. Instances like these could be easily multiplied. They all make sense as "popular," or "vernacular," or "lived" expressions of the well-documented Bible Belt Christianities. All are distinct from normative religious phenomena, such as churches, ministers, seminaries, and denominational publications, yet all were imaginatively possible *within* a context shaped by such normative phenomena. All flourished inside the imaginative canopy of the Bible Belt.[29]

The category of folk religion seeks to get at something different—a religious culture that existed contemporaneously with familiar Bible Belt Christianity yet differed from it in substantive ways. Its imaginative parameters were simply *other* than those of the Bible Belt; it was not simply Bible Belt Christianity with the shadings and inflections of poverty. It was differentiated, at perhaps the most basic level, by its primary technique of transmission: an oral process in which religious content was packaged in stories, songs, proverbs, and other forms that existed by being told and retold, performed and performed again. This oral process did not exist in utter isolation from writing, but it did operate as a powerful medium beyond the reach of writing and literacy. The anecdotes of Lloyd Chandler and Vera Hall are emblematic. Chandler's vision of the moles existed for many years only as a story that he told to others. Late in life, before his death in 1978, he wrote it down to preserve it for his children; but even in the early 2000s, when folklorist Carl Lindahl interviewed Chandler's children at their own advanced ages, the paper copy had been lost, and the children narrated it as they had once heard it. Vera Hall's Christmas story was never written down. Late in her life, in 1959, folklorist Alan Lomax audio-recorded her telling the story. She told it three times, and as one would expect in an oral culture, the basic frame and specific imagery were the same (having long been codified in tellings and retellings), but words and phrases varied with each telling.

In different corners of the New South—the Brazos River bottomlands in central Texas, the Tennessee River valley in north Alabama, and the North Carolina Piedmont—folklorists encountered a proverb: "If salvation was a thing money could buy / then the rich would live and the poor would die."[30] The different tellers of this proverb almost certainly never met one another, yet they were appropriating a shared wisdom by perpetuating this proverb in their telling. Until a folklorist was there to write the proverb down, though, it was an entirely oral form, leaving no paper trail of its own. The "folk" in "folk religion" refers to this largely hidden, underground process of cultural transmission.

*[handwritten margin note: folk = oral culture]*

*[handwritten note in text: is it still folk if it's written down?]*

The proverb contains a pointed insistence. It critiques a too-ready association of Christian belonging with economic position—an association that, as chapter 1 will explain, became a central element in the dominant religious culture of the New South. The proverb insists on the expansiveness of Christianity, on the genuine Christian participation of the poor. This is the second sense of "folk" in "folk religion": it suggests groups on the social or cultural margins. Looking back at Benton's *Arts of the South*, a striking image appears in the painting's lower right foreground. Various discarded items—empty cans and bottles, an old tire, crumpled paper, and rotting wood—compose a sizable cluster. It is a pile of trash. Surely Benton crafted this image to convey the social order's denigration of the impoverished people he painted, the way in which the New South extracted labor from the poor and then discarded them as "shiftless niggers" and "poor white trash," as disposable and dispensable.[31] "Folk" seeks to express the marginalized social position from which the poor of the New South crafted their own religious culture.

The category of "folk religion," folklorist Don Yoder noted in a seminal article, was created in early twentieth-century Germany by formally educated, urban-based Lutheran pastors. They saw substantive differences between the religious culture they inhabited—part and parcel of a world of industrialization, market expansion, and an emergent bourgeoisie—and that of illiterate rural people in older villages, or peasants. These common people, or *volk*, were informed by localized traditions, not a cosmopolitan culture of literacy; they perpetuated their culture through techniques other than literacy, such as orality and imitative action; they had their own sources of authority, rather than formally credentialed professionals; their religious culture lacked official sanction and thus contained seeds of political subversion. In the vision of these forward-looking Lutheran ministers, the *volk* were clinging to increasingly antiquated traditions; they were behind the times. Thus, "folk religion" carried this sense of cultural denigration, of a religious culture that existed in the face of critique and hostility from established authorities.[32]

But the denigration can be reversed, and the category can also carry a strong sense of nostalgia for a more elemental time and a more authentic way of life. From its beginnings, it suggested primitive people living simple lives untouched by modernization.[33] The lives of the New South's poor, however, were intimately tied to regional modernization. Hardly bypassed or left behind by sweeping transformation, their poverty was itself a critical part of that transformation, sitting at the very nexus of the emergent economic order. The folk religion of the poor involved creative engagement with this transformation. Struggle was at its very core.

An aging black tenant farmer in Tennessee reflected on the hardships that had shaped his life. Some of his kinfolk had left the area to labor as migrant workers on the East Coast, and he knew others who had gone seeking industrial jobs in the South's expanding cities. In the late fifties and early sixties he was eking out a living on a rented farm, down a winding dirt path from a paved road. He ruminated, "I can't say it's not a struggle; it is, a bad one. If I had to choose, I'd not choose this life—maybe another one that's easier." Yet such raw candor was intertwined with other thoughts, of a very different spirit: "I've always believed that when we leave our house and start out there on the land, we're meeting God and doing all we can to show Him we can hear Him and we can believe in Him; and the proof is that He's there, helping us with the gift of His land, you see, and His sun you see, and His good, good rain."[34]

A white farm laborer echoed the tenant farmer uncannily as he described his everyday prayer: "I wake up, and I remind myself that this isn't *my* day; this day belongs to God. . . . Oh, Lord, I say, it's your day, and I'll try to meet you the best I can, halfway I hope. It's your sun and it's your sky. It's your rain and it's your wind. The clouds, they're sent over us by you. And I could go on and tell about more of God's miracles!" But his reverent wonder was checked by a vivid awareness of struggle always at hand: "My oldest daughter said to me once: 'Daddy, what about the worms, and what about the drought, and what about the flies and the mosquitoes?'" His reply to her drifted into rich metaphor: "Those flies, they're inside us—landing all over the place. Same with the mosquitoes. . . . I hear your mother bad-mouthing someone, and I know there's a lot of mosquitoes, a lot of flies that have got to her. And to me: I see some people in trouble, and I'll be a fly and land on them." Synthesizing it all, the good that inspired wonder and the evil he had to fight against, he spoke emphatically, "Our religion is hard; it's a hard, hard religion. We're in trouble, and we may not get where we want to be going, but we're going to try, oh are we!"[35]

The tenant farmer and the laborer were both insisting on something that was very much their own, even as the economic means that had defined their working lives were owned by others. What they claimed as their own was a faith that confronted the hardships of their lives, that stared at suffering and confinement and imagined God's good gifts in their midst. This book is an attempt to tell the story of this "hard, hard religion" and the people who crafted it.

## CHAPTER ONE

# The Making of the Poor South

It was the summer of 1936, a bright, hot, dry day. The forty-acre field was full of young tobacco plants, and Harry Crews's father was working his way through the rows, spraying the crop with lead poison to kill the worms. Harry's mother was in the house, a rough, unpainted wooden shack, scrubbing the floors with lye water and a brush made from corn husks. Young Harry was in a separate room, in a little playpen that his father had built for him. The young family seemed, even if slightly, to be moving up: they'd bought their first two cows, and with the future income from the tobacco crop, they hoped to acquire this farm as their own—moving upward from landless tenants to propertied small farmers.

But then Harry's mother happened to look out the screenless window only to see, to her horror, that the two yearling cows were walking toward the large barrel of lead poison. She yelled to her husband, but the air-pressured sprayer strapped to his back drowned out her cries. As the cows moved closer to the deadly poison, she threw down her brush and began to run to the field.

When she was halfway there, she heard screaming from the shack. Harry had turned over his crib, crawled into the room where she had been working, reached into the lye water, and then put his hands in his mouth. He had begun to bleed, and his mother raced back to his screams. Harry's father quickly left the field and hitched up their horse to the wagon, and the young parents rode, fearful and anxious, eight miles into town to the doctor's office.

The report was a comfort: Harry had mild burns on his mouth and hands, but he hadn't swallowed any lye. When the family got back to the farm, however, the consoling relief yielded to a bitter loss: the two cows were lying dead beside the barrel of lead poison. In defeat but also in stubborn endurance, Harry's father strapped the sprayer to his back and resumed his work in the tobacco rows, working until it was completely dark. Then he hitched the horse up a second time, hauling the two stiff cows to the back of the field, leaving their contaminated carcasses for the buzzards to eat.

Ruminating on this story as an adult, Crews wrote of "how tragic it was and how typical." Indeed, for him it distilled the rough core of the world and the people into which he was born. "The world that circumscribed the people I come from had so little margin for error, for bad luck," he wrote, "that when something went wrong, it almost always brought something else down with it. It was a world in which survival depended on raw courage, a courage born out of desperation and sustained by a lack of alternatives."[1]

The 1938 *Report on Economic Conditions of the South*, the work of liberals in the regional elite, painted a broad regional panorama of the context in which families like the Crewses struggled. Prefaced by a letter in which President Roosevelt described the South as "the Nation's No. 1 economic problem," the report carefully delineated Southern poverty and puts that poverty into a wide public consciousness. "The paradox of the South" (the eleven Confederate states plus Kentucky and Oklahoma), the *Report* opens, "is that while it is blessed by Nature with immense wealth, its people as a whole are the poorest in the country." In all quantifiable measurements, the region stood out as far below national averages. Per capita income in the South was $314, compared to $604 outside the region; average industrial wages in the South were 16 cents/hour less than those outside the region; taxable property in the South was $463 per capita, compared to $1,370 in the Northeast; and with 28 percent of the nation's population, the region contributed less than 12 percent of the nation's income-tax collections. For the incipient "consumers' republic" that the New Deal was trying to foster, regional poverty was a glaring national impediment. "The South," the *Report* concludes, "is the Nation's greatest untapped market and the market in which American business can expand most easily."[2]

This was the economic status of the region within the nation. Inside the region, though, there were wide disparities of wealth, and the *Report* focuses especially on those who shared least in it, thereby articulating the defining features of the region's poor. The poor farmed land owned by others; they worked in factories, mills, and mines managed and owned by others; they labored in the houses and shops of others. A small minority owned their own small farms, but in areas remote from market access. Most could not afford their own houses, and the small minority who did lived, like the renters, overwhelmingly in unpainted cabins and shacks with screenless windows. In the towns and cities, the poor lived in overcrowded slums that were "simply a convenient barracks for a supply of cheap labor." Mobility in search of tenuous opportunity characterized the lives of many: "Thousands of southerners shift each year from farm to mill or mine and back again to farm." The sufferings of poverty were manifest in the bodies of the poor. "The low-income belt of the South," the *Report* notes with alarm, "is a belt of sickness, misery, and unnecessary death." In a region of good soil, regular rainfall, and temperate climate, the poor suffered, paradoxically, from pellagra, "a disease chiefly due to an inadequate diet."[3]

At the time of the *Report* there were approximately thirty-six million people in the region, some eight million families. Using the *Report's* "most conservative estimates" that "4,000,000 southern families should be rehoused" and its findings that farm tenants—the largest single group of the poor—numbered 1,831,000 families, the approximate number of people caught in regional poverty was somewhere between 2.5 and 4 million families, or one-third to one-half of the total regional population.[4] They were tenants and sharecroppers, laborers and domestics, coal miners and timber workers, textile operatives and small farmers remote from market access.

In numerical terms, they were by no means marginal or peripheral to the region's population. Nor were they by any means limited to a geographic periphery: they lived throughout the countryside, in mining and timber camps, in remote hollows in the Appalachians, in small towns, and in mill districts in the region's largest cities. With the exception of remote-area small farmers, their lives and labors were in no way peripheral to the regional economy: their labor produced the majority of the cotton and tobacco, the textiles and steel, the coal and lumber, which were the dominant commodities in the region's market economy. They *were* peripheral and marginal imaginatively, however, and a fruit of the *Report* and other products of the New Deal political impulse—like the FSA photographs—was to bring them into visibility and wide public consciousness in the 1930s.[5]

The *Report* contained an uncommon observation. Though it was generated in a Jim Crow culture, on page after page it documented a poverty that knew no color line. There were poor blacks and poor whites. Indeed, of the whole group of farm tenant families, 66 percent were white. Of sharecroppers (a subgroup of tenants who were unable to pay rent to a landlord), about half were white. Reflecting on tenancy, the *Report* claimed that "whites and Negroes have suffered alike," and that white sharecroppers were "living under economic conditions almost identical with those of Negro sharecroppers."[6]

A formative experience in the life of Anne Moody (then called "Essie Mae" by her family) presents striking parallels to Crews's account and gives some concrete shape to the *Report's* claim (the Crewses were white; the Moodys were black). It was 1943, and the Moody family was sharecropping on the Carter plantation in Wilkinson County, Mississippi. Three-year-old Essie Mae and her infant sister were being tended to by their mother's younger brother while her parents labored in the cotton field. Her mother's brother, George Lee, was young—only eight—and he wanted to roam in the woods and hunt, not spend the day babysitting his nieces in a two-room shack of rotting wood. At first he took Essie Mae and her sister into the woods with him, but when their mother later found them covered with ticks, she forbade them from leaving the house. George Lee began to take out his frustrations on Essie Mae, beating her and then heading off to the woods; he would return slyly to the house before evening, when Essie Mae's parents came home. One night, though, Essie Mae's father discovered what had been happening. Enraged when he saw the knot on her head, he confronted George Lee and threatened him. "What happen to Essie Mae here? What happen? . . . If anything else happen," he warned, "I'm goin' to try my best to *kill* you."

The next day, though, George Lee turned the tables. He didn't show up that morning, and Essie Mae's parents reluctantly went to the field, leaving Essie Mae and her sister alone in the house. Then George Lee came by. He began to taunt Essie Mae with kitchen matches, burning pieces of the deteriorating wallpaper, and then putting the small fires out. Having reasserted his power, he brought Essie Mae and her sister to the porch, and he went into the yard to play. But apparently he hadn't put the fire out completely, as clouds of smoke began to billow out the windows and door. Essie Mae heard a loud commotion as her parents and other sharecroppers came racing up from the field. They were able to put the fire out—only the deteriorating wallpaper had burned—but the ending turned violent. Essie Mae's father confronted George Lee, but George Lee was ready with an alibi. He pointed to the bucket he had placed on the porch and insisted that he had been getting water to put the fire out. "Essie Mae musta did it." Weighed down by a drought that had yielded a pitiful crop and the death of his best friend in a work accident, Essie Mae's father believed the lie, and he poured out his frustrations on her: he beat her severely with a small board that had fallen out of a rickety chair.[7]

A hard common ground of tiny margins for error, of human pathos and suffering in a world of circumscribed options, was not a new phenomenon produced by the Great Depression. As the *Report* carefully described, the central factor in creating regional poverty was not the national depression but the absence of basic structural components—sufficient capital, sustainable credit—which made the South's market capitalism stunted and uneven. "The South has not yet been able to build up an adequate supply of credit—the basis of the present-day economic system," the *Report* bemoaned, and this had debilitating ripple effects. Many tenants and sharecroppers were stuck in debt to a local landlord or merchant; industrial workers drew the lowest wages in the nation, since labor costs were Southern manufacturers' key asset in national competition; capitalists outside the region were the primary owners of the extractive industries; and four-fifths of everything the region's farmers ate and wore was bought from well-capitalized industries outside the South.[8]

This economic structure was the product of a distinct historical context, one that began to take shape in the late nineteenth century. Few expressed the economic impulses behind its origins better than Atlanta-based editor and orator Henry Grady. A booster and entrepreneur who became an influential public speaker in the 1880s, Grady told an anecdote of two men, a father and a son. The father was an old man when Grady knew him, an imposing "kingly figure" with "white hair, his lisle thread gloves, his closely buttoned coat." In the antebellum South he had been a planter of great wealth, an owner of a large estate on the Sea Islands. In the postbellum decades, now dependent on the charity of kin, he would entertain Grady for hours with "quaint and courtly talk." Grady recalled that one day he said in rumination, "Do you know, it appears to me that turkeys have lost their flavor? On my island, they fed largely on mast, which gave a nutty richness to their meat. I had thousands every year—the finest birds imaginable." In his innocence, the young Grady suggested that the thousands of turkeys must have brought quite an income in the market. "Income!" the old man sniffed, "Why, my young friend, no Southern gentleman ever sold poultry!"

The old planter's son offered a sharp contrast. He had left college to fight for the Confederacy and came home from the war "a bullet or two heavier." But holding on to the past was not for him. When he returned home, Grady noted, "He went to work. Sell poultry? Well, I should say so! He sells the eggs, then he sells the meat, then he sells the feathers, then he has the soil of his poultry-house scraped up and sold." Whereas the father had disdained certain market activity as beneath his dignity, the son looked even at chicken shit and saw a commodity. Grady moved to the punch line: "From these once despised resources—sold with huckster-like exactness, though in larger spirit— he has rebuilt the fortunes of his family."[9]

Grady was succinctly contrasting the economic logic of the antebellum order with a new logic that was expanding in his own time. Though he didn't coin the term, he became the leading publicist of "the New South," a society whose market capitalism differed substantively from the human capitalism of the antebellum South. Coalescing as the democratic experiment of Reconstruction came to a violent end in the 1870s, the New South advanced as the logic of resource extraction and market penetration suffused the region, incorporating it into a coherent whole more successfully than the antebellum order ever had.

Since the colonial period, the region had been in the vanguard of crop production for international markets, but it was in the New South that this production reached its widest extent. More and more land was devoted to market production, including areas that had once been marginal like the "pine barrens" and alluvial swamps, more and more of the population came directly into the arena of market production, and the New South saw the region's greatest yields ever of cotton and tobacco. As land use intensified for crop production, so too did it accelerate for resource extraction. Areas that had been most marginal in the antebellum order—the mountains and the pine barrens—became the new centers of mining and lumbering. Massive old-growth forests were harvested for timber and turpentine, and minerals that had been underground for eons—coal, iron, and copper especially—were now mined extensively for the nation's fast-expanding industrial economy. Connecting areas of crop production and resource extraction were a host of rapidly expanding cities and legions of new towns. Both the large cities and the innumerable towns served as market centers, gathering the production of their surrounding areas for shipment to distant markets and bringing the mass production of national industries to the region's expanding consumer market. These large cities and small towns also became sites of new factories and mills as the industrial revolution came to the South. Industry was intimately tied to the region's staple crops and extracted raw materials. Textiles were the leading form of this industrial blossoming, but it was also manifest in tobacco, furniture, and steel manufacturing. The gears connecting this network of commodity production, commerce, and industry were the railroads. Though lines had connected parts of the antebellum order, railroad mileage in the region exploded from 7,001 miles in 1860 to 39,108 miles by 1890. Spreading to almost every nook and cranny of the region and moving commodities toward markets near and far, the railroads were a succinct embodiment of the economic logic of the New South.[10]

W. E. B. Du Bois captured the exciting promise of the New South—its new economic logic and new work ethic—in his description of a transforming rural black community in the hills of central Tennessee. In the summers of 1886 and 1887, Du Bois taught school there in an old corn crib of rough hand-hewn logs, where thirty pupils met him daily with "eyes full of expectation" and "hands grasping Webster's blue-black spelling book." "We read and spelled together," he recalled, "wrote a little, picked flowers, sang, and listened to stories of the world beyond the hill." Sometimes he boarded with the Burke family, the head of which, Doc, was "ever-working, and trying to buy the seventy-five acres of hill and dale where he lived." Du Bois also spent hours on the porch with Josie, "a thin, homely girl of twenty," a star pupil in his class and a tireless worker who brought in cash for the family; who dreamed of leaving the hill and making her way to Fisk University in Nashville.[11]

Leading religious voices articulated the ethos of the new order. Bishop and educator Atticus Haygood, a prominent white Methodist, lauded the new order in an 1880 sermon, *The New South: Gratitude, Hope, Amendment*. It would be born through "millions of acts of self-denial, through industry, economy, civil order, and the blessing of God upon obedience," he argued. "Our children are growing up to believe that idleness is vagabondage," he noted in critique of the antebellum order. With hope he looked forward: "The true golden day of the South," he proclaimed, "is yet to dawn."[12] Reverend J. W. E. Bowen, a prominent black Baptist, similarly evoked the new order and its ethos in an 1892 address: "Contemporaneously with the New South," he argued, "the New Negro has appeared upon the scene, the Negro born of schools and colleges, and bent more on acquiring a home, amassing wealth, and the improvement of the social conditions of his home, than the support of the grog shop, the gambling hall, and other institutions of idleness."[13] The old order lauded leisure while disdaining work and productivity; the new order incentivized people to believe that they had no time to be idle and no resources to waste.

Few noticed the symbiotic relationship between the emergent religious ethos and the economics of the New South better than German sociologist Max Weber. A 1904 tour of the United States brought him to Surry County, North Carolina, to visit his wife's relatives. On a crisp autumn Sunday afternoon, Weber found himself watching baptismal candidates emerge from a chilly pond. It was quite an event: a large crowd from both near and far had gathered on the banks of the pond, congratulating the newly baptized as they emerged and comforting their shivers with thick blankets. Weber was especially intrigued by one baptism in particular. During the immersion of one of the young men, Weber's cousin was startled. "Look at him," he said to Weber. "I told you so!" When Weber asked him after the ceremony, "Why did you anticipate the baptism of that man?" he answered, "Because he wants to open a bank in M."[14] Weber came to understand that for this community, the man's moral uprightness—implying his trustworthiness and skill in investing money—was intimately linked to, and publicly declared by, his becoming a Baptist.

From Weber's highly urban perspective, Surry County and its main town of Mount Airy (the "M" of his anecdote) were "the backwoods."[15] Much of the New South landscape, indeed, might seem to fit that description. Yet "backwoods" places like Surry County were intimately tied to far-flung markets. If physically remote, they were not at all isolated and unconnected. With a railroad line running from its terminus at Mount Airy into the quickly expanding tobacco manufacturing city of Winston-Salem, some forty miles away, the county found increased demand for its tobacco crop. The town of Mount Airy, incorporated in 1885, was an emblematic New South market center, with new brick stores stretching along its main streets. There, area farmers would congregate on Saturdays, socializing, enjoying town life, and buying the newly available goods it offered. Mount Airy's development continued in the generation after Weber's visit; by 1940, the town was a distribution center for a large granite quarry, and it had developed typical New South industries: textile mills and furniture factories.[16] Later generations would know Mount Airy as the "Mayberry" of television—a quaint, slow-paced alternative to 1960s America—but at its beginnings and into the mid-twentieth century, Mount Airy was a bustling local instance of the New South's market capitalism.

In the same years as his Surry County jaunt, Weber was theorizing the intimate ties between a distinct Protestant ethic and the development of market capitalism. In fact, he was in the process of publishing his elaborate theory in Germany as *The Protestant Ethic and the Spirit of Capitalism* (1904–5). One need not pursue or even validate Weber's full theory to gain from his basic insight. The new capitalism of the New South was intimately tied to a new evangelical ethos.

The route to this ethos was circuitous and winding. When Baptists and Methodists first appeared in the South in the mid-eighteenth century, they embodied a critique of inclusive, hierarchical, and convivial Anglican culture. They emphasized conversion as a radical break, and they withdrew from official Christianity into small meetings of the truly converted. In these meetings, they used the egalitarian language of "brother" and "sister," and they listened to preachers who had divine inspiration, not the elite privilege of formal education. In striking contrast to their neighbors, Baptists and Methodists displayed a steady austerity in their social life. They shunned the conviviality and frivolity of the tavern, of dancing and fighting, and by doing so sought to display their seriousness and sense of urgent conviction.[17]

By the early nineteenth century, this distinct evangelical culture was moving in two very different directions. As Baptists and Methodists gained converts from the ranks of prosperous yeomen and elite planters, they shifted their emphases and began to accentuate new themes. Similarly, but in a very different direction, as the Baptist and Methodist message spread among slaves and free blacks, especially in meetings away from white supervision, it was creatively grafted onto a framework inherited from West Africa. White Baptists and Methodists shaped their culture in accommodation to existing power in the South—most especially that of white male heads of household. They moved away from their early egalitarian tendencies and instead asserted the prominence of the patriarch, vigilantly defending the household from external threats, setting a serious, austere example for the moral life of its members, yet holding his own in the larger society by displaying mastery of self and dependents. In another movement toward hierarchy, white Baptists and Methodists began to found colleges and seminaries for the formal education of their clergy, their young gentlemen, and their young ladies. Cultivated in this new world of scholarship, some theologians crafted elaborate treatises defending slavery as a divinely ordained institution for the paternalistic edification of slaves. White Baptists and Methodists continued to insist on conversion as a sharp break, but the zeal with which many embraced the Confederate nation suggested that their exclusivist sectarian withdrawal could be pushed to the background to make way for an inclusive nationalism.[18]

As white Baptists and Methodists moved on this trajectory, a very different culture was taking shape below the radar of white visibility. African Americans took the distinct evangelical features and wove them into an African religious framework. They imagined salvation primarily as a communal rather than an individual phenomenon, embracing the well-being and health of the larger community: family, kin, and neighbors. Conversion was conceptualized as an initiation rite, a process of ostracism and alienation one had to go through before becoming a genuine member of the community. With this communal imagination, black Baptists and Methodists developed a strong kinship with the ancient Israelites—God's communal people, whose collective health and well-being were his special concern. Also informed by African religious culture, black Baptists and Methodists did not draw a sharp line between what a European imagination was calling "religious" and "secular." This made their Christianity more worldly, physical, and tangible, in contrast to the ascetic austerity of whites. With this imagination, black Baptists and Methodists could dance with religious zeal and hail the "secular," political act of emancipation as God's great act of deliverance, like the Israelite exodus of old.[19]

In the wake of the epochal events of Civil War and Reconstruction, a great irony emerged in the histories of these two evangelical cultures. Former slaves left the churches of their former masters en masse, and in concert with free blacks (both Southern and migrants from the North), they established new, separate institutions. At the very time that this separation was becoming complete across the region, whites were crafting a new culture of racism, designed to draw a sharp color line between superior and inferior races. The great irony is that as black and white Baptist and Methodist churches became separate institutions and segregation emerged as a new form of white supremacy, black and white evangelical cultures moved closer to each other. Seeking to be in the vanguard of crafting a New South, both white and black evangelicals reformulated their message—and the resulting messages pointed in an uncannily similar direction.[20]

The central feature of this reformulation was a reemphasis on the old austerity. This had never left either culture as they followed their different trajectories in the antebellum era. Temperate, stern Baptist planters had rubbed shoulders uneasily with their jolly, convivial Episcopal peers, and an ascetic, austere Baptist slave like Nat Turner stood out as different from his enslaved neighbors. But the austerity had been pushed aside as other themes—patriarchal mastery among whites, communal well-being among blacks—moved to the center. Dramatic changes in the lives of whites and blacks brought this austerity back to the center. White patriarchal masters had suffered the shame of defeat in war as well as the loss through emancipation of the slaves whom they imagined as needing their paternalistic guidance. In black life, by contrast, the exciting new possibility opened up by emancipation—the free, legally supported coalescence of nuclear households—also meant the decline of a strong communal consciousness. Austerity could point the way forward as an individualized ethic for a new day.

Austerity had originally marked early Baptists and Methodists as religiously serious in the face of what they viewed as merely superficial formal Christianity. It had also established a code of behavior that was deviant in the face of the dominant culture, codifying a clear who's who. Now, as both white and black evangelicals sought to point the way forward into the new incentives of the new capitalist logic, austerity could be more than a differentiating counterculture. It could show both white and black how to prosper in the new economy. With some modifications, it could be an ideal ethic for the New South's market capitalism.

New South Baptists and Methodists could be serious in a different way—not serious as a counterpoint but serious about their time, labor, and resources. They could be productive, thrifty, and frugal. They could shun not just what was superficial and jolly but also what was idle, what was wasteful, what was imprudent. Their austerity could become more than a negative guide to what they didn't do—enjoying the pleasure of alcohol or the sociability of a dance. It could become a positive guide to what they should do: practice self-discipline, hard work, and prudent management of one's resources. Reformulated in this way by both whites and blacks, the old austerity was given new life as an idealized guide for navigating the new economy. A new word appeared in religious discourse, and it quickly became a commonplace, something so apparent that it needed no justification: both white and black evangelicals began to talk about "respectability."[21]

With respectability as the new ideal, time-honored, jolly recreations like drinking alcohol, dancing, playing cards, and enjoying sex were radically reformed. Baptists and Methodists used the force of law to officially prohibit these idle recreations and the power of their culture to push them to the margins as the opposite of respectable—as "trashy." But even as some once-common social customs were banished from the New South's public square, making it seem newly still and quiet, Baptists and Methodists developed new ways of valuing what was public and visible. Weber argued that ascetic, austere Protestants sought tangible confirmation that they had God's favor. In the New South, white and black evangelicals learned to look to property—their home, their farm or business, their clothing—as a clear fruit and demonstration of their genuine respectability.[22] There was a basic optimism undergirding this: right behavior would lead to tangible reward. This was a modern capitalist version of the ancient Deuteronomic two-way schema. As the Deuteronomist imagined it, Israel prospered when it was living righteously, but it suffered invasion and dissension when it fell into patterns of unrighteousness. In the New South's evangelical imagination, the two-way schema was individualized and linked to economic well-being.

Read backward, homes, farms, businesses, and one's own clothes were clear signifiers of religious status, of whether or not one was living respectably. The old austerity, originally a tangible way to differentiate from the Anglican culture of display, shifted significantly in the New South to inform a new culture of display. Possessions that one accumulated—especially a home and clothing—displayed religious standing. The optimism of this two-way schema placed a new faith in the justice of the market. It became the arena in which respectable Christians gained clear, tangible confirmation of their respectability. Surveying this New South scene from the central market center of Atlanta in 1903, Du Bois was alarmed at the new valuations. The material goods threatened to become goals and ends in their own right. The New South, the very society where thrifty, industrious Baptists and Methodists were crafting a Bible Belt, was in danger of falling into a crass "Mammonism."[23]

But it never quite did. Baptists and Methodists, white and black, did not go so far as to sacralize the market. They sought a refuge from its calculating competition and cold logic, and they found that refuge in the home—in domesticity, in the home imagined as a sphere shaped by the softness and nurture of women. This new emphasis on domesticity coalesced in tandem with that of respectability, and like respectability, it signified a new departure. Antebellum white evangelicals had imagined the household as the key site where patriarchs displayed their mastery, while antebellum black evangelicals had imagined the larger slave community (of families, kin, and disparate quarters) as their basic social unit. The new ideal of domesticity was tied to dramatic social changes—the new separation (at least for some) of home and work, and the dispersal of the slave community into more nuclear households. Particularly for whites, domesticity represented an increased power for women: they, not patriarchal masters, would dominate the life of the home. But domesticity had an additional layer of meaning. In a New South where the logic of the market advanced into every corner of the region, the home would be a space exempt from wholesale commodification. It could certainly display goods acquired in the market—fruits of respectability—but its spirit of calm, harmony, and reverence would offer a striking contrast to the rough competition and cold calculation of the market.[24]

The new evangelical ethos of respectability and domesticity pointed the way forward for those who sought to realize the promise of the New South. It idealized a code of behavior that was especially conducive to the market capitalism of the new order. That the Baptists and Methodists formulated a compelling message for the New South seems clearly demonstrated by their notable numerical growth. While the region's population increased by 81 percent from 1890 to 1926, Baptist and Methodist membership increased by 105 percent. By 1926, the Baptists and Methodists accounted for 70 percent of the region's religious members, and 42 percent of all adults in the region belonged to a Baptist or Methodist church.[25] Howard Odum's map of Baptist/Methodist dominance sketched the boundaries of the South—of the nation's Bible Belt—with uncanny precision (see fig. 6).

In the new evangelical ethos, southerners from very different backgrounds could learn to think like Henry Grady's young entrepreneur—seeing resources where they didn't seem to exist, putting a new premium on careful management of time and money, and acquiring status through success in the market. With this new ethos linked to new incentives, a new class coalesced, a middle class that had been a peripheral presence in the antebellum South but now became the ascendant force in the New South: merchants; various

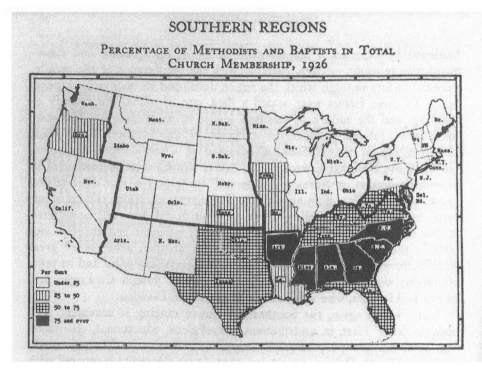

SOUTHERN REGIONS

PERCENTAGE OF METHODISTS AND BAPTISTS IN TOTAL
CHURCH MEMBERSHIP, 1926

FIGURE 6  Map of Baptists and Methodists from Howard W. Odum, *Southern Regions of the United States* (Chapel Hill: University of North Carolina Press, 1936). Used with permission of the publisher.

professionals, such as educators, lawyers, doctors, and journalists; managers in industry, transportation, and finance; and large and small farmers.[26] Touring the Mississippi Delta in the mid-1930s, Reinhold Niebuhr insightfully noted that "the organized church . . . is as middle class in the south as anywhere else."[27] Yet even as this new middle-class ethos taught how to evaluate social status and how to order the household, it offered only a threadbare account of a principal development in the New South: an expanding modern poverty. Despite the optimism of the emergent evangelical culture, something was badly amiss.

Ten years after his initial visit and curious to see its development in his absence, Du Bois returned to the rural community in the Tennessee hills. He found a new schoolhouse of milled boards, but with broken windows. The Burkes had expanded their farm by twenty-five acres and lived in a larger cottage, but they were still in debt and paying for the land, the cottage was but half-finished, Doc and his wife were "showing decline," and one son had left the would-be family farm for Nashville. Violence—white landlords against black tenants and laborers, black men against black women—was a disturbing new staple of community life. Josie, the dreamer, had worked tirelessly over the years but had gained little besides "a face wan and tired." Her aging mother met Du Bois with the news that "we've had a heap of trouble since you've been away," that hard-working, worn-out Josie had died.[28]

The promise had not materialized as hoped; the youthful excitement and energy were gone. Du Bois's rumination on "the meaning of progress" expressed something basic about the New South: while it saw the spread of a new economic logic and an optimistic new ethos, it also became a society of defeated aspirations and new confinements. Amending Haygood's vision of a "true golden day" dawning, what materialized instead was a regional variant of the Gilded Age. There was exciting newness, including genuine new prosperity, but beneath this gilded surface was a widespread new poverty and human stagnation.

The saga of the white Tingle family illustrates the pathos and human cost of this new poverty. Frank, the father, was born into a tenant family in Hale County, Alabama, where the last traces of the Appalachians yield to the fertile Black Belt. He grew up farming and as a young man was bringing income into the household through his job at a sawmill. By the World War I years, when he was in his early thirties, he had established his own household. He was married, raising children, and renting land of his own. When James Agee met the Tingles in the summer of 1936, however, the family was caught in a humiliating spiral of dashed hopes and devastating sufferings:

> Years ago the Ricketts [Agee's protective pseudonym for the Tingles] were, relatively speaking, almost prosperous. Besides cotton farming they had ten cows and sold the milk, and they lived near a good stream and had all the fish they wanted. Ricketts [Frank Tingle] went $400 into debt on a fine young pair of mules. One of the mules died before it had made its first crop; the other died the year after; against his fear, amounting to full horror, of sinking to the half-crop level where nothing is owned, Ricketts went into debt for other, inferior mules; his cows went one by one into debts and desperate exchanges and by sickness; he got congestive chills; his wife got pellagra; a number of his children died; he got appendicitis and lay for days on end under the ice cap; his wife's pellagra got into her brain; for ten consecutive years now, though they have lived on so little rations money, and have turned nearly all their cottonseed money toward their debts, they have not cleared or had any hope of clearing a cent at the end of the year.[29]

FIGURE 7 "Frank Tingle, cotton sharecropper, Hale County, Alabama" (photograph by Walker Evans; Library of Congress, Prints & Photographs Division, FSA/OWI Collection, LC-USF342-T01-008155-A).

In the mid-1930s they were tenants, renting land and a house from a landlord who lived in town, owing him one-third of their cotton and one-quarter of their corn at harvest time, as well as reimbursements for fertilizer and rations money, which the landlord had furnished on credit. This left the Tingles a pittance, even though they owned their mules and farm implements.

FIGURE 8 "Frank Tingle family, sharecroppers" (photograph by Walker Evans; Library of Congress, Prints & Photographs Division, FSA/OWI Collection, LC-USF3301-031322-M5).

The Tingles' poverty was intimately tied to new features of the New South. The family grew staple crops that had value in international markets, and they sold milk in local markets. Even the seeds of cotton had market value, as they were now industrially processed into oil. Finance—cash, credit, and debt—played a critical role, and was central to the family's humiliating descent into dire poverty. To try to escape his widening debt, Tingle was forced to sell his cows in the market, further eroding the family's independence in food production. His wife's pellagra was due to a deficiency of niacin and an overreliance on corn—a crop of high yield that the family increasingly depended on as they sold off their cows and had to buy foodstuffs on their (loaned) rations money. In the South, pellagra was a distinctly modern disease, a twentieth-century malady tied to the intensification of land use.[30] As market logic spread to new corners of the region in the late nineteenth and early twentieth centuries, more and more land was devoted to commercial crops, to the neglect of diversified food. Corn, a staple crop that paid some of the Tingles' annual rent, would have to serve as food too.

Two counties away from the Tingles, some forty miles as the crow flies, granddaughter-of-slaves Vera Hall encountered a similar kind of confined, unforgiving world as she came of age in the early twentieth century. "A woman has to work *so* hard on a farm," Hall told folklorist Alan Lomax in 1948. Though Hall's family had some elements of self-sufficiency that the Tingles had lost—milk cows, a vegetable garden, and a fruit tree orchard—they farmed cotton on rented land and had minimal cash for basic necessities. It was not for lack of industry; Hall eulogized her father in particular as an unusually hard worker, a man who sought out cash-paying work, like cutting hay and selling firewood in off-seasons. But hard work, even on good land, was not enough to provide a family cushion for hardship. Hall's oldest sister died at age twenty-eight, after three years of living with a broken hip for which the family could not afford medical care. Hall and each of her sisters had two dresses a year, one for summer and one for winter, which their mother had stitched from cloth their father was able to buy. When Vera was thirteen, the family was able to buy her first pair of new shoes. Beyond her own family, Hall saw neighbors in even worse poverty, people who came to her father in early summer to weed cotton ("chopping") in exchange for food. One extremely impoverished man who periodically came to her father for work, Rich Amerson, didn't even live in a house but rather in a dug-out hole in the ground, timbered up like a mining shaft, near the railroad tracks.

At the age of eleven, Hall began to work as a cook and nanny for the white family from whom her parents rented land. This meant regular trips to town, to the county seat of Livingston, where the landlords lived. By age thirteen, Hall was spending a month at a stretch with the landlords in the larger town of Tuscaloosa. While there, she met Nels Riddle one Saturday night, and their subsequent marriage seemed to lift her out of the poverty and dependency she had known in her youth. Riddle earned good money working first at a filling station and then in the coal mines. The couple had two children, and Hall and her husband were deeply enamored of each other. "I was just crazy about married life," she remembered.

Then, one fateful morning, Hall's joyful, seemingly secure life was shattered: her husband was shot and killed by another worker in the coal mines. She fainted when she heard the news and remained unconscious for a day. Filled with grief, she moved back to Sumter County, but the old security of family was gone. Her father had died, and her mother was suffering with rheumatism. Hall eked out a living in Livingston, taking her mother in and caring for her even as she struggled to raise her own children. After eight years of suffering, her mother died, and in the struggle to pay her mother's doctor's bills, Hall sent her children back to the family's rented farm, to live with her sister. She continued to work in Livingston, as a cook and maid for white families, but even in the home county of her youth, Hall felt "all alone in this big old world."[31]

From the emergent evangelical ethos that ascended to cultural dominance in the New South, though, impoverished people like Hall and the Tingles could find little comfort. The two-way schema had a harsh, unforgiving side. Prosperity was the fruit of respectability; poverty signified its absence. If people were not prospering, if they did not own their own property and homes, it was because of their own moral failings, their own lack of respectability. Poverty was thus imagined as a moral problem, a problem that rested with the poor themselves. If such people did not demonstrate respectability, it was because they did not will to. Commanding no respect, they could be denigrated and dismissed. They were "trashy" and "shiftless."

As poverty became a staple feature of the New South, the emergent middle class took steps to distance themselves from the poor.[32] Field studies in the region revealed intensely hierarchical class attitudes. In the county seat of Greensboro, Alabama, James Agee heard a volley of ridicule from white townspeople when they learned he was writing about white tenants:

Fred Ricketts [Frank Tingle]? Why, that dirty son-of-a-bitch, he *brags* that he hasn't bought his family a bar of soap in five year. . . .
Why, Ivy Pritchert [Ivy Fields] was one of the worst whores in this whole part of the country: only one that was worse was her own mother. They're about the lowest trash you can find. . . .
None of these people has any sense, nor any initiative. If they did, they wouldn't be farming on shares.[33]

Sociologist Morton Rubin heard echoes of this in Camden, in Wilcox County. "My middle class friends," he noted, "warned me about 'getting mixed up with those wild people'"—with poor whites in the countryside. At the same time, he found that middle-class blacks "condemn lower-class behavior," that "they often isolate themselves from the masses of Negroes because they cannot stand to be near them or to be thought of as associating with them."[34] In Sunflower County in the Mississippi Delta, sociologist John Dollard likewise observed that middle-class blacks sought to distance themselves from poor blacks through education, sexual behavior, "antagonism to spirituals," and women working solely inside the home. He concluded that "the attempt of the middle class to mark itself off from the pilloried lower-class Negroes seems constant."[35] Even members of the small regional elite—planters, industrialists, large merchants—conscientiously sought distance from poor blacks and poor whites. Delta planter William Alexander Percy imagined poor blacks as perpetual primitives, knowing "not whence they came nor what manner of life they led there ... interested neither in the past nor in the future," like a simple animal who "neither remembers nor plans." Of poor whites, on the other hand, he wrote that "the virus of poverty, malnutrition, and interbreeding has done its degenerative work.... I can forgive them as the Lord God forgives, but admire them, trust them, love them—never. Intellectually and spiritually they are inferior to the Negro."[36]

Place of residence in a local geography became a basic form of distance from the poor. Many planters and large farmers abandoned the countryside and moved to the nearest town, separating themselves from the agricultural labor of their tenants and sharecroppers. In many sites of industrial manufacturing and extraction, industrialists and managers isolated their workers into discrete villages and districts. For elite and middle-class blacks, such geographical separation was more difficult to achieve: the residential segregation of Jim Crow, at least in the towns and cities, put blacks of different classes in the same neighborhoods. But given that many poor blacks did not live in towns and cities but rather in the countryside, the urban residence of the majority of elite and middle-class blacks became a partial marker of class distance.[37]

Electoral politics (for whites) and church life (for blacks and whites) had brought disparate classes together in the antebellum South, but in the New South, politics and the churches became sites of class distance. The disenfranchisement campaigns, primarily in the 1890s, stripped almost all African American men, regardless of class, of their voting rights, but the scope of disenfranchisement also meant that white politicians of elite and middle-class status no longer had to feign affiliation with poor whites, since their voting rights were stripped as well. "Demagogues" could and did rally whites on the lower end of the middle class in seemingly "populist" campaigns, but such political dynamics did not involve the poor.[38] Indeed, in a violent demonstration of just how thoroughly poor whites were removed from politics, various Southern states established programs to sterilize poor white women and men. Virginia, North Carolina, and Georgia led the way in stripping almost 20,000 poor whites of their reproductive capacity—against their will, deceived by medical professionals, and with the powerful aura of the law.[39]

Individual churches became spaces of class differentiation: planters, rural merchants, and small farmers attended town churches away from country churches dominated by tenants; mine owners isolated themselves from churches populated by miners; and textile owners and managers established their own churches separate from those of textile workers.[40] The emergent middle class sought and imagined religious differentiation from people whom they disparaged as "backward people" and "simple countryfolk"; as "mountaineers," "poor tenants," "Negroes in the rural districts," "the peasantry," "mill villagers," and "coal diggers" in "rags"; as people who were "constantly moving," people of "ignorance, solid stupidity, thick necks and low brows," "a relatively illiterate mass," and "a landless, homeless people."[41]

In their distancing from the poor, the middle class articulated a contradictory assessment of the poor's religious life. On the one hand, they noted churches composed entirely of the poor and asserted that a deficient, sub-Christian religion was being practiced there. In the early twentieth century, a black minister noted "weird songs," "wild excitement," and "violent physical gymnastics among both sexes" in churches of poor blacks, so foreign to him that it seemed "a species of voodooism imported from the religion of heathen Africa." In 1909, the white Baptist periodical *Our Home Field* lamented religious "destitution [that] in some respects at least is not less than among the heathen"; a missionary echoed the diagnosis, writing, "I know stories of immorality and ignorance that would parallel those told by foreign missionaries occurring all around us." A white denominational official recoiled at the religion he saw in a poor white church in the 1920s: "A number of times the author has occupied a pew in a little church attended by the Bunglers and hoped that something constructive would be said. Each time the preacher, while beating the air, has given the picture of a God that no intelligent being could worship . . . a God with the earmarks of heathenism." In churches of poor blacks in the 1920s, black educator Carter Woodson observed what to him were "manifestations of the spirit resembling paroxysms which could hardly be expected outside of an insane asylum."[42]

On the other hand, middle-class observers asserted that the poor were not religious at all. A white extension agent argued in the early 1920s that landlessness made for a "restless, roving, irresponsible spirit." He lamented, "For the last twenty years in this state we have seen industrious, thrifty, ambitious farmers leaving the country and moving into town for the school, church, and other social advantages. . . . When these thrifty farmers move out they leave renters and share-croppers in possession of the country church and its activities, and soon the church and Sunday school pass out of existence." A white seminary professor echoed with a tight logic that seemed indisputable. "It must be true," he argued, "that religious interest decreases as tenancy increases." Two decades later, a black educator and Tuskegee chaplain concurred with what seemed an established commonplace: "It is now known that tenants and other disadvantaged agricultural people are not overtly given to church membership. Their mobility, their poverty, their lack of 'belonging'" all worked against their capacity to sustain organized religious life.[43]

Weird religion that seemed closer to "heathenism" than Christianity, a pervasive lack of religion—as sweeping assessments of the religious life of the poor, these portraits were mutually exclusive. Both could not be true as comprehensive statements. Yet both make sense as the projection of middle-class valuations onto the poor, projections that contain grains of truth even as they reveal more about the middle class than about those being described. Underneath these projections, though, both portraits convey something important: a palpable sense of difference. The emergent middle class looked at the poor and did not see fellow participants in the ascendant evangelical culture. Beneath the seeming homogeneity of the Bible Belt, of the apparent religious hegemony suggested by Odum's map, there was substantive religious difference *within* the region.

At face value, locating this difference seems fairly easy. Despite the broad allegiance and cultural dominance commanded by the Baptists and Methodists, the New South was not a religious monolith. The Disciples of Christ and some Presbyterians also participated in the new evangelical culture, but liturgical and confessional Protestants—Episcopalians, Lutherans, and most Presbyterians—exerted social power far beyond their small numbers, with their membership among the regional elite. Catholics and Jews appeared in the larger cities, some small towns, and specific subregions, weaving ethnicity and religion together to sustain a strong sense of identity. Reformist movements that began inside the evangelical fold broke out to become their own distinct forms: the Churches of Christ, the Holiness movement, Pentecostalism. Many small groups were born of internecine theological divisions in the large Baptist and Methodist denominations, separating to form their own new denominations such as Regular Baptists, United Baptists, and Two-Seed-in-the-Spirit Predestinarian Baptists; the Congregational Methodist Church and the Reformed Methodist Union Episcopal Church. Most notably, despite the Bible Belt image, approximately 40 percent of the region's adult population did not formally belong to any religious institution.[44]

But where did the religious life of the poor fit into this regional panorama? Certainly not all of the poor were participants in religious institutions; the middle-class portrait of the poor's lack of religion cannot have been complete fiction. Using the broad regional number as a rough guide, as many as 40 percent of the poor may have been uninvolved in religious institutions. But where were the rest? Where were those practicing "sub-Christian" religion? Was their participation embodied in small sects (like the Two-Seed-in-the-Spirit Predestinarian Baptists) and heterodox movements (like Pentecostalism)—as the most common and enduring model in religious studies has framed it?[45] Was it located in specific subregions (Appalachia) or work environments (the coal fields)?[46] Was it tied to specific moments of labor radicalism?[47] The summary report of the Southern Rural Life Council, an interracial group of middle-class ministers and academics, contained a key insight. The council's report found "economic and social stratification . . . *within churches of the same denomination*" (my emphasis). It lamented that "without a representation of a cross-section of the people of the community either as members or participants in its program, the church is severely handicapped in acting as a mediator or integrator in community conflicts." What was at work within these class-divided churches was nothing less than "two kinds of religion."[48]

Seeming denominational homogeneity obscured substantive difference at the local, individual level. Religious difference was housed, then, within the very structures that seemed so uniform and homogeneous: the innumerable Baptist and Methodist churches that dotted the region. The decentralized polity of the Baptists and the Methodists' practice of local preachers meant that individual Baptist and Methodist churches could easily have little to do with the regional denominational structure. Indeed, a massive denominational study conducted by the Southern Baptist Convention (SBC) in 1922 revealed that of some 22,000 rural churches allegedly identified with the SBC, only 12.5 percent sent delegates to state convention meetings, and only 6.3 percent sent them to the annual SBC meeting. In addition, 75.9 percent of preachers serving rural churches had no seminary training, and 90 percent of rural church members had never seen a denominational periodical.[49] Thus, there was plenty of space *inside* seemingly familiar structures for religious difference.

The specific sites of difference were seemingly ordinary, mundane, and ubiquitous. Little on the outside suggested substantive religious difference—or, in some cases, even religious activity at all (see figs. 9 and 10). Yet these spaces housed considerable religious activity. Observers caught glimpses of this and of the people who labored within. In a one-room shack near the house they rented, the Tingle family organized religious meetings on Wednesday, Friday, and Sunday nights. Neighbors would gather until the shack became full. The meetings opened with singing, then shifted to a participatory ritual: each person present, young and old, male and female, quoted his or her favorite Bible verse.

FIGURE 9  "Prayer meetinghouse, Frank Tingle's farm" (photograph by Walker Evans; Library of Congress, Prints & Photographs Division, FSA/OWI Collection, LC-USF342-T01-008149-A).

After that the leader reads a chapter from the New Testament and expounds it, verse by verse; and after that the singing resumes in good earnest.... The leaders are Frank Tingle and his two eldest daughters. Tingle picked up sight-reading in one night at singing-school and has a somewhat fallible talent for harmony and improvisation. His voice is a loud bugling bay and it brackets the whole male register. His daughters, who have learned the tunes and most of the words by heart, strain and tighten their naturally pleasant voices continually.... There is no formal end to the service. The children and men drift out, then the wives: for the last half hour only Tingle and his two girls and Mrs. Tingle (moved, serious, and nearly silent in her deep black) are left in the shack.[50]

In the heart of Appalachia—several hundred miles from the Tingles, who lived on its southwestern edge—a white Baptist official and missionary stum-

FIGURE 10 "Church" (photograph by Walker Evans; Library of Congress, Prints & Photographs Division, FSA/OWI Collection, LC-USF342-T01-008254-A).

bled upon the type of person who periodically preached at churches like the Tingles': "The young man preached to two churches for a year, giving three weeks to revival meetings, for a total salary of $13.20. With his little family he lived in a two-room cottage on thirty acres of land for which he was trying to pay. He worked for a neighboring farmer part of the time, in exchange for a horse with which to plow his own small field of corn, and on Sundays he walked to his churches, six and fifteen miles away."[51] There was no sharp line between clergy and laity, for this preacher was, by all external measurements, scarcely different from the impoverished congregations he served. On the other side of the South, in the Mississippi Delta, Reinhold Niebuhr noted this dynamic: "The sharecroppers are served by lay preachers, who develop spontaneously without religious training. . . . They express the religious protest against social injustice in terms reminiscent of the classical examples of this protest. They know their bible."[52]

John Dollard heard one of these lay preachers when he crept into the back of a black church in Indianola, Mississippi, to observe the service. Despite his scholarly detachment, he found himself moved by the sermon, an evocative oral narrative expounding on the story of Noah and the great flood. He later wrote, with a mixture of condescension and admiration, "After the meeting we talked with the preacher and found him to be a tenant on a plantation some miles away, a typical lower-class Negro worker. His control of English, of course, was nothing like perfect, although it was germane and powerful. I marveled that he could have invented such a sermon and suspected that possibly he had learned the main organization of it from somewhere else."[53] Though he didn't realize it, Dollard was onto something—the far-flung oral networks that connected the innumerable local churches of the poor. This tenant preacher had not crafted his sermon solely out of his own imagination. Amending Niebuhr's analysis, though this preacher (and others like him) didn't have any formal education, he did not develop "spontaneously without religious training." He was "trained" in a folk culture of oral and imitative transmission.

A sermon fragment and its echoes provide a succinct glimpse of how, in this folk culture, religious content was packaged and transported. Benjamin Mays and Joseph Nicholson wrote it down for their 1933 study *The Negro's Church*:

> *Sometimes the devil tries to lead me. I send him away, and call in the doctrine of the Holy Spirit.* God in Heaven will baptize me and He will save me. He will lead me through the chilly waters of Jordan. *If you have the love of God in your heart,* if you know about the doctrines of the Holy Spirit, you will be saved. He knows the plan of my salvation. My Lord! My Lord! I want you to journey on; I do not want you to turn back. *He was pierced in the side. He was nailed on Calvary's rugged cross. I can see them as they hung Him there. I can see them as they laid Him in the tomb.* He brought light out of darkness. He died that we might have eternal life; that we might have a right to the tree of life. *I know His blood has made me whole.*[54]

FIGURE 11  An emblematic lay preacher, "Mr. Buck Grant, preacher and FSA borrower, Greene County, Georgia" (photograph by Jack Delano; Library of Congress, Prints & Photographs Division, FSA/OWI Collection, LC-USF34-044570-D).

A white preacher in the white-majority North Carolina mountains used a variant of the first italicized image in a 1941 sermon and attributed it to a black source: "Colored man said, when the devil comes to my heart's door and knocks on my heart's door, devil comes there and knocks, that I send Mr. Jesus to the door. When Mr. Devil sees Mr. Jesus come to the door he says, 'Pardon me, I'm at the wrong house.'" Vera Hall in the 1940s and a white tenant farmer in the 1930s echoed the second italicized phrase. Hall said that "if you ain't got religion in your heart, you just don't care.... Religion will make you pure and honest in your heart and you'll have the heart and mind to love everybody," while the white tenant said that "a true Christian has the love of God in his heart and all power." The third italicized phrase condenses successive stanzas of "Were You There When They Crucified My Lord," a folk song that originated in 1880s Tennessee and spread among both blacks and whites, while the final italicized phrase lifts the title of Blind Willie Johnson's 1927 song "I Know His Blood Can Make Me Whole."[55] As is expected in a predominantly oral culture, these echoes were not exact or word for word but variations on a phrase.

Small, spartan Baptist and Methodist churches dotting the region, "untrained" preachers who shared in the poverty of their hearers, far-flung oral and imitative networks that transported religious content across wide distances—these were the spaces and mechanisms of the New South's folk Christianity. Like the poor themselves, such spaces and mechanisms did not belong to a numerical or geographic periphery. They were ubiquitously spread throughout the region. But they could be easily missed, by middle-class contemporaries who projected their own valuations onto the religious life of the poor, by scholars trained to look for religious difference outside seemingly uniform denominations.

In their own churches, among people of their own class, through folk techniques, the poor crafted their own Christianity for the circumscribed world of the New South. They found vital cultural space to be more than mere victims of their socioeconomic circumstances. Through this cultural work, they developed a very different account of regional poverty, giving religious articulation to the new confinements wrought by the region's emergent market capitalism. Their folk Christianity spoke to the unfulfilled promise of the New South.

In the hindsight of history, it's clear that children like Harry Crews (b. 1935) and Essie Mae Moody (b. 1940) were born into a regional society on the brink of sweeping transformations: the New South was about to be unmade, and a Sun Belt was slowly being born. The transformations were by no means uniform—some localized areas displayed old patterns well into the 1960s. Yet even with this qualification, from the vantage point of children like Crews and Moody, or of hard-pressed people like the Tingles and Vera Hall, such wholesale, dramatic transformation was unimaginable. Millions of blacks and whites lived in a sharply circumscribed world of poverty, with minimal options and limited horizons. The confinements of this world threatened to destroy them, through the fear, the deception, and the hatred that Thurman eloquently analyzed in *Jesus and the Disinherited*. Yet in their own folk Christianity, in their "hard, hard religion," many found a way to overcome these destructive forces—an alternative vision of the world that infused their everyday lives with transcendent meaning.

# Singing of Death—and Life

In the songs they crafted and sang, folk Christians imagined death as a frightful terror—palpable, personified, and always unwelcome. Death was a grimly adamant census-taker:

> There's a man goin' round takin' names
> There's a man goin' round takin' names
> An' he took my mother's name
> An' he left my heart in pain
> There's a man goin' round takin' names

In each successive stanza, the austere enumerator continues the reckoning, taking father, then sister, then brother, leaving the singer in anguished isolation.[1] A variation on this song insisted that "Death Ain't Nothin' but a Robber":

> Death ain't nothin' but a robber, don't you see
> Death ain't nothin' but a robber, don't you see, don't you see
> Death came to my house, he didn't stay long
> I looked in my bed an' my mother was gone[2]

In successive stanzas, Death continued his theft, taking other members of the household until the singer was left in frightful and bitter solitude.

"The Little Black Train" warned of a certain train "a-comin'," but a train that no one would want to take:

> There's a little black train a-comin'
> Get all your business right
> There's a little black train a-comin'
> An' it may be here tonight
>
> Oh, the little black train is a-comin'
> I know it's goin' to slack
> You can tell it by its rumblin'
> It's all draped in black

It was a mourning train, a modernized version of the traditional funeral procession, but this was a different kind of mourning train. Rather than carrying a distinguished person to a distant grave, it was coming, coming soon, for anyone and everyone. No one could avoid it; everyone had to get on board. Those who weren't ready served as a frightful admonition for others farther down the line:

> Oh, Death had fixed the shackles
> Around his throat so tight
> Before he got his business fixed
> The train rolled in that night[3]

In "Got No Travellin' Shoes," Death came closer, appearing at the door and beckoning people out on a fateful journey:

> Death went out to the sinner's house
> Said, come and go with me
> Sinner cried out, I'm not ready to go
> I ain't got no travellin' shoes
> Got no travellin' shoes, got no travellin' shoes . . .
>
> Death went down to the gambler's house
> Called hi, come and go with me
> The gambler cried out, I'm not ready to go
> I ain't got no travellin' shoes[4]

In "Soon One Mornin' Death Come Creepin'," Death was even closer—not a census taker making rounds, not a train rolling in, but a haunting presence in one's very room:

> Soon one mornin' death come creepin' in my room
> Soon one mornin' death come creepin' in my room
> Soon one mornin' death come creepin' in my room
> O my Lord, O my Lord, what shall I do to be saved?
>
> Death done been here, tuck my mother an' gone
> Death done been here, tuck my mother an' gone . . .
>
> Death done been here, left me a motherless child
> Death done been here, left me a motherless child[5]

And in "O Death!" Death was so close as to be speaking directly to the singer:

> Sinner, I come to you by Hebbin's decree
> This very night you must go wid me
> "O-o death! O-o death!

How kin I go wid you?
Just like a flower in its bloom
Why should you cut me down so soon?
O-o death! O-o death!
How kin I go wid you?"[6]

Or in another song, "Death Goin' T' Lay His Col' Icy Han' on Me," Death could even be felt:

Oh, death, t'row thy sting away, oh, death
Death goin' t' lay his col' icy han' on me
One day, one day I was walkin' 'long
Death goin' t' lay his col' icy han' on me[7]

In his four-stanza "Jesus Make Up My Dying Bed," central-Texas singer Blind Willie Johnson wove the modern imagery of the telephone, the biblical story of the Crucifixion, and the Greek myth of the River Styx together into an austere, haunting statement of hope in the face of seeming abandonment.[8] Johnson began with words that seem to echo the feminized piety of the dominant evangelical culture:

Since me and Jesus got married
Haven't been a minute apart
He put the receiver in my hand
Religion in my heart
I can ring him up easy
Ring him up easy
Jesus gonna make up my dying bed

But the high-pitched, bare sounds of Johnson's guitar and the rough, anguished tone of his singing voice worked to immediately subvert any sense of sentimental piety. Here it is the singer, not Jesus, who is feminized, and the singer's closeness to Jesus, subsequent stanzas quickly reveal, has nothing to do with the stable domesticity of the idealized Christian home. The singer's union with Jesus is a union in suffering and abandonment:

Mourning, weeping
Said, he ain't lost
Late this Friday evening
Hanging on the cross
Hanging there in misery, aah, aah

Hanging there in misery
Jesus gonna make up my dying bed

Late this Friday evening
Before that dyin' moan
Jesus said to his disciples
Come and carry my mother home
Dyin will be easy, aah, aah
Dyin will be easy
Jesus gonna make up my dying bed

Jesus's summons to his disciples to care for his mother—found only in the Gospel of John—heightens the sense of death's terror. It comes unwelcome and unpredictable, subverting the natural order in which mothers die before their children do. In these stanzas, Johnson seems to be drawing on a song that emerged in early nineteenth-century evangelical circles and became widespread among Christian slaves, "Were You There When They Crucified My Lord?" This song meditates slowly and in vivid detail on the narrative of the Crucifixion, and the hearer is brought to the scene to reflect in solemn reverence. The same is true in Johnson's song: the hearer is taken immediately from the early twentieth-century world of the telephone to the climactic event in the Gospels. Even as the song ruminates with awe on the Crucifixion, the singer expresses hope. Dying will be easy because Jesus has gone before in experiencing misery and abandonment in a violent spectacle.

The concluding stanza draws on Greek mythology to chronicle the singer's own death:

I'm dead and buried
Somebody said I was lost
When you get down to Jordan
Ask the ferryman how did I cross
Done gone over
Done gone over
Jesus gonna make up my dying bed[9]

The song reflects on the possibility of ultimate loss—that in death's certain decay, the person ceases to be. Certainly the song moves into the macabre with its narration of death and burial. But the singer insists on hope. Because Jesus has already crossed over, the singer who married Jesus in the song's first line can confidently insist that Jesus will carry the dead over the river of death.[10]

During her fieldwork in the Deep South in the late 1920s and early 1930s, Zora Neale Hurston found that this song (though she heard it called "The Dying Bed Maker") was "easily the most popular of the recent compositions."[11] Indeed, from its beginnings in Johnson's home base of central Texas's Blackland Prairie, the song spread quickly to the Mississippi Delta, the Alabama Black Belt, and the Georgia Sea Islands—a distance of almost one thousand miles. It was an emblematic New South folk song of death.

The pinnacle of this genre—a song powerful in its unrelenting focus, extensive in its geographic scope—was the creation of Lloyd Chandler.[12] Thirty-five years before his vision of the mole monarchy, when he was coming of age in the 1910s, Chandler was known to his neighbors as a dangerous, violent young man. Chandler's violence went beyond the rough brawling that disabled him. It was often darkly theatrical and egregious, intended to leave a disturbed, haunting impression on those who witnessed it. Stories circulated about Chandler's violent and unsettling acts, and a generation after his death they were still being told and retold. One time he bent down to the ground, clenched a hundred-pound feed sack in his teeth, and then reared bolt upright, lifting it off the ground while people watched in disbelief. Another time, while puzzled onlookers watched, he got under a mare and tried to milk her as if she were a cow, even as she kicked back at him and threatened to kill him. Another time, he sat on a hollow log that contained a large yellow jacket nest. He began to beat on the log, and the yellow jackets swarmed out, swirling around him and stinging him. He grabbed them with his fists and crushed them, even as they continued to swirl and sting. He got up from the log only when he had killed all of them with his fists.[13]

Nothing was produced by these acts of violence—except displays of raw strength, and a fearlessness with which Chandler seemed to disregard his own life. Such violence reached a crescendo when Chandler was twenty. With a hefty supply of moonshine, he and a companion disappeared into the woods. It seemed that this time, Chandler really was bent on his own destruction. What exactly unfolded is murky: two weeks into the bender, Chandler lay alone in a barn loft in a remote cove, shivering in the cold and in intoxication. (The companion was later found dead.) Chandler then felt a stark, terrifying presence—icy hands seemed to grab hold of him, and he heard a haunting voice speak: "Oh I am Death, none can excel." Jolted out of his stupor, Chandler found himself pleading and begging for the very life he had disregarded. In his vision, a terrified conversation unfolded. He tried to bargain and reason with Death, but at every turn, Death had a clear and uncompromising rebuttal. The conversation intensified as Chandler felt Death slowly disabling his body, locking his jaw, fixing his feet, closing his eyes. His anxious pleas intensified—"Oh Death, O Death please let me see, if Christ has turned his back on me. . . . Oh Death, O Death please give me time, to fix my heart and change my mind"—but so did Death's unwavering insistence: "Too late, too late, to all farewell!"[14]

Just as his demise seemed imminent, Chandler awoke from the vision, and he stumbled out of the barn a changed man. The vision of Death fundamentally jolted him, and he was shocked into a new embrace of the goodness of life. In place of the dark acts of violence that sought to terrify his neighbors, Chandler began to practice an egregious charity. When a famine threatened his county and the local relief agency was distributing food only to the pinched middle class, Chandler broke in to the depot, said, "Come in here. Lloyd Chandler's filling sacks today" in defiance of the sheriff, and made sure that food reached the vulnerable poor. "If he had two coats and you asked for one," his son recalled, "he'd give you the good one and keep the one with the hole in it." He became a special friend to children.[15]

And he became a Baptist preacher, proclaiming a message of hope and transformation. His preaching began in his Madison County home, but over the ensuing decades, he traveled in a radius of some two hundred miles. The centerpiece of Chandler's preaching was a song he crafted on the heels of his life-altering vision. He called it "Conversation with Death," and it told of a terrified, anxious mortal pleading with Death in an intensifying back-and-forth struggle. Chandler omitted any references to his own individuality, crafting a song that could speak to anyone in the lonely solitude of his or her mortality. He composed ten four-line stanzas, carefully rhyming 8-meter lines in an AABB pattern. It was powerfully succinct, artfully coherent, and stark in its imagery and sound. With his vision of Death in 1916 when he was twenty, and his new vocation as a preacher beginning around 1922, Chandler's song took shape during the late 1910s and very early 1920s.[16]

Tracing the song's spread presents a microcosmic glimpse of the workings of a vibrant oral culture.[17] This is necessarily a suggestive rather than an exhaustive glimpse, though—what survives in the historical record is not the oral culture itself but outside observers' written documentation of it. Who knows how many other singers appropriated the song and made it their own, or how many other sites knew the song as one that was locally performed? The full extent of performers and places is impossible to document at this date. Nonetheless, the suggestive glimpses reveal clear patterns in a flourishing oral culture.

At any early date, the song jumped the mountains, from Madison County in the eastern Appalachian Blue Ridge, to the Cumberland Mountains of southwest Virginia and extreme eastern Kentucky, to the Cumberland Plateau of eastern Kentucky.

Around 1925, most likely from Bell County, Kentucky, or Wise County, Virginia, in the Cumberland Mountains, the following song was heard. The identity of the singers is unclear—they may be people known only as "Uncle Basil" or "old man VanBibber":

What is this that I can see
Death's icy hand taking hold on me
You have fixed my feet so I can't walk
You have fixed my tongue so's I can't talk
Oh death spare me over for another year

I know you are able to open their eyes
For you placed the sun and moon in the skies
Lord spare me over till another year
Lord spare me over till another year

You have made a place for me in heaven
All this I have in your promise given
Lord spare me over till another year
Oh death spare me over till another year

There are so many people with an unbelief
There are so many people, blind and deaf
Lord spare me over till another year
Spare me over till another year[18]

Chandler's opening lines appear here, though not word for word (here the singer *can* see Death), as well as the lines about Death disabling feet and tongue. The basic action is the same—Death beginning to claim a terrified, pleading mortal, with macabre effects—but the singer of this fragment cries out to God to spare him and notes God's power in creation, whereas in Chandler's song the sole dialogue partners are Death and the mortal. This version also expands to a definite sense of triumph over death and to social reflection about other people, features absent in Chandler's song.

Around 1925, the following fragment of a song was heard either in Wolfe County, Kentucky, in the Cumberland Plateau, or "from some preacher who hailed from Wolfe County":

You have fixed my feet till I can't walk
You have fixed my tongue till I can't talk
Lord, spare me over till another year
Spare me over till another year

You have fixed my eyes till I can't see
You have fixed my ears till I can't hear
Lord, spare me over till another year
Spare me over till another year

I know you are able to open their eyes
You have placed the sun and the moon in the skies
Lord, spare me over till another year
Spare me over till another year

I will bind your feet till you can't walk
I will fix your tongue till you can't talk
Until I bring you a sinner unto me
Oh death spare me over till another year[19]

Three of Chandler's lines ("I'll lock your jaw so you can't talk / I'll fix your feet so you can't walk / I'll close your eyes so you can't see") form the core, at least of this fragment. Their order is rearranged, though, and they do not echo Chandler word for word. The song's third stanza echoes the previous song's second stanza, and its refrain echoes that of the previous song (but not Chandler's).

Beginning in the late 1920s in Jackson County, Kentucky—two counties away from Wolfe in the Cumberland Plateau—a woman in her early twenties named Ruby Davidson was singing a lengthy song of thirteen stanzas and a chorus. The chorus echoes the previous songs—"Oh Death, Oh Death, Oh Death / Please spare me over another year"—as does the opening line ("What is this that I *can* see" [my emphasis]). But Davidson's version closely echoes Chandler's in nine stanzas. The echoes are not word for word, and most notably, the order of the stanzas is different. Much more so than the previous songs, Davidson's song follows Chandler's in its unrelenting focus on the anguished conversation between Death and the lonely mortal: God is distant and not implored; the song conveys hopelessness in its certainty of Death's sudden triumph.

*Davidson:*

What is this that I can see
With icy fingers taking hold on me?
I am death, there's none can excel
I open the door to Heaven and Hell

Oh Death, if this be true
Please give me time to reason with you
From time to time you heard and saw
I close the eyes and lock the jaw

Oh Death, please let me see
If Christ has turned his back on me
When you were called and asked to bow
You would not take heed, it's too late
    now

I'll fix your feet so you can't walk
I'll fix your jaws so you can't talk
I'll close your eyes so you can't see
This very hour come go with me

Oh, Death, consider my age
And please don't take me at this stage
My wealth is all at your command
If you will move your icy hand

The old, the young, the rich, the poor
They all alike with me must go
No wealth, no land, no silver, no gold
Nothing satisfies me but your soul

Oh yes, I come to take the soul
To lose the body and make it cold
To drop the flesh off from the form
'Tis sad to you, 'tis an awful alarm

Oh, Death please give me time
To fix my heart and change my mind
Your heart is fixed, your mind is bound
I have the shackles to drag you down

*Chandler:*

Oh what is this I cannot see
With icy hands gets a hold on me
Oh I am Death, none can excel
I open the doors of heaven and hell

Yes, I have come for to get your soul
To leave your body and leave it cold
To drop the flesh from off your frame
The earth and worm both have their claim

O Death, O Death if this be true
Please give me time to reason with you
From time to time you heard and saw
I'll close your eyes, I'll lock your
    jaw

I'll lock your jaw so you can't talk
I'll fix your feet so you can't walk
I'll close your eyes so you can't see
This very hour come and go with me

O Death, O Death consider my age
And do not take me at this stage
My wealth is all at your command
If you will move your icy hand

The old, the young, the rich, the poor
Alike with me will have to go
No age, no wealth, no silver nor gold
Nothing satisfies me but your poor soul

O Death, O Death please let me see
If Christ has turned his back on me
When you were called and asked to bow
You wouldn't take heed and it's too late no

O Death, O Death please give me time
To fix my heart and change my mind
Your heart is fixed, your mind is bound
I have that shackles to drag you down

| | |
|---|---|
| Too late, too late! To all farewell | Too late, too late, to all farewell |
| My doom is fixed, I'm bound for Hell | Your soul is doomed, you're summonsed to hell |
| As long as God in Heaven shall dwell | As long as God in heaven shall dwell |
| My soul, my soul shall be in Hell | Your soul your soul shall scream in hell |

But Davidson's version has four other stanzas, interlaced among the others, that imagine a broader context:

Now, Death, if someone would pray
Can't I just call and charges repay?
God's children prayed, His preachers preached
The time of hope is out of reach

Oh, Mother, come to my bed
And place a cold towel on my head
My head is warm, my feet are cold
Death's putting his shackles on my soul

Oh, Death, how you are treating me!
You close my eyes so I can't see
You stretch my limbs and make them cold
You're ruling my body off my soul

You heard my people sing and pray
You wouldn't take heed but walked away
In your home you wouldn't bow your knee
But now you must come and go with me[20]

These stanzas place the singer inside a Christian context of preaching, singing, and praying that she has willfully neglected, a context that is only dimly suggested in Chandler's song ("When you were called and asked to bow"). But the stanzas remain within the two-party dialogue, like Chandler's song, and the distance of God's people and the singer's mother heightens the very alienation that Chandler evoked.

Documentation indicating that fragments and echoes of Chandler's song first appeared in southern Appalachia, within one to two hundred miles from Madison County, makes sense. Perhaps these early singers heard Chandler sing the song during his travels and made it their own. Or perhaps they heard someone who had heard Chandler, then appropriated the intermediate version. By 1936–43, a new wave of documentation reveals a dramatically expanded scope for the song. The song or portions of it were being heard in the Highland Rim of central Tennessee, the Cumberland Plateau of north-eastern Alabama, the Black Belt of central Alabama, the Piedmont of central Georgia, and the Ozarks of northwest Arkansas—as well as still within the southern Appalachians near Madison County, in the Blue Ridge of east Tennessee, in the Cumberland Plateau of southwest Virginia, and in the Cumberland Plateau of eastern Kentucky.

From Overton County in central Tennessee, a version was documented in 1936 that is almost identical to Chandler's.[21] It lacks the refrain found in the earlier songs ("spare me over for another year"), and it lacks stanzas that diverge from Chandler's. Aside from small differences of a word or phrase, the sole difference between this version and Chandler's is that Chandler's eighth and ninth stanzas appear here in reverse order; otherwise, the stanzas are almost identical. In Jackson County in northeast Alabama, fourteen-year-old Sara Martin was singing a version in 1937 that is even closer to Chandler's: all ten stanzas are in the same order, and there are only slight differences in the words:

| *Martin:* | *Chandler:* |
|---|---|
| With icy hands taking hold of me . . . | With icy hands gets a hold on me . . . |
| Yes, I have come to get your soul | Yes, I have come for to get your soul |
| To leave your body and have it cold . . . | To leave your body and leave it cold . . . |
| I'll dim your eyes so you can't see . . . | I'll close your eyes so you can't see . . . |
| And do not take me in the stage | And do not take me at this stage . . . |

The following year, a young woman in the Smoky Mountains of east Tennessee, documented only as "Miss Gaston," was heard singing the song. The stanzas are all in the same order as Chandler's, but Chandler's ninth stanza is missing. The words of Gaston's version more closely match Sara Martin's and are even closer to the Overton County version, but they still display slight differences (Gaston: "To drop the flesh from off the frame . . . / If God has turned his back on me"; Overton County: "To drop the flesh off from your frame . . . / If Christ has turned his back on me").[22] The striking similarities these three versions bear to Chandler's, and to each other's, is not a function of sheer geographic distance; while the Smoky Mountains were closer to Madison County than places where the song was heard in the 1920s, Jackson County, Alabama, is farther away, and Overton County, Tennessee, is no closer. What does unite these three later locations is their easier accessibility. All were close to major railroad lines and national automobile routes that connected directly to Madison County, while the earlier Kentucky/Virginia sites were not.[23] It's possible, then, that the Overton County singer(s), Sara Martin, and Miss Gaston heard the song directly from Lloyd Chandler. As the song was appropriated, then, there were no intermediaries and no additions or alterations to the frame.

From this later period of 1936–43 comes also the first documentation that the song had crossed the color line. In the Sumter County seat of Livingston, in the Alabama Black Belt, Vera Hall sang a version that echoes the eastern Kentucky/southwest Virginia chorus even as it introduces a new emphasis:

Oh, Death is awful
Oh, Death is awful
Oh, Death is awful
Spare me over another year

Here the singer is not only pleading with Death but proclaiming its terror for hearers to ruminate on. Hall continues with a new stanza, whose metaphors emphasize Death's unpredictable timing and power to destroy the body:

If I was a flower in my bloom
Make Death cut me down so soon
He'll stretch your eyes and stretch your limbs
This the way that Death begins

The first two lines here are almost identical to a couplet in "O Death!" (see page 50), which was heard before Chandler's composition in 1908 in eastern North Carolina from African American singers. Clearly this couplet was circulating independently of Chandler's song, and yet Hall continues with a stanza that more closely echoes Chandler's than any of the previously documented versions, even as two lines are flipped. Unlike the early versions from eastern Kentucky/southwest Virginia, it echoes Chandler's use of three different verbs instead of repeating "fix," and unlike the Overton County, Sara Martin, and Miss Gaston versions, it echoes Chandler's "close" instead of "dim." At the same time, though, matching the ruminating quality of this version, Hall sings of Death in the third person:

| *Hall:* | *Chandler:* |
|---|---|
| He'll fix your feet so you can't walk | I'll lock your jaw so you can't talk |
| He'll lock your jaw so you can't talk | I'll fix your feet so you can't walk |
| He'll close your eyes so you can't see | I'll close your eyes so you can't see |
| This very hour you must go with me | This very hour come and go with me |

Her concluding chorus moves the song back into the dialogue itself, as the terrified mortal pleads with Death:

Oh, Death have mercy
Oh, Death have mercy
Oh, Death
Just spare me over another year[24]

Hall was clearly participating in oral networks that stretched back to Chandler, as well as to eastern Kentucky/southwest Virginia and eastern North Carolina. At the same time, and like others before her, she was weaving new features into the song—here, a stanza and an alternating refrain.

Another version from Sumter County has the stamp of Hall's song, even as it displays new features conveying death's urgency and universal scope. It also incorporates two lines, not found in Hall's song, that echo Chandler's original:

Oh Death, oh Death, have mercy
Oh Death, please don't cut me down so soon
Oh Death, oh Death, have mercy
Just as a flower in my bloom

My name is Death, Heaven sign decreed [Chandler: Oh I am Death, none
    can excel]
I got my writ for to summons thee
I'm travelin' through every city and town
I must make my report before the sun go down

Oh Death, consider my age and leave off [Chandler: O Death, O Death
    consider my age]
I am just a little flower in my bloom
Oh Death, oh Death have mercy
What make you want to cut me off so soon?

Oh Death, this is the way death begins
He'll stretch your eye and stretch your limbs
Oh Death, oh Death have mercy
Oh Death, just spare me over another year[25]

A third version heard in Sumter County illustrates both the fluidity and the fixity of an oral culture. Its first stanza is almost identical to the second stanza of the Sumter County version just discussed ("My name is Death, Heaven sign decreed"), and its second stanza mixes the first two lines of the first stanza and the first two lines of the third stanza from that version, but its chorus is identical to Vera Hall's, and its third stanza narrates Death's disabling of the body slightly differently from both Chandler's and Hall's versions:

> Let me tell you what old Death will do
> He'll lay his cold icy hands on you
> He'll stretch your limbs so you can't walk
> He'll lock your jaws so you can't talk
> He'll close your eyes so you can't see
> Oh come, he'll say, and go with me[26]

In the Piedmont of central Georgia, the black gospel quartet the Middle Georgia Singers was singing a chorus that clearly echoes Hall's: "Oh, Death / Oh, Death is awful / Oh, Death / Just spare me over another year." Their first stanza echoes Hall's ordering: "Fix your feet / lock your jaw / close your eyes"—and yet they are closer to Chandler's version by having Death speak in the first person ("*I'll* fix your feet") as opposed to Hall's third person. Their second stanza then echoes Chandler's most frightful stanza:

> Too late, too late, to all farewell
> My doom is fixed, I'm sent unto hell
> As long as the Father in heaven shall dwell
> My soul my soul is gonna burn in hell[27]

There are slight variations here ("My doom is fixed" versus Chandler's "Your soul is doomed," "the Father" versus "God," "My soul" versus "Your soul"), but the line order is identical and the stanza's stark theme is the same. The Middle Georgia Singers' song is the sole African American variation to include this stanza of Chandler's—a striking instance of how in an oral culture, knowledge, once packaged in memorable forms, can be transported over time and distance, persisting intact to reappear in individualized variations.

In these same years, back in the southwest Virginia/eastern Kentucky area where the song first appeared, a number of variants were heard in the late 1930s and early 1940s. In Floyd County in Kentucky's Cumberland Plateau, the opening stanza introduces a new line and tone:

> What is this that I can see
> Cold icy hands taking hold on me
> For death has come you all can see
> Hell gate is open wide for me

But the following stanza imitates Chandler's song (though with a varying last line), not the version that had earlier been documented in eastern Kentucky:

I'll lock your jaws till you can't talk
I'll bind your legs till you can't walk
I'll close your eyes so you can't see
I'll bring you unto me

The singer then cries out to Death, not God, to be spared:

Oh! Death. Oh! Death. Can't you spare me over for another year.[28]

The "I'll" (as in Chandler's song) instead of "You'll" heightens the sense of Death's power, as does God's absence from the drama.

In Wise County, Virginia, Laura Hunsucker was singing a version that is almost identical to Ruby Davidson's. It is only six stanzas as compared to Davidson's thirteen, but the six stanzas are in the same order as Davidson's first six, and the words display almost no differentiation—the lone exception being the second and third lines ("With icy hands taking hold on me / I am Death, none can excel"), which are almost identical to Chandler's. Wise County and Davidson's Jackson County, Kentucky, are some 125 miles apart, and the two singers' documentation is some fifteen years apart, but the almost-exact echoes are striking: just like Davidson's version, Hunsucker echoes exact stanzas of Chandler's song, but adds new stanzas establishing some social context and concludes each stanza with the refrain "spare me over till another year."[29] Also in Wise County, Polly Johnson was singing a version almost identical to Davidson's. Johnson's version was longer than Hunsucker's—it has ten of Davidson's stanzas, all in the same order—but, like Hunsucker's, is closer to Chandler on the occasional line ("To drop the flesh from off the frame / the earth, and worms, both have a claim").[30]

In the Cumberland Plateau of eastern Kentucky (the specific location is unclear), a version was heard that echoes those first heard in the area but with new features that are entirely its own. Its opening stanza has the "Hell gate is open wide for me" line. As the song continues, it echoes stanzas previously heard in the area, as well as the refrain:

You have fixed my feet till I can't walk . . .
Lord spare me over till another year . . .
There's so many people so blind and deaf
I know you are able to open their eyes . . .
You have made for me a home in heaven . . .

But entirely new stanzas appear, grafted on to the familiar refrain:

> You have healed the sick and raised the dead
> There is lambs in the desert a-cryin for bread
> Lord spare me over . . .
> Go feed my lambs, go feed my sheep
> When this comes to me it makes me mourn and weep
> Lord spare me over . . .
> Go feed my sheep and them take care
> Step out on the promises and never fear
> Lord spare me over . . .
> We see the faithful was Abraham
> If they ask you who sent you tell them the great I AM
> Lord spare me over[31]

This has the narrative effect of not only proclaiming God's power over death but of commissioning the now-rescued singer for a mission of preaching and proclamation. Indeed, attached to this version of the song, folklorist Jean Thomas heard a remarkable framing story. She was in a small church in a "remote section" of the mountains. After finishing a hymn, the church elder told this story:

> Come a preacher here on the first Sunday of May, twelve month past, and norrated this tale: "There was a man who lived on the edge of Morgan or Breathitt, I can't rightly ricollict which, but nohow he turned a deaf ear to the call of the Lord upon him to preach. He said he would not preach and by some cause his life were taken from him, so far as they could see. He lay there in this fix, cold as a rock for some time. He were laid out for dead. And after a long spell he were revived up with this song on his lips: 'You have fixed my feet til I can't walk / You have fixed my tongue til I can't talk . . .' Some folks call the piece *Oh Death*, and suit in the words 'Oh death, spare me over till another year.' But a body's right to beg of the Lord to spare 'em."[32]

As documented, the song is at three steps removed: Thomas heard it from a church elder, who heard it from a traveling preacher, who was telling a story about the song's original singer, a man who lived in Morgan or Breathitt (counties in Kentucky's Cumberland Plateau). The story about this man resembles the story of Chandler and the song's origins in some ways—the singer confronts Death/seems to die; the song emerges on the heels of this terrifying encounter—but there are also substantive differences. Though he became a preacher on the heels of his encounter with Death, Chandler was not shirking a call to preach when he disappeared into the woods with a drinking companion. And the song that follows, of course, is different. In itself, Chandler's song gives not the slightest hint that the overpowered mortal will be imbued with new life as a traveling preacher. But the framing story that Thomas documented does provide insight into the workings of an oral culture: telling and retelling, packaging knowledge in story and song so that it could be remembered and passed on.

The broad reach of this oral culture is suggested in documentation of this song in the Ozarks of northwest Arkansas in 1941. Arlie Freeman had learned the song "from singers near his home," and it had become a regular feature in his life. He and his wife sang it at what folklorist Vance Randolph called "Holy Roller" meetings—church services of one of the various Holiness-Pentecostal groups. Freeman's version—like those from Overton County, Sara Martin, and Miss Gaston—is almost identical to Chandler's. Freeman's song is Chandler's ten-stanza, four-line-stanza song, with only slight changes of words and phrases. The slight differences that do appear ("with icy hands taking hold of me"; "yes, I have come to get your soul"; "I'll dim your eyes so you can't see"; "And don't take me in this stage"; "They like you will have to go") match those of Overton County, Sara Martin, and Miss Gaston in differing from Chandler.[33] Clearly the lines of the slightly varying version that was documented in 1936–38 in southern Appalachia served as better packaging for the song's extended transmission—in this case, for a distance of over 550 miles. Were the singers that Freeman learned the song from traveling? If so, perhaps they traveled from southern Appalachia on major east–west railroad lines or automobile routes to the vicinity of Freeman's home (at least as of 1941) in Natural Dam. Or perhaps they learned it from an intermediary, someone undocumented in the wide space between southern Appalachia and the Ozarks. Or perhaps there was a chain of numerous intermediaries, as Thomas's anecdote suggests. It's impossible to uncover the exact networks of such oral transmission. What does come through clearly, though, is the powerful capacity of an oral culture to package and transmit knowledge over wide distances.

This is not to suggest, though, that the knowledge being transmitted orally was static. As the preceding evidence suggests, from an early date, people heard Chandler's song and made it their own. They borrowed pieces of it, punctuated it with a refrain, and crafted their own new stanzas or lines and worked them into it. Both the geographic sweep of oral transmission and the adaptability of oral forms come through in two documentations of the song from the 1950s, which again show how Chandler's song crossed the color line and was actively appropriated by African Americans. In a 1953 Miami recording, Anderson Johnson of Newport News on the Virginia coast echoed Chandler and the early Ruby Davidson version, even as he worked in his own lines and stanzas. Johnson's version also includes his own framing techniques— short narrative glimpses that complement portions of the song:

> *Well, it makes no difference what part of the world a man or woman are /*
> *when Death lays hands on you my friends, you'll think about dear old*
> *mother of yours / and when you arrive to mother's door she won't pass you*
> *by / she'll do all the good she can / can mother say no?*
> Well, the doctor driven up to my gate
> Believe my child you have waited too late
> Fever now is a hundred and two
> You have a narrow chance he'll ever pull through
>
> Please, Death
> Please, Death in the morning
> Please, Death
> Well, spare me a little longer, just another year
>
> *Well, just like a child will do / think about mother when you get in trouble /*
> *I heard the child say*
> Mother, mother won't you come now to my bed?
> Place a cold towel all over my head
> My head is warm, my feets is cold
> Death got a shackle all over my soul
>
> *Mother ran screamin' and crying / Oh Death, my child is young / haven't had*
> *any pleasure in life / spare him a little while longer / I heard Death saying*
> Mother, mother, the old and young, the rich and poor
> To the judgment they must go
> Says, all your silver and all your gold
> Nothing can satisfy but his soul
>
> *Mother ran away screamin' and crying / Death and the child stood alone /*
> *I heard the child sayin' to Death*
> Look a here, Death, at what you're doing to me
> You're fixing my eyes so I can't see
> Chewed my tongue where I can't talk

Fixed my feet when I can't walk
Foldin' my arms, you're leavin' me cold
Robbin' my body of my poor soul

*I heard Death sayin' to the child / I know your number / seen your days pass*
  *and gone / you had your chance*
You heard God's people out singin' and prayin'
You wouldn't hear, you walked away
You wouldn't give your hand, you wouldn't bend your knee
Now you've got to come and go with me[34]

Johnson's shifting speakers—himself as the outside observer and comment-
ing preacher, Death, the mother, the child, the doctor—create a different conversation than the other versions. But the cacophony of voices conveys the
same basic impression: that of confused helplessness in the face of death. The
mother's quickly changing presence accentuates this: she is summoned in,
pleads and begs with Death, and then disappears, leaving the child to face Death
alone. Similarly, Johnson's alteration of the refrain ("Death in the morning")
presents a disorienting paradox: the sun is rising and a new day is dawning, but
Death upsets this comforting natural rhythm with his unexpected, unwelcome appearance.

In 1959 on St. Simons Island on the Georgia coast, Bessie Jones sang a version
that clearly borrows from Johnson's version. It has essentially the same paradoxical chorus as his ("Oh, death in the morning / spare me over in another year")
and stanzas that evoke a pessimistic physician and a helpless mother:

Well Death walked up to the sinner's gate
Said, believe me I waited now a little too late
Your fever now one hundred and two
Have a narrow chance that you'll ever pull through . . .

Oh mother standing by the bed
Well a aching heart and a hung down head
And the doctor looked around very sad
Say, it's the worst old case I ever had . . .

Like Johnson, Jones has a stanza that echoes Ruby Davidson's version ("You
heard God's people sing and pray"), and like Davidson, the song features the
figure of the mother. But other stanzas of Jones's don't appear in Johnson's
but do echo Chandler's (and the early versions heard in eastern Kentucky/
southwest Virginia):

What is this I see?
Cold icy hands all over me
He said, I am Death no one can excel
I open the doors of death and hell ...

Well I'm gonna fix your feet so you cannot walk
I'll fix your tongue where you cannot talk
Close your eyes and you cannot see
You got to come and go with me ...

Well Death consider my age
And do not take me in this stage
Because all of my wealth is at your command
If you just move your cold icy hand[35]

Johnson (born in 1915, originally from the Virginia Piedmont) and Jones (born in 1902, originally from southwest Georgia) lived peripatetic early lives on the East Coast before settling, respectively, in Newport News and St. Simons. Unlike many of the other documented singers who were more stationary, their travels may have brought them to Chandler's song (or fragments of it, or variations on it), as opposed to the song being brought to them by traveling but undocumented singers. Either way, the geographic base of Johnson and Jones reveals the widest extensions of the song—from the Virginia coast to the Arkansas Ozarks (just under 1,200 miles) and from the Cumberland Plateau of Kentucky to St. Simons on the Georgia coast (just under 600 miles).

The later dates of the recordings of Johnson (1953) and Jones (1959) highlight a basic issue in the historical recovery of the workings of an oral culture: the date that the song was documented (either written down or audio-recorded) is only the date that a folklorist or some other observer captured the song, not the date when it was first learned or appropriated. Certainly the song was learned and appropriated before that date—but how much before? How long had each singer been singing it before its documentation? The accompanying notes of folklorists provide few clues. Folklorist Vance Randolph believed the song to be "recent" when he recorded it in 1941 in the Ozarks; perhaps it had recently reached that area. The ages of a few of the singers are suggestive: because they were young when they were recorded singing the song, the earliest possible date that they picked it up can be established. Sara Martin was fourteen when she was recorded in 1937, and Miss Gaston was "a young woman" when she was recorded in 1938. Sara Martin surely didn't learn the song until the 1930s, and Miss Gaston (depending on what exactly "young" means) probably didn't either. In the case of Bessie Jones, though, accompanying documentation muddies the water. Folklorist Alan Lomax recorded her singing a wide catalog of songs on his 1959 field-recording trip, and in 1961 he recorded an extensive narrative of her life. In obscurity, Jones had learned and carried a host of songs with her long before she met Lomax. It's probable that she was singing "Death in the Morning" in the 1930s and 1940s.

On this same field-recording trip, Lomax traveled back to Livingston, Alabama, where his father John had first recorded Vera Hall in 1939. Hall's 1959 recording of "Death Have Mercy" sheds light on these undocumented ellipses in an oral culture. The 1959 recording has striking echoes of the 1939 song, even as it omits lines from the earlier song and includes lines that did not appear in the earlier version:

Oh, Death have mercy
Oh, Death have mercy
Oh, Death
Just spare me over another year

Like a flower in my bloom
Make death cut me down so soon

What is this that I can't see
Cold icy hands all over me
Stretch my eyes and stretch my limbs
This is the way that death begins[36]

In this latter version, Hall doesn't sing the stanza that so closely echoed Chandler in the 1939 version ("He'll fix your feet . . ."). And yet she does sing the two opening lines of Chandler's song—lines that did not appear in the earlier version. The twenty-year distance between the two recordings shows that Hall carried the song with her simply in her memory, through singing it over and over again. Lacking the fixity of writing, the versions display alterations over time, even as they are clearly versions of the same core song. Hall's selective use of lines echoing Chandler's suggests that she stored song fragments in her memory and only worked them into the song when she wanted to. In 1939, "He'll fix your feet" was what she wanted to sing, and in 1959, "What is this" was her choice. It's very likely that before the first recording, she knew more of Chandler's song than the recording suggested, and that she carried that knowledge with her and chose to use a different part of it in the later recording. The documentation of these two versions emphasizes what is also the case, more broadly, with the documentation of Chandler's "Conversation with Death" and its echoes: the documentation is but a glimpse, episodic and incomplete, of the workings of a creative, far-flung oral culture.

Alan Lomax's 1959 field-recording trip overlapped with a final period of documentation of the song, in the early 1960s. This was the work of the folk revival, and the goal was to locate and record older singers and the songs they carried with them before it was too late. Berzilla Wallin of Madison County, North Carolina, was recorded singing the song in 1962, Dock Boggs of Wise County, Virginia, was recorded singing the song in 1963, and Sarah Ogan Gunning of eastern Kentucky was recorded singing the song in 1965. Also in 1965, folk revivalist John Cohen made his way to Madison County, North Carolina, where he tape-recorded Lloyd Chandler singing "Conversation with Death" on his front porch. In each case, folk revivalists were curious to learn the origins of the song, and the accounts they received provide a strong complement to the earlier documentation. They also show how, as with Vera Hall, the codification of knowledge into oral forms (in this case, song) is a powerful vehicle for perpetuating it—as long as the song continues to be sung over time.

Berzilla Wallin's version is almost identical to Chandler's, with slight alterations of a few words and the mere omission of one line. The remarkable similarity makes good sense: she was Lloyd Chandler's sister, and she said that she had learned the song from him.[37] Dock Boggs's version is closest to Ruby Davidson's (and to Laura Hunsucker's, which is almost identical to Davidson's). The chorus is a close echo ("O Death, O Death / Won't you spare me over till another year") and the eight stanzas of Boggs's song echo Davidson's thirteen stanzas, though in an altered pattern and with some of Davidson's stanzas missing: B1—D1, B2—D5, B3—D10, B4—D4, B5—D6, B6—D9, B7—D7, and B8—D8.[38] Boggs's version's closeness to Davidson's and Hunsucker's also makes good sense: Laura Hunsucker was Boggs's sister, and he said that he had learned the song in the 1930s from her husband, Lee. And yet some words and phrases in Boggs's song (my emphasis), differ from Davidson's version and where they do, they echo Chandler.

*Boggs:*

Well what is this that I *can't* see . . .
To drop the flesh off *of the frame*
*The earth and worm both have a claim* . . .

*Chandler:*

Oh what is this I cannot see . . .
To drop the flesh from off your frame
The earth and worm both have their claim . . .

*Davidson:*

What is this that I can see . . .
To drop the flesh off from the form
'Tis sad to you, 'tis an awful alarm . . .

Perhaps in the years after he first learned the song from his brother-in-law, Boggs heard other versions in the eastern Kentucky/southwest Virginia area, where so many were documented—versions that were more directly traceable to Chandler. The song he sang in 1963, then, would be drawing from different variations. Sarah Ogan Gunning's version, like Boggs's, closely echoes the Ruby Davidson/Laura Hunsucker version, though again, as with Boggs, it is a shortened version (in this case five stanzas) and with an altered order: G1—D1, G2—D7, G3—D8, G4—D6, G5—D3/5. Gunning's final stanza draws from two different stanzas in the Davidson version:

*Gunning:*

Death, oh Death, please let me see
If Christ has turned his back on me
God's children prayed, his preachers preach
The time of hope is out of reach[39]

*Davidson:*

Oh Death, please let me see
If Christ has turned his back on me
When you were called and asked to bow
You would not take heed, it's too late now

Now, Death, if someone would pray
Can't I just call and charges repay?
God's children prayed, His preachers preached
The time of hope is out of reach

Gunning, born in 1910, remembered hearing her mother sing the song. Because Gunning left her parents' house when she married at age fifteen, her mother must have been singing the song before 1925, but how much earlier is impossible to determine. It's also unclear how much earlier Ruby Davidson was singing the song before her nephew Homer heard her sing it when he (born in 1915) was a boy. Gunning's parents in Knox County, Kentucky (some forty miles from Davidson in Jackson County), were closer to Chandler's Madison County, and Knox County borders Bell County, where the earliest version was likely documented, around 1925. Whatever the exact lines of transmission were, Gunning's memory complements what was established in the beginning of this analysis: in its spread out from Madison County, the song's first movement was to jump the mountains and move into southwest Virginia/eastern Kentucky.[40]

The documented sites of the song's reach are only the documented sites— the full scope of the song's reach is impossible to determine. Perhaps it was sung in areas for which no documentation survives. Nonetheless, with this caveat, the documented sites are revealing about the social patterns of folk Christianity. As has already been emphasized, this social world was not determined by the color line. Whites and blacks appropriated and sang the song; it was neither an Anglo-American nor an African American song but became the cultural property of both whites and blacks. Though of Appalachian origin and strongly associated with Appalachia through the work of the folk revival, the song was not uniquely Appalachian but spread to different corners of the South. It came to appear in a variety of places: in small farming areas on the regional economic periphery, in coal-mining areas experiencing rapid industrialization, in cotton-producing areas at the heart of regional agriculture, and in coastal areas with close connections to long-distance trade. The song thus appeared in the "many Souths" that constituted the regional society of the New South.

The unifying factor in the song's social basis was neither race nor regional geography but class position. Where individual singers' names were recorded, a rough sketch of their biography can be assembled. A clear and definite pattern then emerges. What comes through collectively is a series of glimpses into the world of the poor of the New South. Lloyd Chandler was born into a small farming family in Madison County, North Carolina, in 1896. By 1910, though, the family's independence had declined—they were now tenants, as they would be again in 1920. As Chandler married and established his own household by 1930, he too labored as a tenant farmer, though he also brought in cash wages through periodic work at a sawmill. Ruby Davidson was born in 1905 in Kentucky, and was still a single woman living in her parents' household at the time of the 1930 census. Her parents were small farmers in the marginal area of the Cumberland Plateau, moving from one small tract to another in the years of her youth. In 1910 they were in Booneville in Owsley

County, in 1920 they were in Sturgeon in Jackson County, and in 1930 they were in Horse Lick, also in Jackson County. Sara Martin, born in 1923 in Alabama, was the youngest of the documented singers. Her parents had been small farmers, at least for a time—at the time of the 1920 census her father was paying the mortgage on a farm in the marginal area of the Cumberland Plateau. But by 1930, even that minimal security had fallen apart. Her father was now recorded as a farm renter, in a different part of the county. In the late 1930s, Martin's family was eligible to participate in a New Deal program for landless tenants and sharecroppers, a resettlement community called Skyline Farms. But by 1940, the family seems to have moved out of Skyline Farms. They were farm tenants again, and Sara's older sister was working at a hosiery mill.

Vera Hall's biography is outlined in chapter 1. Laura Hunsucker, born in 1891 in Virginia, was the daughter of a blacksmith who owned his own home. By 1910, though, her family had moved to a different part of the county, her father was renting a house, and her older brother was working in the coal mines. By 1920, she was married to a coal miner, a wage laborer who rented a house. In 1940, she and her husband were back in the Virginia county of her youth, and he was working for the WPA in road building. Polly Johnson, the oldest of the documented singers, was born in 1866. In 1900, she and her husband were tenant farmers in Wise County. In 1920, he was working as a wage laborer, and in 1930, she and her husband were living in their daughter's household. By 1940, she was a widow, and her son had found work with the WPA. Arlie Freeman was born in 1905 in Arkansas, to small farmers in the marginal Ozarks. Per the 1930 census, as a young man he had moved to a different part of the Ozarks, was boarding with a family, and was working as a laborer in a sawmill. Ten years later, he was boarding with another family and working as a day laborer.

Anderson Johnson was born in 1915 to a family of tenant farmers in the Virginia Piedmont. In 1920, his father was working as a wage laborer at a lumber plant, but by 1930, his parents had divorced. His father was then boarding with another family and working as a farm laborer, and his mother was working as a cook in a boardinghouse—though young Anderson, it seems, was no longer with them. He had begun a peripatetic life as a traveling preacher up and down the Atlantic coast. Bessie Jones was born in 1902 in Georgia and grew up in a tenant-farming family. By 1920, she was married to a tenant farmer in the newer agricultural frontier of southeast Georgia. After they separated, she worked in various sites in Florida in the late 1920s and early 1930s as a cook, laundress, and child nurse. By 1940, having remarried, she was settled on St. Simons Island on the Georgia coast, where her husband's family had roots. She worked as a domestic, he drove a truck for a hardware store, and they lived in a rented house. What comes through in all of these glimpses is a clear pattern: landlessness or marginal property owning, frequent mobility, and extractive manual labor for someone else's benefit.[41]

That these impoverished southerners (and many others whose names were not recorded) were participating in networks of oral transmission is clear from the preceding analysis of the spread of "Conversation with Death," yet how exactly these networks operated is difficult to discern. Preachers and singers carrying the song can be glimpsed in a few of the folklorists' accounts. The circa 1925 Kentucky account was heard either in Wolfe County or from a traveling preacher based in Wolfe County. Jean Thomas's anecdote portrays another traveling preacher—"come a preacher here"—who brought the song (and a framing story) to a church elder. In the Ozarks in 1941, Arlie Freeman learned the song from what were presumably traveling singers who passed near his home. Memories of kin and neighbors paint a clear portrait of Lloyd Chandler traveling out from his Madison County home by foot, train, and bus to preach and sing.

In the majority of cases, however, women and men who were not preachers or singers were bearers and carriers of the song. The participation of at least some of these men and women in regional labor flows is a likely mechanism through which the song spread. The case of Vera Hall is especially suggestive. As noted in chapter 1, Hall was born into a tenant-farming family in Sumter County, but her work as a domestic took her to Tuscaloosa. There, at age fifteen, she met and married Nels Riddle, who was then working in the coal mines—the southwesternmost edge of an extensive coal seam that stretched far up the Appalachians into West Virginia and Pennsylvania. After Riddle's death in a fight, Hall continued to live in Tuscaloosa, working as a domestic before returning, several years later, to the Sumter County seat of Livingston, where she remained for the rest of her life. Hall's years of married and widowed life in Tuscaloosa (1917–30) are the likely time when she encountered Chandler's song, a variant of it, or fragments of it. Coal-mining families moving from southwest Virginia/eastern Kentucky into the Tuscaloosa area seeking better prospects may have carried the song—or perhaps a chain of coal-mining families moving southwestward down the Appalachians. From the coal-mining world of Tuscaloosa, Hall then carried the song to the Black Belt, where she had returned to live with and care for her family. This hypothetical account would explain how the song moved from coal-mining

Appalachia to the cotton-producing Black Belt. It would also show the intimate connection between religious culture and the work life of the poor—in Hall's case, from tenant farming, to domestic service, to coal mining, and back again to domestic service. The mobile world of Southern labor and the oral transmission of religious content operated in a symbiotic relationship.

"Conversation with Death," its variants, and the other songs of death circulated throughout a distinct cultural milieu; in a close analysis of hymnals and gospel songbooks published by the leading regional denominations and gospel publishing houses, not a single instance of "Conversation with Death," its variants, or the other songs of death is to be found.[42] As religious culture that flourished outside the channels of the regional religious establishment, these songs of death carried a vision that was very much their own. This vision was generated out of the life experience of the poor; it emerged from the grassroots and was circulated and sustained through folk techniques involving hearing, codifying in memory, and repeated singing. And yet the vision was not entirely sui generis. Through these very same folk techniques, the poor of the New South were drawing on deep layers of tradition that stretched back to late medieval Europe. They were crafting a modernist version of the Dance of Death.

Emerging in the early fifteenth century in the wake of a crisis of religious authority opened up by the Great Schism, the Dance of Death presented a stark, macabre visual and textual spectacle. Massive mural paintings in churches, cemeteries, chapels, and cloisters depicted a jarring procession. Figures from all the varied ranks of the elaborate medieval hierarchy were walking slowly in this procession: from the pope, emperor, king, and knight, on down to the priest, peasant, child, and hermit. In front of each figure, a skeleton or decaying corpse was dancing wildly—a provocative juxtaposition to the slow, almost still members of the procession. Painted into the murals underneath this strange procession was lengthy text, articulating each individual figure's fearful, anxious conversation with Death (represented by the skeleton or decaying corpse). These dialogues featured pleas for life and begging for time, but Death's rejoinder was always the same: this was the time of death. The procession could not stop if it wanted to; every figure was moving inexorably and unwillingly to his or her irreversible demise. The Dance of Death thus also carried a potentially subversive social message. Even as the elaborate social hierarchy was represented, it was on a flat horizontal plane. Death was the great leveler, annulling social distinctions and claiming everyone, from pope to peasant, as helpless, isolated mortals.[43]

In the course of the fifteenth century, the Dance of Death appeared throughout Catholic Europe, in sites ranging from Paris's central Cemetery of the Holy Innocents to the small village church in Meslay-le-Grenet, from the Bern convent's cemetery church to the Chapel of St. Anthony in Reval (modern-day Tallinn, Estonia). Prints of images and the lengthy poetic text also circulated in book form, such as John Lydgate's *The Dance of Death* and Antoine Vérard's *La Danse Macabre*. After the fifteenth century, though, new versions of the carefully stylized Dance of Death ceased to appear. Hans Holbein the Younger drew on the tradition but also broke significantly from it in his 1538 *Les Simulachres and Histories Faces de la Mort*. Fragments of the Dance continued to appear on facades, chests, gates, and sheaths. The defining conventions of the Dance were carried on not in visual or textual art but rather in song, in a variety of European languages, in the form of written ballads, published broadsides, and folk songs.[44]

The two scholars who have explored this sizable world of song have uncovered remarkable connections. Henri Stegemeier traced the Dance of Death in a host of folk songs, in German, English, French, Czech, Slovak, and Dutch. Two songs in Stegemeier's vast collection appear outside Europe: a circa 1770 broadside published in Boston, *and* "Conversation with Death" as performed by Miss Gaston in 1938 in the Smoky Mountains![45] Likewise, Susan Barks traced the Dance of Death's imprint from sixteenth-century English broadsides to folk songs heard in early twentieth-century England—and in the early twentieth-century American South: Kentucky, North Carolina, Georgia, Louisiana, and Arkansas. One of the English folk singers, ninety-two-year-old Henry Burstow, was documented in 1908 singing a long ballad almost identical to a broadside published some two hundred years earlier. Burstow's folk performance added one concluding stanza, though—a critique of the valuations of an emergent capitalist economy: "The grave's the market place where all must meet / Both rich and poor, as well as small and great / If life were merchandise, that gold could buy / The rich would live—only the poor would die."[46] Writing in the late 1930s, Stegemeier noted that this stanza was "often found inscribed on tombstones in village churchyards in all parts of England."[47] A variation on Burstow's concluding couplet, "If salvation was a thing money could buy / then the rich would live and the poor would die," was heard (as noted in the introduction) by folklorists in the early twentieth-century South—in central Texas, north Alabama, and the North Carolina Piedmont. Both Stegemeier's and Barks's findings, then—that echoes of the late medieval Dance were still being heard in the early twentieth

FIGURE 12 *The Dance of Death*, ascribed to Bernt Notke, ca. 1463–93, in Chapel of St. Anthony of the Church of St. Nicholas, Tallinn, Estonia.

century—offer strong evidence of the durability and scope of tradition. The folk culture of the New South was participating in oral networks of transatlantic reach.

Lloyd Chandler, then, was drawing on the inherited cultural material of the Dance of Death when he crafted his own song of Death. (There is also strong, though not certain, evidence complementing this claim. The English folk-song collector Cecil Sharp recorded a Floyd or Lloyd Chandler—Sharp's handwriting is unclear—singing the traditional English ballads "Young Hunting" and "Matty Grove" in 1916, during his fieldwork in Madison County. More broadly, Madison County was a site where Sharp found a number of early modern folk songs being actively sung and thus sustained.)[48] Chandler's song, while very much his own artful composition, preserves the defining conventions of the Dance of Death, even as it gives them a modernist twist. First, Death is personified—a terrifying, unwelcome, formidable foe. Yet in Chandler's song, Death is felt, not depicted: its "icy hands" grab hold of the singer, but the song shows the hearer no skeletons or rotting corpses. Second, the basic drama is an anxious, fearful conversation. In the Dance of Death, this conversation appeared underneath the mural procession; in Chandler's song, lacking by definition a visual element, the conversation is the whole piece. Chandler's conversation, like those in the Dance of Death, narrates a give-and-take whose intensity rises as it proceeds. Death's dialogue partners increase their pleas, yet Death remains firm, insistent, and unmoved. Third, a basic isolation or alienation is powerfully portrayed. Though the procession of the Dance was social, the encounter with Death was not. Each member of

the procession had to confront Death individually, without anyone to help. Chandler's song heightens this alienation: no third party is even remotely present. The conversation involves one lonely mortal and Death, whose entire focus is on taking this lonely mortal's life. Both the Dance and Chandler's song exaggerate isolation by making it not only social but also religious. God is notably and remarkably absent from the encounter with Death. Note that the larger context is not Christian: in many of the Dances of Death, a preacher appears outside the scene, serving sometimes as an opening narrator. In Chandler's song, the mortal pleads for time, to see "if Christ has turned his back on me." But both the preacher and Christ are distant presences, unavailable for help in the encounter with Death. Fourth, Death is a tangible, physical, bodily event. The Dance starkly depicted the decay that was soon to overtake the procession by placing each member with a dancing double, a skeleton or corpse who showed them what they would soon be. Chandler's song doesn't feature the dancing double, but Death is physically felt, and Death narrates the decay that will soon consume the mortal: "I'll lock your jaw." Death is no spiritualized experience but the earthly, macabre demise of the finite body. Fifth, Death is the great leveler. In the Dance, this was depicted dramatically through the procession of the social hierarchy that is then subverted. Chandler's song doesn't display social hierarchy but instead has Death insisting that old, young, rich, and poor must all confront it, on their own, without any of their social attachments but simply as lonely mortals. Indeed, what seems like social vagueness in Chandler's song has a powerful effect: because the singer has no distinguishing social characteristics, he or she could be anyone—any mortal who must necessarily face the great and terrifying leveler.

It is this latter element that is perhaps most revealing of the song's modernism. "Conversation with Death" presents an isolated, solitary individual about whom the hearer knows nothing other than that the individual is mortal. The individual is alienated from all social networks that typically define identity: family, kin, community, geography, occupation. Nothing in the song identifies the singer's gender, class, or race. The singer is cut adrift, forced into an existential encounter with Death without any sure supports. Certainly the late medieval Dance conveyed isolation. Each member of the procession had to pair off to dance and dialogue with Death alone. At the same time, though, the dramatic depiction of the social hierarchy reminded viewers of an identity rooted in a seemingly stable, fixed social order. The hierarchy was exposed as fragile—it proceeded to an encounter with the great leveler Death—but its members retained their social identity in that encounter. "Conversation with Death" knows no social identity. Its lonely individual knows only the fearful encounter with Death. Likewise, though the late medieval Dance emphasized religious isolation (God is nowhere in the Dance; the preacher stands outside the procession at a distance), the context of its viewing necessarily reminded viewers of the framing power of the Church. It was viewed in churches, chapels, cloisters, and cemeteries named for characters in the biblical story. The Dance suggested God's distance, but the religious context of viewing surely suggested God's presence, or the role of the Church as presider and interpreter of the experience of death. "Conversation with Death" was sung in churches, and Lloyd Chandler and other preachers carried the song to new places. Thus, it was framed by an institutional Christian context. And yet, as the documentation reveals, the song was also sung outside churches, by many people other than preachers. Lacking the fixity of a mural painting, "Conversation with Death" (as well as other death songs) had wings. It could move outside "religious" sites and figures, and be sung in a variety of spaces by a variety of people. Surely in those moments, singers and hearers alike confronted a frightening possibility inherent in its tight, unrelenting dialogue: God seemed far, far away, and the community of Christians was nowhere in sight; Christ may very well have irreversibly turned away. No religious mediator was at hand. The solitary individual was left to face death in anguished isolation. Though emerging out of a very different milieu, this alienated, solitary individual resembled that of philosophical/literary modernism of the same era.

"Conversation with Death," then, drew on distant tradition to fuse the medieval and the modern in provocative ways. It wove the earthly, macabre late-medieval ethos together with a modernist sense of alienation. In this, its kinship to Blind Willie Johnson's "Jesus Make Up My Dying Bed" is instructive. Jesus is intimately close and present in "Jesus Make Up My Dying Bed," in sharp contrast to his notable absence in "Conversation with Death." "Conversation with Death" presents a terrified mortal who has failed to heed Christ's help and is now being consumed by Death; "Jesus Make Up My Dying Bed" knows no help but that of Jesus in the face of death's certain oblivion. And yet both are songs of death that articulate modernist alienation. Jesus in "Jesus Make Up My Dying Bed" is a rejected and isolated figure, distanced from kin and followers, hanging in misery at the moment of death. The singer's union with Jesus is a union in isolation. Like "Conversation with Death," the song features no intermediaries. It is only the singer, in first person, married to Jesus. No kin, friends, neighbors, or church community appear to minister or comfort at the moment of death. The lonely, isolated singer draws comfort solely from the persistent knowledge that Jesus was also lonely and isolated—and yet crossed over to conquer death. Clinging to Jesus, the dying individual insists on hope in the face of alienation and abandonment. No one else may be present even to care for the singer's dead body, but Jesus will make up the dying bed.

The creative fusion—traditional material, modernist cast—at play in songs like "Conversation with Death" and "Jesus Make Up My Dying Bed" had no parallel in the dominant religious culture. More broadly, the sensibility articulated in folk songs of death was at odds with the religious vision of the dominant culture. This is readily apparent from a careful survey of songs commonly appearing in hymnals published by the leading regional denominations and in gospel songbooks published by small-scale regional companies. The songs in these hymnals and songbooks convey their own very distinct vision of death.

Yet examining the dominant religious culture's songs of death immediately reveals a notable absence. What appear on page after page are not songs of death per se but songs about life *after* death. "There's a land that is fairer than day / And by faith we can see it afar / For the Father waits over the way / To prepare us a dwelling place there," "Sweet By and By" begins, and then sings hopefully in its chorus, "In the sweet by and by / We shall meet on that beautiful shore." "O they tell me of a home far beyond the skies," "The Unclouded Day" opens expectantly, "O they tell me of a home far away / O they tell me of a home where no storm-clouds rise / O they tell me of an unclouded day." "Shall we gather at the river," "Beautiful River" invites, "where bright angel feet have trod / With its crystal tide forever / Flowing by the throne of God?" and then answers joyfully in its chorus, "Yes, we'll gather at the river / The beautiful, beautiful river / Gather with the saints at the river / That flows by the throne of God." "When our work here is done / And our life-crown is won / And our troubles and trials are over," the last stanza of "Where We'll Never Grow Old" imagines, "All our sorrow will end / And our voices will blend / With the loved ones who've gone before." "Some day my earthly house will fall," "Saved by Grace" expects, "I cannot tell how soon 'twill be," and yet the singer has no fear: "But this I know—my All in All / Has now a place in Heaven for me / And I shall see Him face to face / And tell the story—saved by grace." In "Higher Ground," the singer is eager for death's release: "My heart has no desire to stay / Where doubts arise and fears dismay," one stanza begins. The next stanza opens with "I want to live above the world / Tho' Satan's darts at me are hurled," and the following stanza continues, "I want to scale the utmost height / And catch a gleam of glory bright."

In "The Home over There," the expectancy has intensified. "I'll soon be at home over there," the final stanza foresees, "For the end of my journey I see / Many dear to my heart, over there / Are watching and waiting for me." The chorus amplifies the message: "Over there, over there, I'll soon be at home over there / Over there, over there, over there / I'll soon be at home over there." "Safe in the Arms of Jesus" goes further, envisioning a peaceful postmortem rest as if it were already manifest: "Safe in the arms of Jesus, safe on His gentle breast / There by His love overshadowed, sweetly my soul shall rest / Hark! Tis the voice of angels, borne in a song to me / Over the fields of glory, over the jasper sea." "When We All Get to Heaven" echoes this vision of the impending future: "Onward to the prize before us! / Soon His beauty we'll behold / Soon the pearly gates will open / We shall tread the streets of gold / When we all get to heaven / What a day of rejoicing that will be!" "Dwelling in Beulah Land" likewise narrates the triumph over death from the incorruptible home that the singer has already reached: "Let the stormy breezes blow, their cry cannot alarm me / I am safely sheltered here, protected by God's hand / Here the sun is always shining, here there's naught can harm me / I am safe forever in Beulah Land." The chorus sings jubilantly, "I'm living on the mountain, underneath a cloudless sky / I'm drinking at the fountain that never shall run dry / O yes! I'm feasting on the manna from a bountiful supply / For I am dwelling in Beulah Land."[49]

Life *after* death is imagined in these songs in sharp and striking contrast to life before death. Before death one faces troubles and trials, doubts and fears, storms caused by Satan's assaults. But life after death holds peace and rest, safety and joy, beautiful vistas and fair skies that no cloud darkens. Indeed, the predominant image of life after death in these songs is of a glorious family reunion—of meeting again, gathering again, singing together again, rejoicing together again, feasting together again, telling the story of salvation again. And the predominant metaphors are distinctly feminized: sweetness, fairness, beauty, brightness, beholding Jesus's beauty, resting safely on Jesus's gentle breast. All of these lyrical themes bring out the core message of the songs: to die is to be delivered into one's true home. Like the idealized home of domesticity, the longed-for heavenly home is a space of safety and refuge, suffused by gentle femininity, a place of genuine belonging and fellowship. Some of the songs say explicitly what is implicit in all: death is a joyful release, the beginning of a glorious homecoming. One later song rolled all these metaphors into a succinct question with a ready answer: "Why should we weep when the weary ones rest / In the bosom of Jesus supreme / In the mansions of glory prepared for the blest? / For death is no more than a dream," as its chorus repeated triumphantly, "Only a dream, only a dream / Of glory beyond the dark stream / How peaceful the slumber, how happy the waking / For death is only a dream."[50]

The vision of these songs of life after death belonged to an epochal shift in Western culture. In his magisterial *The Hour of Our Death*, Philippe Aries argued that in the eighteenth and nineteenth centuries, the medieval terror of death was being supplanted by a new conception of death as a radical break— but a positive one. "Death," he argued, "now ceased to be sad. It was exalted as a moment to be desired." For death was newly imagined as deliverance out of limitation and finitude. In this ascendant vision, "the next world becomes the scene of the reunion of those whom death has separated but who have never accepted this separation: a re-creation of the affections of earth, purged of their dross, assured of eternity."[51] In this shift, domesticity as a cultural value was mythologized into a clear vision of life's ultimate telos. By imagining a postmortem heaven as home, the idealized Christian home was imbued with sacred status: it is a foretaste and intimation of eternal life. Unlike the fragile, finite home of this world, though, the reconstituted home of the world after death is delivered from all those antagonistic forces that could destroy it. It is reconstituted for eternity.

Such a vision offered powerful sanction for the evangelical ethos—for the idealized Christian homes that middle-class evangelicals were seeking to craft. What they were crafting, it said, was not a finite good but rather the one thing that would evade death. It fortified this cultural project by imagining life after death as the Christian home writ large for all time. And yet there was a central paradox here. If death is release to one's true home, then there is a strong *otherworldly* impulse at work. Death is not a formidable foe or an awful terror but a welcome liberator from a world of troubles and trials to an impregnable world of peace and rest. The Christian has no doubt that death means joyful triumph and blissful deliverance; personal immortality is an unquestioned premise. With the assurance of a life after death of perpetual, unshakable domesticity, life before death seems inadequate by comparison. The fragile, finite goods of this life cannot satisfy—and so, in song after song, religious longing centers on a world other than this.

The folk songs of death present a sharp and striking contrast. Death is a formidable foe, an unwelcome visitor whose appearance terrifies. For death is a great power, not only personified but able to snatch life away and snuff it out. In the encounter with Death, the singers appear as lowly, humble, defenseless creatures who must beg and plead with Death (or, in some songs, who must insist that God/Jesus will rescue them from Death's awful power). Death's power is most evident in its destruction of the body, narrated in many songs in macabre detail. Death is thus a deeply tangible experience. The soul is the life force that animates the body; Death simultaneously claims the soul as it destroys the body. There is no release of an immortal soul from a limiting body (as the dualism of the dominant culture's songs imagine). Indeed, in so many of the songs, there is no release at all. Death triumphantly and irrevocably claims the person. When hope does appear, infrequently, it is hope that God/Jesus will deliver the helpless mortal from Death's power. In "Jesus Make Up My Dying Bed," this hope clings to a Jesus who has already suffered death's alienating abandonment. "Conversation with Death," by contrast, envisions the frightful possibility that the time for Christ's help has already passed.

No folk song of death sketches a portrait of life after death, or centers longings in that afterlife. The songs dwell, by contrast, on this life in this world—a life that they don't want to lose. They make anxious pleas for it, and they insist that to encounter death is to face the anguished loss of something good. Indeed, in the encounter with Death, the songs portray a profound and unsettling alienation. The lonely mortal is cut adrift from family, kin, neighbors, religious community—from those networks that sustain life and locate identity. Dying is severance from these, not reuniting with them in a perfected eternal condition. The folk songs thus display a strong *this-worldly* orientation. Death means loss and destruction. It is fearsome, terrifying, an unwelcome yet inescapable foe. The encounter with Death reveals humans in their most basic, stripped-down identity; as lowly, lonely mortals. Through stark negation, Death's appearance highlights the good things of this life in this world: finite but fragile goods, such as speaking, seeing, walking, enjoying the fellowship of others, and building networks of human community.

The catalog of folk songs of death thus presents a vision very much at odds with that of the dominant religious culture. As the dominant culture sacralized the Christian home even while it looked to a heavenly home for satisfaction of religious longings, so too did the folk culture contain a basic paradox: in seeming to dwell morbidly on the terror of death, folk Christians exaggerated the goodness and value of *this* life in *this* world—especially in the fragile, finite body. But the cultural distance at play here makes sense in the context of what the dominant religious culture was saying about the lives of the poor.

Chapter 1 documented the routine distancing and denigration that the poor of the New South faced, and how this distancing and denigration were both imagined and fortified by the ascendant evangelical culture. Two classic sermons from the late nineteenth and early twentieth centuries articulated the logic of this evangelical culture to its dark extreme. Neither sermon was a Southern cultural production, and yet in tracing the full extensions of evangelical tropes, they provide crisp, clear insight into dynamics that were powerful but rarely elaborated in raw prose. Russell Conwell's "Acres of Diamonds" (1915) patched over the nation's wide disparities of wealth with an ebullient optimism. "There is not a poor person in the United States who was not made poor by his own shortcomings," Conwell proclaimed. Seeking to help the poor, then, was not only useless but actually in defiance of God's clear judgment on the moral character of the poor. "To sympathize with a man whom God has punished for his sins," Conwell insisted, "thus to help him when God would still continue a just punishment, is to do wrong." In their very poverty, the poor were suffering God's punishment, but no sentimentalist should intrude—it was their own fault.

A generation earlier, Henry Ward Beecher's "Individual Responsibility" (1870) expressed the ascendant spirit of the Gilded Age, the dramatic shift in American Protestantism from sweeping postmillennial reform to the glorification of individual wealth accumulation. Everyone possessed the crucial means for living, Beecher argued: "Men are equipped with all necessary faculties for their guidance, both in the physical and moral world, and they are practically held responsible, in consequence, for the right use of their faculties." The poor, then, deserved not charity or sympathy but condemnation. "The least valuable thing in this world is life, frequently," Beecher argued. "If you could only make a good selection of men, there would be nothing so good as killing, in this world." But mass killing, historically, was rarely an example of eugenics: "The trouble is that promiscuous killing generally goes from the bad toward the good." Beecher closed by lamenting the presence of the still-living poor. "The earth," he insisted, "is burdened with worthless population."[52]

The ascendant evangelical culture of the New South rarely articulated itself with such succinct logic, but it didn't have to: through a variety of ways, many not even verbal, it sent powerful messages to the poor. Their own poverty was a badge of their moral failure, a tangible display of God's just punishment. Having made so little of their lives, the poor could be reckoned as literally "worthless." It would have been better if they had never been born.

The well-preserved stories of Lloyd Chandler before his encounter with Death make sense within this context of utter devaluation. Chandler's acts of theatrical, egregious violence left a haunting, disturbing impression on his neighbors. In some of the acts, he seemed to be trying to insist on his self-worth through violence: lifting the feed sack with his clenched teeth, milking the mare. These were displays of brute strength to awe and impress, but there was also a wild, dangerous element. The acts contained the possibility of severe self-inflicted injury, perhaps even death in the story of the mare. Even as violence might display self-worth, self-destruction was close at hand, heightening the puzzled fear of onlookers. His destruction of the yellow jacket nest was especially paradoxical. It was simply nihilistic destruction: nothing was produced by this violent act except to display raw strength—and the fearlessness with which Chandler disregarded the value of his own life. When he and a drinking companion disappeared into the woods with their hefty supply of moonshine, it seemed as if he might finally realize the possibility inherent in his previous acts of violence and destroy himself. Two weeks into this bender, Chandler seemed to have reached the point that he'd threatened to. He lay shivering and alone and began to feel himself dying. It was at this moment, at the end of a nihilistic pattern of violence that had almost played out, that Chandler had his terrifying encounter with Death.

This origin story as a frame deepens the meaning of "Conversation with Death" and provides insight into the countercultural messages at work in the various folk songs of death. The story contains a series of radical reversals. Chandler, the wild man whose displays of raw power sought to inspire fearful respect in others, was here overpowered and terrified by Death. He is transformed from the violent agent of his own destruction to a lowly, fearful mortal. The dark nihilism embedded in his acts of violence is here upended by a pleading insistence on the goodness and value of life. Having flirted with death and finally sought his own demise, Chandler is shocked into a passionate longing for life. The life that he had denigrated to the point of willfully destroying he is now terrorized into seeing as a fragile, finite good, to be honored and cared for. It matters—it is weighted with ultimate significance.

With "Conversation with Death" as the pinnacle of the genre, the folk songs of death crafted in the New South sought to terrify their hearers into a profound and abiding appreciation of life. They needed to do this because the dominant religious culture of the New South sent powerful messages that told the poor that their lives did not essentially matter. They clearly displayed none of the fruits of respectability—they were dispensable and worthless. In the face of this culture of denigration, the folk songs articulated an alienating, leveling vision. They isolated every human being from all markers of social identity and depicted each as a lowly, lonely mortal, cut adrift from kin and community to face death in anguished solitude. Everyone met death on the same terms, "the old, the young, the rich, the poor," and despite the pleading attempts to buy off death, property was irrelevant: "no wealth, no silver nor gold" would appease insistent, uncompromising Death. As a terrifying, unwelcome foe, Death cast this life in stark relief. Unpredictable, threatening to appear without warning, Death's closeness heightened the meaning of each moment in this finite life. Its macabre conquest of the body highlighted the goodness of the material—precisely what, in the lives of the poor, revealed poverty more than anything else. Its destruction of life exaggerated the value of life, of *this* life in *this* world.

## CHAPTER THREE

# Tales of Conversion and Call

For Florence Cheek, a white woman in the Traphill community at the edge of the North Carolina Blue Ridge, the decisive moment came in a tobacco barn in the mid-1930s. Built of logs, daubed with red clay, and utterly dark inside, the barn resembled thousands of such buildings in the tobacco-growing areas of the South. For her, though, this particular barn at this specific time had become a place of holy retreat. She was "down . . . down on that floor, dirt floor, beside that old rock furnace," in a posture of humility and lowliness. She was praying for an epiphany—for a manifestation of God in her own time and place.

Suddenly the scene was transformed. The barn "just disappeared," it seemed, because the once-dark place was filled with light. The mundane became mysterious. "Then that place was just so gold," and Cheek was overcome by the stunning, unexpected brightness. Such a dramatic shift should surely have hurt her eyes, she knew, but instead she was caught up in a more sweeping transformation. "That hit my body, something did, and that light, it wasn't, it didn't hurt my eyes at all. It just come right to me, and it come to me just like that there, and it just went all over me, and from that, I just, I just felt different. I didn't even . . . I just . . ." She struggled to fully articulate what had happened to her, and recounting the experience some forty years later, her voice trailed off into the ineffable.[1]

For an African American man, a Georgia native living in central Tennessee in the late 1920s, the crisis came around 1890, when he was in his early twenties. He had fooled around and not taken life seriously when a strange sickness left him immobilized in bed. Looking up at the ceiling, he suddenly saw a heavenly hand reach out and hit him in the face, and a thunderous voice said, "I am a doctor." Shocked, he ruminated on the voice for a long time. But when he got better, he returned to his old ways. Several years later he was struck by sickness again, and this time he became so ill that he could not move his hands or feet, having to depend on others to move him into different positions on his sickbed. Suddenly, lying on his back and feeling sicker and weaker than he ever had, the heavenly hand appeared again. It slapped him in the face, and he heard the same thunderous voice say, "If you are sick, behold, I am a doctor!" At once the man regained his strength, rose from his bed and dressed, and walked out determined to obey the voice.

FIGURE 13 Florence Cheek (Blue Ridge Parkway Folklife Project Collection [AFC 1982/009], Archive of Folk Culture, American Folklife Center, Library of Congress).

But his saga was not over. One night around midnight, while his wife and daughter lay sleeping, he saw "heaven spread out before me. It was so bright up there that I couldn't look at it." The mysterious hand appeared again, and this time it completely overpowered him. "It was like lightning; it came so quick I was killed dead." All of a sudden "I was standing on the brink of hell. I was in two bodies: there was a little William and the old William. Little William stood looking down on old William, my earthly body." Terrified at the awful sight of his "old body lying at hell's dark door," he pleaded with God for rescue. Suddenly he felt himself turned to the east and saw before him a "little white path." A heavenly voice spoke to him gently now, urging him to walk along the path to deliverance, promising him that divine presence would be with him to guide and protect him. As he started on the path, he heard angels singing, "Canaan, Fair and Happy Land." It was "the prettiest song" he had ever heard, and he knew that his route was now sure and certain. Rescued and reconciled with his old body, he "came back" to himself "as the clock struck one. I was shouting and crying all night; I was so glad."[2]

Susanna Springer, an African American woman in New Orleans, heard the decisive word of revelation in the privy in her backyard, in the early twentieth century. She was used to praying—she'd "prayed and prayed"—and yet she didn't truly know how to pray. She had even seen visions—numerous visions, "vision on top of vision"—and yet something in her resisted. She just "wouldn't believe." Now, in that place of literal self-emptying, she was praying for a transformation, for a special manifestation of God to her. Suddenly she heard the voice of God, beckoning her: "I plant my feet in the sea, follow after me." This time her resistance began to come undone. She sprang out of the privy and took off running, and the word chased her.

Then, mysteriously, she found herself lying down, and a man "all dressed in white" came to her. Was he a messenger of God? Or a physician? Or a mortician? He stretched her out on a table and clipped her breath. Then he did it again, and then a third time. This was surely a strange surgery, for after the third time, Springer got up from the table and found herself traveling to a church. It was a mysterious scene, not an ordinary church. In front of the church door was a weeping willow, and beside it was a "four-cornered garden." Three people were kneeling to pray in the corners, and seeing this, Springer's resistance ended. She "had to pray, to send up a prayer," and so she joined them. She completed the outline of corners, and in this place of new life and growth—so different from the privy in which she had started praying—she found genuine faith.[3]

Richard Young, a white man in Franklin County in the Virginia Blue Ridge, was working in the coal mines in West Virginia in the 1930s when his decisive moment came. He was too sick one morning to work. His brothers wanted to stay and care for him, but he urged them to go on anyway. He was lying in bed when all of a sudden a mystical man appeared in the room: "He was just as white, as white as snow. And he walked right up over me, astride my legs, and looked right down in my face. And his hair was as white as lamb's wool, flowing out over his shoulders. And he had a white cloth over his head. And his eyes was just flashing like fire. And he was white, he was so white, his garments were so white." Was this Jesus? An angel? Something dangerous? Young lay there motionless, struck with awe and terror.

Then he felt a dreadful sensation. His feet began to get numb, and he realized that he was beginning to die. But death—like the mystical man hovering over him—was no abstraction. It was tangible, an awful force that "crept on up, crept on up" from his feet. As death began to slowly claim him, the mystical man kept looking him in the face. "His eyes was revolving, just like fire in his eyes. I couldn't get my eyes away. I wanted to turn my head but I couldn't.

I had to look right at him." But was the man in concert with death? Why didn't he stop it? "Death come on up," and Young knew that when it reached his heart, he would surely die. But somehow it skipped his heart. The terror did not abate, however. "It passed on up to my eyes. My eyes, they felt like they was full of sand, and I was about to close them." Death was claiming him, and he knew his end was near.

Just then, though, the mystical man performed a violent but lifesaving surgery: "He reached right under there and he got a spear out. It flashed like lightning. A little dagger about that long. And it was gold, and it just flashed like lightning. He come down on me with it. I didn't know nothing then for a long time." This mysterious dagger proved to be the man's deliverance from the death that seemed sure to claim him. He came to, and though he was still in the same room in which he'd first lain down, he was now lying on a little bench on the other side of the room. A voice spoke to him and said, "Arise now and shine, for the light has come, and the glory of the Lord is risen in you." Death and sickness had left him, and he got up and walked out of the house—only to see a dramatically transformed panorama. "It was a dark and dreary morning when I went in my room, but when I come out, everything looked new, everything was summertime, and the trees was green all around. The little birds was sitting out in the ends of the twigs of the trees, chirping just like they were offering thanks to God. I ain't never seen a morning so bright."[4]

Vivid symbolism, dramatic change, awful isolation, expansive reconciliation—these themes and a number of others characterize these four experiences, from people who lived in different corners of the region and almost surely never met one another. Yet what we have here is not experience per se but experience articulated, codified, and passed on in a stylized oral form: the conversion narrative, or testimony. Folklorist Zora Neale Hurston recalled the telling of such narratives in the early 1900s in the rural community of black day laborers and domestics where she grew up, in the center of the Florida peninsula: "The first thing was to hear their testimony or Christian experience, and thus the congregation could judge whether they had really 'got religion' or whether they were faking and needed to be sent back to 'lick de calf over' again. It was exciting to hear them tell their 'visions.' "[5] In the mountains of western North Carolina in those same years, home missionary R. P. Smith heard similar stories from white mountaineers. To his admonitions that initiates to church membership need not recount dramatic stories of conversion, he encountered opposition: "They objected because the applicants had not given sufficient evidence of real conversion. They had not mourned, and wept, and agonized in prayer over their sins. Without that experience there was no heartfelt religion."[6]

As a stylized oral form, the conversion narrative necessarily existed through telling and retelling. It was written down or recorded not by its own practitioners but by outside observers, people who moved in a culture of literacy and sought, for a variety of reasons, to document the presence of this oral form. From the New South era, the most extensive documentation of stories like these comes from African American communities in disparate parts of the region. Hurston collected some of these stories during her fieldwork along the Gulf Coast of Florida, Alabama, and Louisiana in the late 1920s, and published three in the 1934 *Negro: An Anthology*. Fisk graduate student Andrew Watson gathered a large body of stories in central Tennessee in the late 1920s. Rich and extensive as Watson's collection was, however, the twenty-eight stories did not reach a wide audience until over a generation later, when they were published in 1969 as *God Struck Me Dead: Voices of Ex-Slaves*.

Northern-born schoolteacher Rossa Cooley, who taught on St. Helena Island, South Carolina, in the first three decades of the twentieth century, recalled rituals that mirrored the basic frame of the stories collected by Hurston and Watson. She remembered that "in our community the 'Seeker' must 'see visions and dream dreams' which are interpreted to him by a 'Spiritual Father' or a 'Spiritual Mother,' who is chosen after having been seen in a dream. . . . I have known young people to go into the woods and stay on their knees for hours."[7] In the mid-1930s, Tuskegee graduate student Nathaniel Colley found such stories to be a ritualized feature in the black community of Gee's Bend in the Alabama Black Belt. "To the outsider," Colley wrote, "one of the most interesting features of the church services in Gee's Bend is the telling of conversion experiences. These stories, which are a very definite part of the religious experiences of these people, are very fascinating. Of twenty-one people interviewed by the writer, each one expressed the conviction that if a person is really converted he will have some experience which he will be anxious to tell publicly."[8] Educator Carter Woodson found such experiences to be so prevalent that, writing in his 1930 study *The Rural Negro*, he summarized them into an emblematic occurrence:

> While in a state of prayer for deliverance from sin, he [the initiate] falls into a trance, prostrate like a man in dying condition. . . . He gradually awakens from his stupor, usually saying with a peculiarly primitive intonation: "Thank God! Thank God! Thank God I was born to die! He

snatched me like a brand from eternal burning and saved me from hell's dark door." . . . All the candidate needs to do is to convince the brethren that he had some such experience as they themselves had—that he saw a light, heard a voice, had a vision, outwitted the devil, or received a visit from Jesus. With such a straight story they find ready acceptance in the church.[9]

Woodson's cultured condescension is evident, of a piece with Colley's sense of himself as an outsider viewing exotic customs or Watson's characterization of the stories he gathered as belonging to "Negro primitive religious services." The perception of significant difference is evidence for the distance between the world of formal education and that of folk creativity, but what is important now is that these observers documented a folk practice in time and place.

The stories and story summaries traverse the region, from central Florida, to the Sea Islands, to the Gulf Coast, to the Alabama Black Belt, to central Tennessee. They are a cultural production of regional scope, not unique to a certain subregion. The stories were observed and recorded (if not immediately published) in the period from approximately 1895 to about 1940 (from the earliest of Hurston's personal memories to the latest date of Colley's field research). They are a New South cultural production. This is a point worth emphasizing because Watson's rich and extensive collection of stories has been used as a window into slave religion in the antebellum era.[10] The subtitle of the 1969 publication of the stories collected by Watson ("voices of ex-slaves") fosters this association, yet Watson's fieldwork was done in the years 1927–29, some sixty-five years removed from the twilight of the antebellum period. Some of Watson's interviewees were very elderly and had indeed been born in slavery, but the stories Watson collected were a basic part, in his own framework, of contemporary (1920s) "Negro primitive religious services," not antebellum ones. Internal evidence in Watson's stories also suggests their New South context: Fisk University, train tickets, a fertilizer plant, women's work as domestics.

The extensive documentation of such stories from African American communities can suggest (along the line of inquiry that imagines these as manifestations of slave religion) that this New South cultural production was uniquely African American, a pillar of a distinct African American Christianity rather than a folk Christianity born of interracial exchange. Though the evidence is not as extensive as one would hope—nothing like the treasure trove that Watson collected—folklorists, missionaries, and sociologists documented these types of stories and their corresponding rituals among predominantly white communities as well. Teacher-minister John C. Campbell lived in the southern Appalachians for twenty-five years (1895–1920), traveling extensively throughout the region in the 1910s. Writing around 1920, he observed that "visions, dreams, and omens have a part in the life of the people," and that for white mountaineers, "usually the 'conversions' have, or are supposed to have, some impressive preliminary experiences, and when these do not occur it is sometimes a matter of deep anxiety to the waiting one."[11] In the Appalachian foothills of north Alabama, in a predominantly white community, an older man told sociologists Paul Terry and Verner Sims of a regular practice in his boyhood, in the 1880s or 1890s. "Those were the days of real religion," he said. "Folks would go off into the woods to pray late in the afternoons, the men going off to one side and the women to the other. Along about dusk after they had got religion they'd come out of the trees shouting so loud the woods would ring. You couldn't hear your ears."[12] Clearly, by the mid-1930s, when the older man was reminiscing, the practice no longer existed. Perhaps the newly established, seminary-educated minister had put an end to it.

In the late 1930s, three folklorists working independently along the rugged eastern Kentucky/southwestern Virginia border recorded stories in their full form, like those recorded by Hurston and Watson. In 1937, John Lomax recorded a story as told to him by an eastern Kentucky mountain woman. In 1938, Mary Elizabeth Barnicle recorded three stories told during church services in eastern Kentucky. In 1939, Herbert Halpert recorded stories as told to him by two men, one in eastern Kentucky and one in southwestern Virginia. The scope of these, and of the descriptions from both Campbell and Terry and Sims, is more contained than the documentation from African Americans: it is limited to a broad swath of Appalachia. One wishes for much more in the form of sound recordings or written transcriptions, both in scope and in volume, but these gleanings and glimpses do suggest the presence of such stories and their attendant rituals among whites in the New South era. The stories were not unique to Appalachia nor to African Americans but part of a cultural milieu that encompassed blacks and whites.

Consider excerpts from the previously quoted narrative of Richard Young, a white man in the Virginia Blue Ridge, as juxtaposed with excerpts from the story of an African American woman recorded in *God Struck Me Dead*:

Long about nine o'clock, I laid down across the bed. And being laying there, a man appeared over me. He was just as white, as white as snow. . . . And I felt myself getting numb down in my feet, and death crept on up, crept on up. I was just sure I was dying. . . . It passed on up to my eyes. My eyes, they felt like they was full of sand, and I was about to close them. . . . When the Lord brought me to, I was laying on a little bench. . . . And I hear a voice . . . and it spoke like this: "Arise now and shine." . . . When I come out, everything looked new, everything was summertime, and the trees was green all around. . . . I ain't never seen a morning so bright.

At eleven o'clock on Wednesday . . . God took me off. I experienced death, the way I'm going to die. I was flying in the air. He throwed me down stiff. I was standing up ironing one morning, and I felt death creeping up on my toes, then to my knees, and finally I was waist-deep in death. Then I lost my sight, and God throwed me on the bed. . . . My fingers were like candlesticks. The next morning everything was white. My hands were like snow. They just shined. They looked like the sun was on them. . . . Then he led me into the green pastures. I never heard such preaching in my life.

A feel for what existed but was lost because it was not recorded or transcribed comes through in the story of Lloyd Chandler's conversion. Chandler, it will be recalled, had his decisive experience in 1916, and in the decades that followed, he told his story to legions of people, accompanying it with his signature song. But it was only in the early 2000s, a generation after Chandler's death and a world removed from Chandler's own context, that the story was written down and published by folklorist Carl Lindahl. Lindahl heard the story and felt its power from many of the thirty or so people he talked to in Chandler's Madison County. The story and its power had existed up to that point only in oral form—known and valued by being told and retold. Though it acquired a place in written scholarship only relatively recently, its operative place was in a definitively earlier context (and as people descended from that context remembered it). Put differently, the story is a cultural production of New South vintage, though it was written down long after the unmaking of the New South. Despite its recent date of publication, it belongs to that older world.[13]

In a similar vein, folklorists and oral historians in the 1970s—and into the 1980s, 1990s, and early 2000s—encountered stories among blacks and whites in the Virginia Blue Ridge, western North Carolina, the Mississippi Delta, the Texas Blackland Prairie, the Florida panhandle, and the South Carolina Sea Islands. They were working independently of one another and, in many cases, not initially looking for these stories. The stories they recorded for posterity constitute a rich document that complements the early material from the 1920s and 1930s. The wide gap of intervening time may seem to be too much for meaningful cultural continuity, but three things are important to note. First, all the people recounting stories in the latter part of the twentieth century were elderly; their lives had been formatively shaped by the society of the New South. Second, with one exception, the experiences they recounted had all happened at a much earlier time—all in the period from about 1900 to around 1945. Third, the stories recounted had solidified long before they were narrated to a recording folklorist.

Just how solidified the stories had become—allowing them to survive intact over significant stretches of time through regular retelling—comes through in field notes about the narrative of Edgar Cassell, an eighty-year-old white man in Meadows of Dan, Virginia, who told his story to folklorist Patrick Mullen in 1978: "One of the informants, Edgar Cassell, when re-visited nearly a year after his story was taped, repeated the story almost word-for-word, nuance for nuance, for a different fieldworker." Indeed, the liner notes of the *Children of the Heav'nly King* album noted that "when permission was being sought to use these recordings on the present album, every individual contacted knew immediately what 'story' was in question, just as they might recall a particular song or instrumental performance. There was nothing casual about the telling of any of these stories."[14] Similarly, historian Albert Raboteau described the endurance and power such stories held in a different corner of the South in the 1980s and 1990s:

> I travel to the low country of Georgia and the South Carolina coastal islands to talk to elderly black Christians about their experience of conversion, about a process called seeking they underwent many years ago. Led by the Spirit into the wilderness to pray, each had a spiritual father or mother to examine dreams and visions and to serve as a guide in the way of salvation. Now in their eighties and nineties, these are hard-pressed people who've been poor all their lives. They've been through the fire and refined like gold. When they speak about their conversion experiences of sixty and seventy years ago, their faces light up with joy.[15]

Raboteau does not explicitly say that the stories took on a decisive shape on the heels of the occurrence of the events they describe, but the striking similarity between these stories told by elderly African Americans on the Sea Islands and those heard by Rossa Cooley on the Sea Islands from about 1905 to 1930 suggests as much. The stories had taken on a definitive shape many decades before they were recounted in the 1980s and 1990s. Their definitive shape preserved them—like the stories that Mullen and the *Children of the Heav'nly King* album documented—and fortified their power, making an experience of the distant past seem alive and contemporary when it was told and retold.

Material that was recorded long after the unmaking of the New South—material that had existed in oral form for quite some time before its recording—is thus a vital complement to material recorded in the New South era itself. Taken as a whole, the stories represent a distinct cultural production: a specific understanding of initiation into Christianity. The orality of the stories is therefore double edged. On the one hand, it made them vulnerable to being lost in the historical record, forgotten and unknown to later generations (unless, of course, they were recorded). On the other hand, it meant that they could become vehicles for a distinct theological understanding, the organizing point around which various ideas and themes could coalesce. Oral cultures survive through repetition, through "formulaic thought patterns," because "knowledge, once acquired, had to be constantly repeated or it would be lost."[16] Through the workings of orality, then, a distinct understanding of Christian initiation took shape, became normative, and operated (subconsciously or unconsciously) as the lens through which participants in folk Christianity imagined and articulated their religious experience.

Reflecting on the stories she had heard in the central Florida community where she grew up in the late nineteenth and early twentieth centuries, and surely thinking of the stories she had collected in her late 1920s fieldwork, Zora Neale Hurston wrote, "These visions are traditional. I knew them by heart as did the rest of the congregation, but still it was exciting to see how the converts would handle them. Some of them made up new details. Some of them would forget a part and improvise clumsily or fill up the gap with shouting. The audience knew, but everybody acted as if every word of it was new."[17] Hurston was writing here as a folklorist, not as an autobiographer. She understood the stories to be a communal production, through the terms of which individuals learned to imagine and narrate their religious experience. The body of stories above illustrates that there was clearly room for innovation—individuals did not narrate *a* normative story. Instead, they narrated diverse stories through the frame of a normative type.

Hurston linked the conversion narrative with another oral form that closely paralleled it in its basic features: the call narrative. "The vision . . . almost always accompanies conversion," she wrote. "It almost always accompanies the call to preach. . . . In conversion, then, we have the cultural pattern of the person seeking the vision. . . . In the call to preach we have the involuntary vision—the call seeking the man."[18] Conversion narratives told how an initiate entered into Christianity; call narratives described how the one clergy figure of importance—the preacher—came to be an authoritative proclaimer of Christianity. The purposes were different, yet the two oral forms informed and fortified each other. A sense of this comes through by comparing the following two call narratives with the four conversion narratives at the beginning of the chapter.

Tom Bronner, a black sharecropper in Bolivar County in the Mississippi Delta, began to be troubled by an inner sense that he was being called to preach. Though his inner turmoil grew, he steadfastly resisted the feeling. Bronner engaged in contested conversations with God. "I talked to God," he recalled. "I said, 'I ain't gonna preach.' But something was within me, was . . . . saying, 'I mean for you to preach.' I say, 'I ain't got sense enough to preach. You get after someone else. Let me do what I'm doing.'" One day, as he was walking in solitude and seclusion along a dirt road next to a canal ditch that led into the small creek on whose bank he lived, he was overcome by an unexpected and undesired visitation. "I was walking, stepping," he remembered. "As I was stepping I got paralyzed. . . . I couldn't move. I had my same mind. I had my same eyes. I could see my same person sitting on the bogue. I couldn't lift my feet." Bronner tried to argue with God as he had in the past, but he kept hearing a persistent voice as he was stuck motionless: "I say preach." Trapped, he made a reluctant bargain with God: "Well, if you let me go home, I'll preach." Suddenly, "it looked like I come to my sense. . . . My legs started walking, [and] I walked up to the house," taking up the calling that he had been successfully evading for some time.[19]

Quincy Higgins, a white small farmer in the mountains of Alleghany County, North Carolina, also resisted a growing inner sense of his vocation. "I didn't aim to become a preacher," he remembered. "Law, no, I, I was a— they's something in here that kept knocking and knocking and knocking." To this summons Higgins had a ready response: "I wasn't the man; I wanted to put if off on good men. . . . I wasn't the man." One night, though, Higgins had an intense experience, in the course of which his resistance crumbled. His wife woke him up with a frightful message. "This youngun's a dying, this youngun's a dying," she cried. It was their second child, an "awful sweet little boy" that Higgins was especially close to. "He'd come way out to the road to meet me, to get on the wagon and ride back to the house." Higgins darted out of bed, made a fire to light a lantern, and in the light his wife looked over the boy. "Quincy, you better get a doctor here, as quick as you can," she urged. "This baby's gonna die." He raced out of the house, saddled up his horse, and rode through the dark night. Alone and in intense anxiety, he made a bargain with God. "Lord, if you let that baby live," he prayed, "I'll take that Book and do the best I can." Then he continued on to the doctor's, and they made their way back together to the house—to find a transformed scene: the boy was now well. Higgins's wife said that the child had begun to breathe clearly an hour after he left. This was precisely the moment, during his anxious horseback journey, that he'd made his promise to God. With his favorite child unexpectedly and dramatically restored to health, Higgins took up the call that he had previously shirked.[20]

The call narratives are products of the same era as the conversion narratives. They display many of the same features, and they were sometimes narrated by the same person (an individual speaker who told both a conversion and a call narrative). Though their rhetorical purposes were different—to describe and define initiation or authority—their ultimate function was similar: to present a common, specific understanding of Christianity, either as an initiate enters into it or as an authoritative figure proclaims it. They are stylized oral forms containing a distinct vision of Christianity and its meaning in the world of the New South.

In the conversion and call narratives, the speaker was always *alone* at the decisive moment of the story. Often this solitude was literal. Lloyd Chandler was alone in a barn loft after his drinking companion disappeared, Florence Cheek was praying by herself in the seclusion of a tobacco barn, Susanna Springer was in the privy in her backyard. An African American woman in Midway, Florida, insisted that when she first "got religion," "I didn't get it in church; I got it all by myself. . . . The Lord often calls you when you are by yourself." Quincy Higgins was by himself, having hurriedly left his family but not yet at the doctor's; Walter Evans found a solitary place of prayer on a remote mountaintop; Edgar Cassell was traveling alone to new work that he had picked up; and Floyd Roe was riding his mule on a country road after his wife had left him. But the solitude could also be psychological— the speaker was surrounded by others yet overcome by a powerful feeling of isolation and alienation. Rosie Reed was in church and yet felt herself pushed into the floor, unable to "hear them singing or nothin." An African American man in southwest Virginia remembered "a lot of people were mingling out there," but he felt himself standing "about 30 inches off the ground."[21]

Closely connected to the speaker's solitude was the site of the story's main drama: a *place*, literal or psychological, *of removal and isolation*. Lloyd Chandler was secluded in a barn loft; Walter Evans was roaming remote mountaintops and forests; Eddie House was in the middle of an alfalfa field; Tom Bronner was at his "praying ground . . . under a pecan bush on the bogue bank"; Rachel Franklin had gone out into the open field to pray; Roosevelt Fields's father was praying down in the bottomlands of the Brazos River; an African American woman in Midway, Florida, was at her praying place near the swamp; and Leonard Bryan had gone out in the woods to pray. G. W. Blevins was out on a remote stretch of the Norton Road, "an old wagon road, a little snow on the ground, just a little bit, wagon ruts and mud"; Jessie Jefferson remembered that "in that swamp where that graveyard was there was catamounts and panthers and wild beasts but not a one of 'em touched me and I laid there all night"; Edgar Cassell was on a lonely winding stretch of mountain road between Floyd and Roanoke; an African American woman in central Tennessee was in a blackberry patch; and Elihu Trusty was lying in muddy water deep in the coal mines, praying for an experience of God.[22]

The tangibility of the literal places, the fact that they were all staple elements of the New South, is strikingly mixed with *rich symbolism and mystical language*. With a short turn of phrase, the stories move from the tangible and mundane to the mystical and mysterious. Death personified appeared to Lloyd Chandler, so palpable that he could feel it grabbing hold of him. In the ensuing encounter, he had a long, terrifying conversation with Death—a haunting back-and-forth of pleas and taunts. An African American woman in Gee's Bend, Alabama, was "called to go 'cross the river of hell on a spider web.'" Quincy Higgins was in the midst of an everyday task when his scene was dramatically transformed. "I's plowing the corn over yonder at the old place," he recalled. "And I had spoke to that horse that evening after dinner. I just pulled the lines. And he'd turn. Let him take his time and do as he pleased, just so he stayed in the row. And went on, and about three o'clock they's a whirlwind appeared somewhere in the firmament. And I went blind. I went deaf. And automatically the horse stopped. And when I come back to myself, the line was laying over on the cultivator. And I'd stomped my hat in the ground, and I'd stomped the corn down in both rows."[23]

Samuel Adams was hoeing corn in the field with his wife and their child. It was the middle of the day when all of a sudden everything "looked as dark to me as the darkest night I ever seed in my whole life, no light or nothing." Then he saw a mysterious light, and it came toward him, getting "larger and larger" as it approached. It struck him down with its power, but he found himself jumping back up, shouting and praising God—so much so that his wife thought he had gone crazy. Susanna Springer "laid down and a white man come to me all dressed in white and he had me stretched out on the table and clipped my breath three times and the third time I rose and went to a church door and there was a weeping willow. There was a four-cornered garden and three more knelt with me in the four corners." An African American man in southwest Virginia was standing, waiting for a train to appear. When it did, it "didn't be moving on no track, but sailing through the air. And it come right up to me." Lavere Walker saw an awful place of otherworldly destruction, where "they're dumpin' them in that fire, and there's all the screamin' and hollerin' you ever heard. And it's burnt black as far as 'tis from here to that door." He then saw Lazarus and the rich man, in painful separation. Then he saw three moons. He asked Abraham what this meant, and "Abraham said, 'That's not the moon. That's the Father, Son, and Holy Ghost. You just stay in the rim of the lights.'" Jessie Jefferson came to and "was standing naked beside the table and there was three lights burning on the table. . . . They told me to reach forth with my right hand and grasp the brightest one and I did. It was shining like the Venus star. And they told me it was to be my guidin' star." Later, a heavenly voice clarified the meaning of the three lights: "You got the three witnesses. One is water, one is spirit, and one is blood. And these three correspond with the three in heaven—Father, Son, and Holy Ghost."[24]

Ernest Huffman was hanging over hell "by one strand of hair," with "flames of fire leaping up a thousand miles to swallow [his] soul," when he cried out to Jesus for rescue. All at once "[I was] on solid ground and a tall white man beckoned for me to come to him and I went, wrapped in my guilt, and he 'nointed me with the oil of salvation and healed all my wounds. Then I found myself layin on the ground under a scrub oak and I cried, 'I believe, I believe.'" Edgar Cassell was just at the top of Bent Mountain on his way to work in Roanoke when he "never remembered not one thing a-taking place. I left this world as far as I'm concerned." Suddenly he was standing before the mirror at night, shaving before he went to bed. But he looked at the mirror and "nobody had never seen no such a face as I saw in there." Then he heard a stark warning: "If you don't pick up your calling, this is your last night on earth." Floyd Roe was riding his mule on a country road when he saw a strange light whose source he could not discern: "I stepped off my old mule and looked down at the gravels and I could see a border, a sharp border, between the light and the shadow. Finally I just stepped into the light and, when

I did, it just seemed like something come up my leg, just like when your foot goes to sleep. . . . And I knelt down in the light and prayed."[25]

James Benton was struggling to preach his first sermon. On Sunday morning at the Dry Holler church, he looked out the window only to see the sun go black. The moon began to drip away in blood, the earth began to quake, and people began to run for their lives. Suddenly he was there on the day of Jesus's crucifixion. Then, in the flash of a moment, he was back in the church, where preaching seemed to burst out of him, and all the congregation was suddenly on its feet. Thomas Claytor was shunning his call to preach, working in a coal mine, when the river began to speak to him, and the hills began to echo. Three men came to visit him at night, and he was taken to hell on a black horse before finally submitting to the call. An African American man in central Tennessee "went off in a trance" one night while he was praying at a big beech tree near his house. "I saw myself going up a broad, hilly road through the woods," he remembered. "When I was nearly to the top I saw a big dog. I got scared and started to run back, but something urged me on. . . . Though she tried to get me, I passes out of her reach. I came then to a tree like a willow, and there I heard a dove mourn three times."[26]

The rich symbolism and mystical language is of a piece with the *vivid drama* of the narratives: though feelings and emotions, inner states of guilt or repentance, are aspects of the narratives, each narrative involves action—tangibly felt, experienced with one's own body. The basic plot structure that frames most of the narratives is a dramatic story of *death and rebirth*. Not only was Lloyd Chandler on a wild binge, with self-annihilation as the apparent goal, but he also felt Death grabbing hold of him, pulling him into decay. His emergence from the barn was as nothing less than a newly born man. Richard Young echoed Chandler: he told of how death "crept on up, crept on up"; of how he "knowed when it hit my heart, I'd die." And yet even as he seemed to die, to "know nothing then for a long time," the drama continued. He heard a voice saying, "Arise now and shine," and when he came out of the room, he heard angels singing, "He done died one time, ain't gonna die no more." An African American man in Gee's Bend, Alabama, tersely recalled the basic drama of his conversion: "I dies and raised again, and then I knowed I was converted." When Rosie Reed came to after feeling herself "mashed down lower and lower," haunted by an "awful feeling," she knew she was a new person. "Never after that did I doubt my experience," she recalled. "I know I was born again." An African American woman in Midway, Florida, told of her experience similarly. She was "struck down and shot through to the bone by the quickening light of the Spirit." Fifty years later, that experience was still etched in her mind, for it meant nothing less than that she was "born again of the Spirit." An African American woman in Nashville recalled how "when his power struck me I died. I fell out on the floor flat on my back. I could neither speak nor move, for my tongue stuck to the roof of my mouth; my jaws were locked and my limbs were stiff."[27]

In the call narratives, the drama is a variant on that of death and rebirth. Death looms as the certain fate of those who do not take up the call. When they do, they find themselves with capabilities that they did not in any way have before. Samuel Adams was "struck" by a stark voice telling him, "You've got to preach the gospel, or die." Tom Bronner was paralyzed, and Floyd Roe felt something deadening creeping up his leg. Edgar Cassell was warned that if he did not heed the call, it was his "last night on earth." Walter Evans was convinced that his death was imminent, and so he climbed to a mountaintop to try to pray "one more time." For Quincy Higgins, it was not his own impending death but rather his favorite son's. In a similar fashion, for the preacher of Vera Hall's youth, it was the sudden, mysterious appearance of his deceased mother that caused his shift from resistance to acceptance of the call. On taking up the call, though, preachers found themselves "born anew" with a gift they didn't have before. Floyd Roe was barely present for his first sermon. "It seemed like something had a holt of me," he remembered. "When I kind of come to myself, the people was sheddin tears all around me. I couldn't say what I'd done, but the old deacon told everybody that I had preached just about as fine a sermon as he'd want to hear." Similarly, G. W. Blevins was asked to read from the Bible at an evening church service. He was still resisting his call, but when he opened the Bible and began to speak, he lost consciousness and was caught up in an ecstatic experience. When he came to some time later, his first sermon had been delivered, and the Bible was lying on the floor.[28]

The basic posture of the speaker was one of *incapability* and sometimes outright *resistance*. Samuel Adams was a "vile sinner" who cared nothing for religion when the bright light struck him. Lloyd Chandler was in a state of severe intoxication, shivering in a barn loft, immobilized by the Death that crept up his body. Of Christianity, Ernest Huffman said that he "never paid it no mind. I was hard." He was "walkin' in my sins, wallerin' in my sins," when Jesus touched him with just "the tip of his finger and I fell right where I was and laid there for three long days and nights." Even when he walked over hell on a narrow log, though, he still "wouldn't believe." Quincy Higgins "hadn't run just exactly the race, straight path, like I's commanded." After his mother's death, he began praying in earnest—for forty days—but still experienced no change of heart. Walter Evans "cared nothing for God nor his people" and was "satisfied with my big times attending places of worldly pleasures." G. W. Blevins was suffering from tuberculosis, "down til I was just a skeleton nightmare walking on the earth," coughing and spitting up enough to "cover a place as large round as a large washtub." He was an angry man, to the point that he thought "something just infest my mind." When he would try to pray, he felt that he "couldn't pray, didn't seem like a prayer would go higher than my head." Later, after his conversion, "the burden fell on [him] to preach." He was deeply resistant: "I tried to get out of it, and I prayed and I done everything in the world, and it just followed me up and followed me up." As he slept, he would be seized by dreams of himself preaching to "great crowds of people," but when he woke up, he would plead with God, insisting, "I'm too ignorant, I don't know anything, I don't know anything about the Bible."[29]

Susanna Springer felt similarly: she "had done prayed and prayed but didn't know how to pray . . . had done seen vision on top of vision, but I still wouldn't believe." Lavere Walker knew he was going to die: after a tree fell and crushed him, "they amputated my leg, five doctors all givin' me up not to live through the night." Though he was only twenty-one, Jessie Jefferson felt that he was going to die. People told him to go to the graveyard to pray, but he was scared and did not want to go despite their repeated insistence. But then "the Lord sent Death after me and when I knowed anything I was on my way to the graveyard. And when I got there I fell. I fell right between two graves and I saw Him when He laid me upon a table in my vision. I was naked and He split me open." An African American woman in Gee's Bend was walking across a spiderweb above the river of hell. When she was halfway across, she began a terrifying plummet as she lost her footing.[30]

Tom Bronner adamantly resisted the call to preach, carrying on a running dispute with God—until paralysis made him concede. Quincy Higgins felt the call, but he insisted that "I wasn't the man." Floyd Roe had felt called to preach but simply did not want to. In a strange encounter in the train station in Oklahoma City, a white landlord insisted that Roe come out to his farm to preach to his tenants. "But I'm not a preacher," Roe replied. "Well, you're Jonah then," the man said in taunting response. "You remember how God sent Jonah to Nineveh and he tried to run away and what happened to *him*." "I can't read, how can I preach," Elihu Trusty said three times as a counterpoint to the command he heard—"You go and preach"—and John Reynolds tried to run away from the call even as he heard his name. Henry Truvillion and Thomas Claytor both resisted the call adamantly—for eighteen and twenty-five years! The preacher of Vera Hall's youth, Reverend Giles, had a series of dreams in which he heard the command, "I want you to preach." He simply didn't believe the first dream, but in the second dream, when a mysterious person handed him a Bible and opened it for him, he simply refused the summons: "I don't want to be a preacher and I'm not gonna preach," he told the unwanted messenger. In a third dream his deceased mother came to him. She shook him, and when he opened his eyes, it seemed as if he were looking right into her face. "She was smiling and she says, 'You've got that to do . . . you've got to preach." At this his resistance crumbled. When he woke up he prayed, "Lord . . . I can't read, can't write. I don't know a word in the Bible. I don't know how to *be* a preacher, but I promise you I'll preach till I die."[31]

Many of the stories conclude not only with a transformed person but with a dramatic glimpse of what the person's new life entails. It is a vision of *loving community* and the *beautiful goodness of the world*, a vision that is tangibly seen, touched, and in some cases even tasted. When he was caught up in the whirlwind, Quincy Higgins had a vision of his recently deceased mother: "There she was, and I knowed her, reaching down like that, with them hands, didn't have a wrinkle in them—everything was just as perfect. Looked young and tender and reaching down there." When Rosie Reed came to after the awful alienation that seemed about to crush her, "everything was as bright as sunshine," and as she looked around the church, "I thought they was the prettiest people I'd ever seen in all my life." Rachel Franklin looked around her to see that "the sun was just at the top of the trees and that sun just went reeling and rocking and going up and down." The dark, dirty tobacco barn where Florence Cheek was praying suddenly disappeared, and a brilliant light suffused the area, "and then that place was just so gold." Walter Evans was at the top of a mountain on a dark night when "suddenly there shined a light around me, a complete circle fifteen feet in diameter, or more, the resemblance of a rainbow's many colors but brighter. Such as this I had never seen nor felt." An African American woman in central Tennessee "saw a beautiful green pasture, and grazing there were thousands of sheep, and they turned towards me and all in one bleat cried out, 'Welcome! Welcome to the house of God!' "[32]

Richard Young saw an utterly different day: "It was a dark and dreary morning when I went in my room, but when I come out, everything looked new, everything was summertime, and the trees was green all around. The little birds was sitting out in the ends of the twigs of the trees, chirping just like they were offering thanks to God. I ain't never seen a morning so bright." An African American woman in Midway, Florida, followed Jesus across a body of water even though she was scared. On the other side was "a beautiful white church." An African American man in southwest Virginia saw a little white train coming through a cutaway in the mountains, which "didn't have too many coaches behind it. And it was pretty as a doll. White as snow." At a mysterious white house, a woman welcomed Jessie Jefferson in. Once inside, "as far as mortal eye could behold, the robes was hanging level and touched my head as I passed under. Then I found myself robed in the color of gold." G. W. Blevins found himself with a wholly restored body. He had been wasting away with tuberculosis and was debilitated so badly that he needed to hold a stick with both hands when trying to walk. He was lying on the ground beside a rock where he had been praying fervently when "all at once the misery left me, every pain left my body. My lungs quit hurting me. And after I'd said all that I could think to say—I guess I stayed there maybe two or three minutes—I made an effort to get up. I forgot all about the stick. I went hollering and screaming up that hill." An African American man in central Tennessee came out of his trance and "felt a great love in my heart that made me feel like stooping and kissing the very ground." An African American woman in central Tennessee echoed him: "I came to myself, and it looked like I just wanted to kiss the very ground. I have never felt such a love before." After the stark voice told him to take up his call or die, Edgar Cassell fell across his bed. But something was radically different: "Ain't no human being ever, never has nor I don't guess ever will, lay on the bed that I laid on. It was just like downy feathers. . . . And I looked out at the window, and there's a bright star a-shining, and all at once that changed, and there He was. In another scripture He says, 'I am your bright and morning star.'" After she was delivered from hell, an African American woman in Nashville saw Jesus "standing in snow—the prettiest, whitest snow I have ever seen." Later, Jesus led her to what looked like a grape arbor and invited her to taste the strange snow. "I took some," she recalled, "and tasted it, and it was the best-tasting snow I ever put into my mouth." An African American man echoed her. A mysterious man in white offered him water to drink, and "it was the best-tasting water I ever drank. I can't say what kind of water it was, but I never tasted anything like it."[33]

Being alone and in a place of removal and isolation, using rich symbolism to convey a vivid drama of death and rebirth, emphasizing human incapability and resistance, concluding with a tangibly transformed world shot through with love and beauty—these stylized features give shape and form to the diversity of individual experience. They mark a normative oral type through which different individuals learned to imagine their encounter with Christianity.

At the same time, they have radically condensed the struggles of an individual's life into a single dramatic moment. Folklorists have noted the importance of this radical condensing in oral cultures. When knowledge has to be continually told and retold to be remembered, it is typically packaged into a form that allows for this continued retelling. The continuum of life is rhetorically shortened into ripe moments and emblematic episodes, and the struggles that pervade a lifetime are imagined into a decisive, once-and-for-all drama. Furthermore, as stories (in this case conversion and call stories) become communal property, known and told by a network of people far beyond the original speaker, the stories crystallize the phenomena that the community sees as truly significant. They "continually mix the godless and the holy," folklorist Carl Lindahl argues, allowing their tellers and hearers "to experience both halves of their lives at once through narrative."[34] This does not mean that the narratives are untrue or fiction. Certainly at some basic level, a real experience was the focal point around which a story began to take shape; thus, there is a historical or biographical truth at the heart of the story. But the stylized features and rhetorical conventions that transform a core experience into a memorable story go beyond this historical/biographical truth to poetically convey theological or religious truth; by the standards of the community of which they are a part, the stories express truth about initiation into and authority in Christianity.

Walter Evans's interwoven conversion and call account sheds light on the radical condensing at play in the narratives. Alone among the various speakers whose New South conversion and call narratives survive, Evans personally wrote down his own narrative. The original story had taken shape as an oral form in the 1930s, on the heels of the experiences it recounts. Forty years later, in the 1970s, Evans wrote the story down as part of a longer account of his life. Evans's written account is not an extended meditation on a single decisive experience but rather stretches over the course of five years. It moves from the mystical and mysterious to the ordinary and mundane, back-and-forth again several times. It includes stages of uncertainty and regression—not an irreversible clean break with the past. At the same time, though, it displays all the characteristic features of the other (entirely oral) narratives: solitude, places of removal and isolation, rich symbolism and mystical language, the initiate's incapability, a vivid drama of death and rebirth, and a tangible vision of loving community and the beautiful goodness of the world.

Evans's written account begins in November 1930, just before he turned twenty-one. Though he "cared nothing for God," he attended a Baptist service at his parents' insistence. There he was overcome by "a strong power," so much so that his body "trembled under the weight like a leaf on a tree shaken by a mighty wind." He heard a voice say, "You are lost without God or hope in this world," and an "awful feeling" came over him. He struggled under this new burden, growing increasingly more disturbed, yet the prayers of his parents and of other church members brought no relief. Evans began to pray fervently himself, kneeling beside his bed in the lonely darkness of the night. Finally, after three days and nights of desperate prayer, lying on the floor exhausted, he experienced God's presence. He felt himself raised to his feet and found himself in church, joining in a song of hope and thanksgiving. Evans felt himself to be "in a new world," and he became a prayer leader in the church.

Four years later, though, Evans had a disturbing experience that seemed to sharply weaken his faith. It was a dark night, and he was standing alone outside the church after the meeting had ended. He went inside to find an incredibly bright room, though the kerosene lamps were not lit. He made his way up the aisle, looking on either side at rows of dark faces and then at a smaller section of white faces. When he got to the front, he was deeply troubled by the austere presence of a gray casket. A powerful sadness overcame him, and when he woke up from the dream, he was so disturbed that he stopped leading prayers in church and then stopped attending altogether.

He took to roaming "the mountains and rock cliffs" in anguished solitude, becoming so convinced that he was about to die that he told his wife he had only three weeks to live. But he tried to pray again and wandered out into the cornfield late in the day. As he passed through the field, the corn "appeared to be mourning with its blades bending toward the earth." Roaming on into a pasture, he passed cattle who also seemed to be mourning. Finally he ascended the top of a mountain, but it was so "dark and gloomy" that he looked for a safer place. He turned down the ridge and stumbled into dark woods, roaming "among the trees, trying to find some place to pray . . . . such a burden was I carrying." But his prayers brought no relief, and he went back to the top of the mountain. Then something dramatic and decisive happened: "Suddenly there shined a light around me, a complete circle fifteen feet in diameter, or more, the resemblance of a rainbow's many colors but brighter. Such as this I had never seen or felt. Every doubt and fear left me quick as a flash. I felt so light in my feelings. . . . I started singing: I thank you Lord, for every blessing." He walked down from the mountain a transformed man, and as he passed the cattle, they seemed ready to shout for joy.

But rather than continuing this religious trajectory, Evans's written narrative falls back to the hard struggles of his life as an impoverished man in the

New South. With his wife and son, he labored on a farm owned by an elderly man. The landlord was a miserly capitalist, paying Evans 60 cents a day and resenting it when Evans would stop to take a drink of water. Evans became preoccupied with finding a new tenancy arrangement, and after he gathered the corn that fall, he moved to another farm offering better conditions. Meanwhile, though, he had felt an increasingly heavy burden that he must take up preaching. This burden gave him no new lease on life, however, but began to consume him with a feeling that he was about to die. In the quiet of the night he began to see his grave, certain that he would soon be in it.

In anxiety and depression, he headed back to the mountaintop where he had experienced his apparent earlier transformation. It was raining that morning, and certain that his death was near, he was going "to try to pray one more time." As he made his way, he stumbled upon a mysterious scene that brought him great comfort: in a thicket of briars, he saw two fallen trees, "one across the other crosswise." Drawn in by this woodland sign of the cross, he wrote, "I parted my way through the briars until I came to where the trees had crossed." This richly symbolic, isolated place suffused Evans with a new sense of life. "Between these two trees and in the briar patch," Evans realized his vocation and gained a new confidence in God's power. The place became for him a sacred site that resolved a five-year internal struggle. Rather than dying or praying one last desperate prayer, Evans found new life. He emerged from the thicket a preacher, a calling that would occupy four decades of his life, emboldened by the "power" God gave him "to speak of the wonders of his grace and love toward the children of men."[35]

Evans's circuitous written account draws out the gray areas and detours that have been rhetorically condensed in the oral form, and it shows how religious transformation was connected to economic struggles in his everyday life. Yet all the stylized elements of the oral narratives are there—indeed, in even more elaborate shape. The stylized elements enable a codifying of the diversity of individual experience, and they package a distinct understanding of Christianity for the New South. But the oral narratives were not created from scratch. Like songs of death, they were crafted out of inherited tradition to articulate something new for their own time.

Two independent strands of tradition inform the narratives: the early evangelical conversion narrative and the traditional initiation rites of West Africa. In their earliest appearance as oppositional reform movements in the eighteenth-century British Atlantic, Baptists and Methodists sought to deepen and disrupt the inclusive framework of established Anglican Christianity. Theoretically and legally in the Anglican system, the boundaries of church and state were coterminous; all citizens were incorporated into the church, and its rituals gave shape to time throughout the year and over the course of individual lives. The Baptists and Methodists criticized this framework as the mere form of Christianity, not its genuine substance, and they sought to call individuals away from the inclusive established church and toward small groups of the truly devout. The inwardness of feeling and experience would mark the truly devout, but more than anything else, the experience of a dramatic break with one's everyday way of life and the ordinary workings of society—a conversion experience—would identify the genuinely Christian.

The insistence on a conversion experience did two things. First, it established imaginative space for different types of Christianity within an ostensibly Christian society. It summoned people away from what was critiqued as the merely formal church and into the genuine church, whose membership was confined to those having the conversion experience. Second, the insistence on a conversion experience dramatically intensified individual feeling and inward experience. No one else could have this experience for you; only you could truly know, in the depths of your own inwardness, if you had experienced a genuine change of heart.

This logic moved the process of Christian initiation out of the church and into the uncharted waters of individual experience. The rituals of the Anglican system—the same for everyone, codified in the written script of the Book of Common Prayer, overseen and administered by the tangible community of the parish church—established a normative process that gave objective shape to the variety of individual lives. Precisely in attacking this system as mere form rather than substance, Baptists and Methodists opened the door to a potentially infinite variety of individual experiences, without the safeguards of normative ritual or communal sanction. The logic of Baptist and Methodist critique thus placed an intense burden on the individual, an anxiety born of imaginative isolation: If only I could know genuine Christianity in the inwardness of my individual experience, what objective supports could I look to for verification?

Even as they opened the door to this intense individuality, Baptist and Methodist leaders sought to codify a normative morphology of conversion. Central to this undertaking were stylized narratives of conversion that presented the experience in its succinct, normative type. These narratives were told in gatherings, published in periodicals, and central to preachers' autobiographies. This narrative from an English Methodist is typical:

From twelve at night till two it was my turn to stand sentinel at a dangerous post. . . . As soon as I was alone, I kneeled down, and determined not
to rise, but to continue crying and wrestling with God, till he had mercy
on me. How long I was in that agony I cannot tell: but as I looked up to
heaven, I saw the clouds open exceeding bright, and I saw Jesus hanging
on the cross. At the same moment these words were applied to my heart,
"Thy sins are forgiven thee." My chains fell off; my heart was free. All guilt
was gone, and my soul was filled with unutterable peace. I loved God and
all mankind, and the fear of death and hell was vanished away.[36]

The other strand of tradition shaping narratives of conversion and call
were the religious patterns of eighteenth-century West Africa. In the king-
doms of Kongo and Dahomey, among the Yoruba and Ewe and others, people
practiced an initiation ritual with common features. To become true and genuine members of the community, boys and girls had to be properly initiated
into adulthood. The process began with their seclusion from the group into
the wilderness, or bush. Accompanying the literal seclusion were conscious
deprivations, like fasting and bodily suffering: the initiate was stripped of the
good things that make up life, alienated into a place and a state like that of
death. The mood was somber, and the initiate entered seclusion in focused
prayer. From the outer limits of human experience, the initiate made his or
her way back to the world of community, returning from seclusion to the
dancing and feasting of a great celebration. The mood was now one of joy.
Now the youth was an adult—truly alive as a proper member of the community.
Time and space were both critical to the ritual. Initiation happened regularly
during the threshold between youth and adulthood, and the seclusion of the
initiate could continue for several months. The dramatic contrast between
the ordinary, positive space of community and sociability and the special,
negative space of seclusion displayed the antinomies of life and death, of belonging and alienation.[37]

Enslaved Africans carried the core of this cultural practice across the Atlantic, and in areas with significant slave majorities, with a critical mass of
slaves concentrated in quarters separate from the masters', and with plantation stability over time, they were able to sustain the practice to a great degree. On the Sea Islands of South Carolina in the 1840s, a white Methodist
minister engaged in plantation missions observed:

The word *travel* . . . is one of the most significant in their language, and
comprehends all those exercises, spiritual, visionary and imaginative,
which make up an "experience." . . . These travels may differ in some

things; and in others they all agree. Each seeker meets with warnings—
awful sights or sounds, and always has a vision of a white man who talks
with him, warns him, and sometimes makes him carry a burden, and in
the end leads him to the river. When the teacher is satisfied with the
travel of the seeker, he pronounces "he git thru"; and he is ready for the
church.[38]

By the late antebellum decades when this minister was writing, West African
initiation rituals had been synthesized with Christianity. But precisely in his
concern, the minister emphasized the extent to which the frame of African
initiation rituals remained largely intact. Christian ideas had been grafted
onto a durable frame; slaves had woven pieces of their new Christianity into
an older cloth of African tradition.

Both traditions—the evangelical conversion narrative and West African
initiation rites—were common, non-class-specific cultural property in the
nineteenth century. But over the course of the century, and especially in its
latter decades, evangelical leaders, white and black, took active steps to push
this cultural property into the distant background.[39] They did this because
the understandings once expressed by these forms no longer fit their self-
understanding. The forms seemed at odds with the middle-class ethos that
evangelical leaders were seeking to foster.

Conversion hardly fell out of the dominant evangelical culture. Legions
of gospel hymns sang of the joys of conversion, prominent ministers saw
their task as one of "soul-winning" and getting their hearers to make a "decision for Christ," large revival meetings were perennial events in New South
towns and cities, and newspapers printed precise statistics of conversion
in the wake of these revivals.[40] Even as it remained an evangelical staple,
though, conversion was imagined in new ways. Most basically, it became
willful individual appropriation of the values of the evangelical community—a self-conscious identification with the ideal of respectability. To
convert was not to undergo a strange, mysterious experience of spiritual
transformation; rather, it was essentially a moral choice, a declaration that
the initiate wanted to live with upright self-control and disciplined productivity. The spirit of the declaration needed to match the values being appropriated, so mysterious stories of self-abandon had to be pushed to the
"primitive" past.

At the same time, conversion became closely identified with the idealized
Christian home. To self-consciously appropriate the ideal of respectability
was to identify with the stable and secure sphere of domesticity. In popular

gospel hymns of the late nineteenth and early twentieth centuries, middle-class evangelicals sang:

> I've anchored my soul in the "Haven of Rest"
> I'll sail the wide seas no more . . .

> Softly and tenderly Jesus is calling, calling for you and for me
> See, on the portals He's waiting and watching, watching for you and
>     for me
> Come home, come home, ye who are weary come home
> Earnestly, tenderly, Jesus is calling, calling, O sinner, come home![41]

With its safe domesticity, the home was imagined as the antithesis of the wild, rough, dangerously uncertain world. To join the Christian community was to reject the roughness and wildness of the world, to find a refuge from danger-ous uncertainty.[42] By identifying Christianity with safety and security, the dominant evangelical culture put wildness—either the uncharted waters of individual experience or initiation into literal wilderness—in its distant back-ground.

The oral narratives of conversion imagine Christian initiation in very much the opposite direction: it is in a place removed from the solid, secure supports of the home—often tangibly—that one encounters Christianity. What is stable and familiar drops dramatically from view; the initiate is brought into danger and mystery, and it is here where the genuine Christian experience takes place. The movement is not a conscious appropriation of the familiar and not an identification with the stable supports of order and harmony; rather, it is an experience of being led out into the uncharted and the unknown: to a graveyard in the swamp, to a sheltering rock beside the river, to a solitary place in the field, to the muddy Norton Road, to a barn loft in an isolated cove, to a mountaintop, to a pecan bush on the bogue bank. Even when the narrators are literally in their home, surrounded by the familiar—like Susanna Springer in her backyard privy, Florence Cheek in her tobacco barn, the Midway woman and Richard Young in their beds—the place becomes radically unfamiliar through the experience of strange myste-rious visions.

In the oral narratives of conversion and call, the traditions of the evangeli-cal conversion narrative and West African initiation rites have been synthe-sized into a new whole. The conversion narrative focused on an individual's movement from formal Christianity to genuine Christianity, and the empha-sis was on inward feeling and personal transformation. Initiation rites marked a temporal passage from youth to adulthood after time spent in the secluded isolation of the wilderness, and the characteristic tropes were tangible movement and reincorporation into community. In the New South oral forms, these two understandings were fused together: the New South narratives articulate decisive personal transformation, not reincorporation into the existing community; the tangible movement of place and materiality, not inner states of feeling. In their creative fusion, the oral narratives embody a clear message: it is in isolation from the everyday that one finds genuine Christianity. Late in the antebellum era, slaves in the South Carolina Sea Islands had sung, "If you want to find Jesus / go in the wilderness."[43] The New South conversion and call tales echo this sense and display it in a variety of iterations. They imagine the encounter with Christianity in disruptive separation from the ordinary, in spaces (literal or psychological) that humans have not tamed.

Based on his early 1950s fieldwork with the Ndembu people of northwestern Zambia and Arnold van Gennep's theory of *rites de passage*, anthropologist Victor Turner developed the idea of liminality (from the Latin *limen*, meaning "threshold"). Turner especially had in mind the initiation rites he observed, "complex initiation rites with long periods of seclusion in the bush." The initiate was on the edge of adulthood and proper belonging, and the space of seclusion was the necessary threshold that he or she had to cross. Liminality, Turner theorized, is a blend of "lowliness and sacredness, of homogeneity and companionship. We are presented, in such rites, with a 'moment in and out of time,' and in and out of secular social structure, which reveals, however fleetingly, some recognition (in symbol if not always in language) of a generalized social bond that has ceased to be." Turner expounded on the meanings contained in rituals of liminality: "as a time and place of withdrawal from normal modes of social action," liminality "can be seen as potentially a period of scrutinization of the central values and axioms of the culture in which it occurs."[44]

In their creative synthesis of inherited traditions, the oral narratives imagine Christianity in liminality—on the far edge of the familiar, distinct from ordinary experience. It is in liminality that one gets religion, has his or her experience, and finds God. That liminal space may be quite tangible (a lonely mountaintop, a secluded swamp, a hidden spot on the riverbank), more familiar (a cornfield, a country road, a barn), or psychological (a vision in one's room), but in every case, Christianity is imagined as other, as foreign. It is not to be identified or associated with anything familiar or common. Symbolic, mystical language is thus the appropriate vocabulary for talking about it, for neither words nor metaphors drawn from the ordinary can rightly express its essence. The narratives thus establish a categorical, qualitative difference between Christianity and society—or any element of the social order. To enter into Christianity is not to willfully affirm the stabilizing, solidifying forces of the social order but to be led, in a posture of incapability or resistance, away from what is familiar and into another world.

This other world, however, is neither postmortem nor a heavenly escape. It is a deeper reality that appears disruptively amidst the familiar, often so tangible that its force is felt in one's own body. This qualitatively other world is experienced, but it is experienced in a way that pushes the initiate back into the (now-transformed) familiar. Put differently, the narratives follow the classic pattern of African initiation rituals: the initiate is led away from the familiar, toward the liminal and the secluded, and then back again to the familiar. The liminal is a threshold or boundary, not the stopping place. The narratives do not leave the initiate with a wistful, heavenly gaze, nor is the initiate focused or fixated on a postmortem hereafter. Rather, the initiate returns from the boundary to live in the familiar but in a transformed way. The basic plot of death and rebirth imagines new life as a possibility *within* this world—after the initiate has found Christianity in liminality.

This understanding of Christianity was opaque to middle-class observers; they understood the oral narratives as strange, mystical stories told by primitive people and did not hear their critical edge. But they could not as readily dismiss the liminal figure of the folk preacher. Indeed, they seemed genuinely bothered by him. "Who, then, is this high priest in the rural community?" Carter Woodson asked in his 1930 study *The Rural Negro*. He answered with dismissive sarcasm:

> He is not the man required to direct the religious work of an urban center, but "an inspired man" whom the fates have superimposed. He had a vision and he heard a voice which called him to preach. He had "to answer this divine call lest God might strike him dead." Such an inspired creature may have the rudiments of education or he may be illiterate; for in spite of his lack of mental development he can find a following sufficient to maintain a church. . . . For the special task in which they are engaged their formal preparation is practically blank. They do well to be able to read and write intelligibly.

White seminary professor Jefferson Ray recorded a common sarcastic aphorism about the folk preacher: "He does enough farming to spoil his preaching and enough preaching to spoil his farming." A white Georgia doctor echoed this aphorism in a written critique of the Baptist policy of congregations or-daining their preachers. "An unlettered plowman of forty has a dream and thinks he hears a voice," the doctor lamented in the pages of the denomina-tional periodical *Our Home Field*, "and we ordain him, spoiling a good plow-man to make an incompetent exhorter." A white Baptist home missionary in the Ozarks wrote with concern of "preachers of limited capacity and vision" shaping religious life in "undeveloped places," while an educated black minis-ter in southwest Georgia wrote that the majority of preachers in the field were "unlearned and ignorant men, ignorant in the sense of fitness for leadership." Black minister-educators Benjamin Mays and Joseph Nicholson argued in their 1933 study *The Negro's Church* that "the establishment of churches by a relatively illiterate mass has been unrestrained," and they traced the problem to the preachers' lack of proper credentials: "In the majority of Negro churches there has been no standard allowing men to enter the ministry. If a man says he is called to preach, he can usually be ordained."[45]

All that was wrong in folk Christianity seemed to be crystallized in the figure of the folk preacher. "Occasionally a 'poor weak servant of the Lord,' as he aptly describes himself, straggles into the settlement and preaches in the log school house in an effort, he announces, 'to help save his own soul,'" a white Baptist home missionary wrote from the mountains of east Tennessee. She simply reinterpreted the preacher's theological self-description into a cultural description, arguing that the Christianity she encountered among mountaineers was "poor" and "weak." Similarly, in his sweeping study of rural black churches, Tuskegee chaplain Harry Richardson wrote that the typical preacher he encountered delivered a sermon that was little more than "a heated hodge-podge of emotional shibboleths mixed with bits of common sense." The wide scope of such sermons and their preachers, he argued, "jeopardizes the whole task of propagating and transmitting Christianity in enlightened and practicable forms."[46]

These middle-class critics were judging folk preachers by standards that had become ascendant in their own time. In their earliest appearance in the late colonial–post-revolutionary era, Baptists and Methodists had given cru-cial sanction to the idea of "inspired" preachers without any formal training or official credentials. But some leaders were quickly taking steps to shut the door on the heterogeneity and idiosyncrasies that this sanctioned. They sought to establish a normative pattern of ordination through stages of trial and apprenticeship. By the late antebellum period, they were going a step fur-ther, establishing seminaries to ensure proper training of their clergy. The seminaries expanded significantly in the postbellum–early New South decades, and by 1900, they had come to be pillars of the region's dominant evangelical culture, gathering future clergy into a central locus, training them through a normative process, and disseminating a common religious culture as their graduates fanned out into the region's churches.[47]

The seminaries were also crucial sites of professionalization in the New South. Other areas of life—medicine and law being the most obvious— followed a similar trajectory that reflected the rising nineteenth-century process of credentialization, culminating in normative, centralized professionalization in the New South era. "As the people advance in intelligence there must be a corresponding advance in preachers," North Carolina's white Baptist newspaper argued in 1894, and some forty years later, state Baptist leader Edwin Poteat depicted an idealized version of that advanced, professionalized preacher in his 1935 *The Reverend John Doe, D.D.* Black minister-educators Benjamin Mays and Joseph Nicholson found reason for optimism when they examined some of the region's largest urban churches in their 1933 study *The Negro's Church.* "A minister is respected in the community now," they wrote happily, "not because he claims to be 'called' by God to preach, but because as an individual he has admirable qualities, merits recognition, and has a unique contribution to make to life." Professionalization was not just replacing the inspiration of an earlier era; it was being appreciated and valued by the laity too.[48]

Professionalization of religious authority was indeed about ensuring a normative message, but it was about more than that. Professionalization imagined the leading authority figure—the minister—as being at home in the world, properly credentialed by an institution of human construction and a rightful member of a class of professionals, alongside doctors and lawyers. Studying the highly industrialized textile town of Gastonia, North Carolina, in the 1930s, Liston Pope found that in the churches of mill owners and management, a pervasive belief was that "a minister ought to be a leader in all community enterprises" and "be a good fellow in his private life, joining civic clubs, attending baseball games, and the like."[49] As the exemplar of what Christianity ought to look like, the professionalized minister who complemented and fortified the social order succinctly embodied Christianity's constructive, socially solidifying role. Though it involved very different gendered imagery, then, professionalization went hand in hand with the ascendant ideal of domesticity. Imagining ministers as respectable professionals and the home as a sacralized haven were ways of demystifying Christianity, of envisioning it as a constituent piece—a crucial one—of the social fabric.

The call narratives, which took shape in stylized oral form in the same era as the ascendant drive for professionalization, present a consistent counterpoint. They exaggerate the would-be preacher's lack of capability and active rejection of the vocation. The folk preacher, they insist, was the antithesis of a properly trained professional, master of a body of knowledge and a figure commanding social respect. The preacher was ignorant, sometimes illiterate, and shirked the unwelcome call. At a certain level, the narratives reveal the social reality behind them: folk preachers were neither full-time preachers nor recognized professionals but impoverished people who labored as small farmers, tenants, coal miners, and timber workers. Hard labor filled their week, but on Sundays they entered the church to act out their vocation.

A white Presbyterian missionary wrote in 1930 of the "backwoods" preachers he encountered in the North Carolina mountains: "Being illiterate themselves and serving illiterate congregations, they were not able to pen and keep records of their labors. . . . These men worked on their little, rugged, sloping farms six days of the week, and then preached on Sunday, often serving two or three congregations the same day. . . . When a preacher did not own a horse or a mule, and could not borrow one, he went afoot, often walking eight to twelve miles during the day. In most cases no definite salary was promised and but little ever given." Similarly, an educated black minister depicted a folk preacher he encountered in a middle Georgia county in the mid-1940s as emblematic of the type: "The pastor is approximately forty-four years of age, has a fourth grade training, is married and has six children. He is farming as a share-cropper on an 85-acre farm just two miles from the church. He has three other churches with a combined membership of about 500. . . . The minister gets no money at the regular services but he is allowed three rallies per year." Neither occupation, nor a record of formal training, nor patterns during the week set such preachers apart from the congregations who listened to them. In the literal sense of social reality, they did not live as professionals, nor were they recognized as such.[50]

The narratives' insistence on preachers' inability was doing more than speaking out of social reality, though. Emphasizing just how unprofessional the preacher was operated as a rhetorical strategy to articulate a different ideal: not professional competency but mystery; the preacher not as a socially solidifying professional but as a strange, liminal figure. The narratives' trope of inability took the focus off the preacher and put it on the source of the call and the message that the preacher bore. "I just felt the Lord wanted me to deliver this message," an eastern Kentucky folk preacher said in closing his sermon. "I'm ignorant, I'm unlearned—of course, I'm no fool, not by any means—I'm just a fool for Christ's sake."[51] His direct statement was of a piece with the self-presentation found in the narratives. The preacher was the humble bearer of a message, not its master or possessor. Discernibly no different from his hearers, he nevertheless appeared before them with a message that, properly speaking, had taken hold of him rather than him taking hold of it. The message, like the locus of initiation in the conversion narratives, came from outside the ordinary structures of society—from a liminal place to which the preacher was a simple witness.

The preachers' call narratives complemented and fortified the conversion narratives in the most basic sense they sought to convey: a conception of Christianity as a mysterious, liminal presence. Just as professionalized ministers did, so too folk preachers embodied in their own person some of the core sensibilities of the culture to which they belonged. Their lives had been disrupted by an unbidden call, just as Christianity was a disruptive, unexpected presence. Through the force of a mystically received message that took hold of them, they became authority figures, just as initiates only truly experienced Christianity when their own capacities had been exhausted.

As mutually reinforcing oral forms, the conversion and call narratives imagined an enchanted cosmos—a seemingly mundane world that could suddenly be disrupted by the mystical and the mysterious. Tangible elements of everyday life—a tobacco barn, a railroad track, a cornfield—could be supplanted by strange phenomena, such as a large rainbow-colored circle, robes the color of gold, or a sharp light that paralyzed. Enigmatic, richly symbolic objects—such as two fallen trees forming the sign of the cross in a briar patch, a weeping willow and a four-cornered garden in front of a church door, or a train white as snow snaking through the mountains—could appear at a moment's notice as vivid beacons of the sacred in one's midst. Personal transformation was at the heart of each narrative, but the transformation was less about inner feelings or moral change than about tangible, action-based change: the speaker is yanked out of the ordinary and caught up as a participant in a strange, sacred drama, filled with such characters as a white-clothed man with eyes flashing like fire, a mysterious man handing off a Bible, a deceased mother appearing as she did in youth, Jesus at his crucifixion, Abraham and Lazarus, angels singing of triumph over death, a mysterious man offering the best-tasting water, or thousands of sheep singing a song of welcome.

These themes had special meaning for the poor. The dominant evangelical culture allowed market logic free reign in the society of the New South: except for the sacred haven of the home, the world was understood as a bundle of resources. No one confronted this thoroughgoing commodification more than those in poverty. The land that surrounded them was devoted to crop production or resource extraction or rendered peripheral by its distance from the market. In extractive industries and in manufacturing, employers squeezed long hours of labor out of their workers. A money economy touched such basic elements of life as food and clothing, with the poor struggling for adequate subsistence, plagued by chronic debt and limited sources of credit. The bodies of the poor and their immediate surroundings became casualties of commodification. The poor suffered from malnutrition, and they wore meager clothing. Their minimal subsistence was just enough to maintain what for the dominant culture was the lone resource they contributed: their labor. The land surrounding them also bore scars, with common scenes like eroded and depleted fields, denuded forests, and heavily dusted coal camps.

Of tenants—the largest single group of the poor—an Atlanta banker wrote, "Every two years . . . they move from one place to another. They build no homes, they live in rude huts, no flowers about their dwellings, no trees to shade them from the sun, consumed by the summer's heat and the winter's cold, no lawns about their houses, no garden fences, and with the accursed cotton plant crowding the very threshold of their rude dwellings."[52] It was a pitiful portrait of people beaten down by their material lack, isolated from social connections and surrounded by ugliness.

In their oral narratives, folk Christians—tenants, sharecroppers, small farmers, coal miners, timber workers, domestics, and day laborers—articulated a different vision of their world, one that allowed them to be more than simple victims of their circumstances. Imaginatively, they gained breathing room to explore an identity other than that taught by the dominant culture. Dramatic personal transformation was at the heart of the narratives, but another critical transformation was at work too: the transformation of the mundane and the material. As they listened to others' tales of conversion and call, as they told them themselves, or as they reflected on them in memory, folk Christians were continually reminded of how the mundane and material were shot through with the mysterious and mystical. The sacred was not removed in some distant other world, nor was the mundane, material world a flat, secular plane. Rather, folk Christians imagined the disruptive, liminal presence of Christianity in their very midst, in ways that they could see and touch. A place in the swamp, a lonely bedroom, a cornfield, a barn loft—these common spaces could become holy sites of sacred encounter.

As with the songs of Death, there was a paradox at play here: people defined most basically by material lack sought tangible, earthy, material contact

FIGURE 14 The barn of Lloyd Chandler's encounter with Death (photograph by author).

with the sacred. They saw and touched Christianity in liminality, and from that encounter, they were propelled to proclaim the beauty and goodness of the mundane world and the people who composed it. "Everything was summertime, and the trees was green all around"; "that sun just went reeling and rocking"; "my hands . . . shined . . . like the sun was on them"; "they was the prettiest people I'd ever seen in all my life"; "a beautiful green pasture, and grazing there were thousands of sheep"; "it was the best-tasting water I ever drank"—materiality was powerfully affirmed, perhaps most vividly by the two speakers who echoed each other: "I felt a great love in my heart that made me feel like stooping and kissing the very ground"; "I just wanted to kiss the very ground. I have never felt such a love before." In the transformation imagined and recounted in their narratives, folk Christians gained new eyes to see an enchanted world and a new heart to practice love in community.

## CHAPTER FOUR

# Sacramental Expressions

Across the New South, from the Atlantic coast to central Texas, strange, enigmatic displays punctuated the landscape. A puzzled observer stumbled upon one such display spread over the jagged bluffs of the Congaree River on the edge of Columbia, South Carolina. Carefully arranged sea shells marked the outlines of individual graves, and amidst the shells was "a most curious collection of broken crockery and glassware. On the large graves are laid broken pitchers, soap-dishes, lamp chimneys, tureens, coffee-cups, sirup jugs, all sorts of ornamental vases, cigar boxes, gun-locks, tomato cans, teapots, flower-pots, bits of stucco, plaster images, pieces of carved stone-work from one of the public buildings destroyed during the war, glass lamps and tumblers in great number, and forty other kitchen articles." One set of graves was differentiated by its objects: "Doll's heads, little china wash-bowls and pitchers, toy images of animals, china vases, and pewter dishes" marked the graves of children.[1] A decade later, another observer to the same graveyard noted a "large number of medicine bottles," and twenty-five years later, in Columbia and in Ridgeway in the Piedmont, a folklorist found "bits of broken crockery, lamps or toys" covering graves.[2]

In Lowndes County in the Alabama Black Belt, a rough graveyard on a bleak, gullied hillside displayed "a goodly number" of graves "decorated with bits of broken glass and china and old bottles."[3] To the east, in Pike County and in Lee County at the Piedmont's edge, graves were covered with a wide variety of ornaments, including tin tobacco cans, butter dish covers, medicine bottles, electric light bulbs, porcelain wash basins, pepper shakers, and small stone sheep and lambs. One half-acre graveyard in Lee County displayed twenty-three lamps, some with the chimney still intact and some still partially filled with oil.[4] On the Black Belt's western edge, in Columbus, Mississippi, china, glassware, medicine bottles turned upside down, and "the cup and saucer used in the last illness" marked graves—as they did almost identically on the Sea Islands of South Carolina, with the addition of conch shells.[5] In south Georgia, favored possessions of the deceased adorned graves: "certain things they liked to eat out of or certain things they liked to drink out of."[6] In disparate parts of North Carolina—the Atlantic coast, the central Piedmont, the foothills of the Blue Ridge Mountains—graves were decorated with sea shells and large white flints, bottles with the necks sticking out of the ground, broken lamps and vases, medicine bottles, and cups and saucers.[7]

Extensive documentation from the mid-1930s and early 1940s, both written and photographic, reveals the broad scope of such decoration and distinct variations on the idiom. On Sapelo Island on the Georgia coast, numerous alarm clocks were on display in one graveyard, while graveyards in nearby mainland communities were decorated with "the bottles and dishes and other possessions" of the deceased, with "all the things what they use last, like the dishes and medicine bottles." In another graveyard in neighboring Glynn County, "lamps and electric-light bulbs are as popular as cups and pitchers."[8] In Savannah and in other towns on the Georgia coast, graves were covered with "broken bits of blue china and glass, blue plates and vases." In other parts of the state, favored toys of children, medicine bottles and pill boxes from the deceased's last sickness, and the crutches of cripples and walking sticks of old men were placed on graves.[9] In Ocilla, in the center of the state's coastal plain, "old knives, medicine bottles, tools, jugs, plates, shoes, sewing baskets, and similar personal paraphernalia of the deceased" appeared on graves. One grave, the intrigued folklorist wrote, "is even covered with a bedstead, and a walking cane protrudes from another."[10]

In Copiah County in southwest Mississippi, "cups and saucers and bottles" adorned graves of adults, while "some play-pretties, little doll heads, small cups, or toy animals" marked the graves of little children. "Frequently one finds a broken lamp," a folklorist noted, and "a cripple's crutch is always placed on his grave." A recently deceased elderly man's cup and saucer, medicine bottles, walking stick, and pipe were gathered to decorate his grave.[11] In a cemetery in Barataria, Louisiana, in the lower delta of the Mississippi, one grave was adorned with "a vase, a vinegar cruet, and a whiskey jigger turned upside down," another with "a half-filled bottle of medicine, a deep saucer filled with oil, a purse mirror and a tiny white elephant."[12] Graves in central and south Texas were covered with "bleached sea-shells, softly colored glass, doll-heads, medicine bottles, empty Colgate's Tooth Powder cans, broken dishes, and light globes." A "small conch shell provided with a wick" was the oil lamp atop one grave in Pilot Point, while shells adorning a grave near Corpus Christi were arranged to spell the deceased's name. In a cemetery near Denton, light globes had been carefully placed in the centers of three graves, with size and wattage being proportional to the person's age at death.[13]

The most extensive written accounts come from writer James Agee and folklorist Julia Peterkin. Agee composed a vivid description of a graveyard he observed in central Alabama's Bibb County. Many of the pine headboards

FIGURE 15 "Negroes' graveyard. Macon County, Alabama" (photograph by Arthur Rothstein; Library of Congress, Prints & Photographs Division, FSA/OWI Collection, LC-USZ62-13780).

FIGURE 16 "Negro graveyard on abandoned land in the Santee-Cooper basin near Moncks Corner, South Carolina" (photograph by Jack Delano; Library of Congress, Prints & Photographs Division, FSA/OWI Collection, LC-USF34-043572-D).

FIGURE 17 *Beaufort County, South Carolina* (photograph by Doris Ulmann; Library of Congress, Prints & Photographs Division, LC-USZ62-92907).

FIGURE 18 "Sharecropper's grave. Hale County, Alabama" (photograph by Walker Evans; Library of Congress, Prints & Photographs Division, FSA/OWI Collection, LC-USF342-T01-008176-A).

had been cut "into the flat simulacrum of an hourglass." Over the graves themselves, there were a variety of decorations. A "line of white clamshells" was placed on the ridge of some graves, while on others, the rim of the grave was traced by these shells. In the exact middle of one grave, a "blown-out electric bulb" was screwed into the clay, while on another, a blown bulb had been placed in the center of a horseshoe, which lay flat on the ground with its feet touching the headboard. Several other graves were decorated with "insulators of blue-green glass." In the center of some graves, "the prettiest or the oldest and most valued piece of china" had been placed, while others were festooned with "small and thick white dishes of the sort which are used in lunch-rooms." On yet another grave, a corncob pipe had been placed "carefully" just next to the headboard. The decorations on children's graves were the most poignant: "On the graves of children there are still these pretty pieces of glass and china, but they begin to diminish in size and they verge into the forms of animals and into homuncular symbols of growth; and there are toys: small autos, locomotives and fire engines of red and blue metal; tea sets for dolls, and tin kettles the size of thimbles: little effigies in rubber and glass and china, of cows, lions, bulldogs, squeaking mice, and the characters of comic strips."[14]

Folklorist Julia Peterkin observed the process by which such a display was created in Calhoun County in the South Carolina Midlands. Attending the funeral of an elderly woman, she noted how "when the low mound of earth was smoothed and the Bury League white paper flowers laid on it, things she prized on earth were put with them: a clock that had not ticked for many years, the cup and saucer she used, a glass lamp filled with kerosene, and a china vase holding fresh blossoms from those growing around her doorstep." This elderly woman was the first to be buried in the "new" graveyard, for the old graveyard had become too full. Peterkin penned an evocative description of it:

> The old graveyard . . . [sits] on the edge of a hill that drops to the river with a steep fall called "Lover's Leap." Below it lie untamed miles of swamp where the river bends into the Devil's Elbow, or swollen by rains, makes a vast yellow lake that uproots and drowns the swamp's undergrowth. Yellow stains high on the trunks of tall trees mark the height of its flood long after it has passed. But no flood can reach the old graveyard. Spring shows early in the tender, misty green of willows that mark the river channel. . . . Tangles of yellow jessamine drop golden bells and crab apple thickets send down showers of fragrant pink petals to lie among the

carved wooden heads of wheat placed on some of the graves long ago. Nobody knows who carved them or why the wood lasts so long.[15]

Even as the region began to change dramatically in the decades after 1940, instances of this suggestive practice were still being documented in different corners of the region, along the Georgia and South Carolina coasts and in the Piney Woods region of northwest Louisiana and east Texas. On St. Simons Island, Georgia, in the 1940s and early 1950s, newer consumer items were making an appearance amidst older materials: "The articles on the graves include every kind of container or utensil—sea shells, salt and pepper shakers, pickle bottles, shaving mugs, moustache cups, piggy banks, the interior mechanism of a radio, alarm clocks, lamps, automobile head lights, electric light bulbs, flash lights, combs, cold cream jars, plates, cups, saucers, ash trays, milk bottles, and chamber pots."[16] Popular culture was also on display (see figs. 19 and 20).

In coastal South Carolina in the 1960s and 1970s, innovations—like an overturned toilet tank and a stainless steel pot—adorned graves. But traditional staples were there too, like a glass pitcher set down over a conch shell. Innovation and tradition were readily mixed, as on one mounded, clamshell-covered grave with a new granite headstone.[17] Similarly, in the Piney Woods in the 1960s, old staples were apparent. "Shells are common," a folklorist observed. But so were telephone-line insulators, plastic bleach bottles, glass canning jars, and coffee cans. Graves of children displayed significant diversity, with "marbles, toy cars, airplanes, light bulbs, metal-tipped vacuum tubes from radios and television sets, and broken pieces of colored glass."[18] In Cass County in the Piney Woods in the 1970s, a folklorist found graves adorned with shells, dishes, pipes, toys, and brown snuff bottles, while one grave commemorating a teenager was "decorated with a soda fountain lever and a drugstore light fixture."[19]

Decorating graves with the broken belongings of the deceased—household possessions and other suggestive paraphernalia—was a folk practice of wide scope, documented from the Atlantic coast to central Texas. In the society of the New South, it was sufficiently exotic to attract the curious attention of folklorists, documentary photographers, and others in search of cultural difference. Yet it was also sufficiently enigmatic to be overlooked or dismissed by many who lived in close proximity to such displays. Even a professional archaeologist, sent to investigate a site near Charleston, South Carolina, in the late 1960s, reported "that there didn't appear to be anything there other than some late nineteenth century and twentieth century junk scattered throughout the area . . . late period garbage of no interest."[20] The graveyard this

FIGURE 19   Statue of Jackie Coogan as a child, from Margaret Davis Cate and Orrin Sage Wightman, *Early Days of Coastal Georgia* (St. Simons Island, GA: Fort Frederica Association, 1955).

archaeologist dismissed, like others that appeared across the landscape of the New South, was in fact a material display containing powerful symbolic meaning. With his literary insight, William Faulkner evoked this in his 1940 story "Pantaloon in Black." As the grave of a sawmill worker's wife was slowly filled, "the mound seemed to be rising of its own volition, not built up from above but thrusting visibly upward out of the earth itself, until at last the grave, saw for its rawness, resembled any other marked off without order about the barren plot by shards of pottery and broken bottles and old brick and other objects insignificant to sight but actually of a profound meaning."[21]

This practice originally had meaning in the societies of west and west central Africa. In roughly the same era that it was being documented across the South, it was being documented by travelers and anthropologists in an arch stretching from the Ivory Coast and Ghana, to Benin and Nigeria, to Gabon

FIGURE 20 Statue of Superman, from Margaret Davis Cate and Orrin Sage Wightman, *Early Days of Coastal Georgia* (St. Simons Island, GA: Fort Frederica Association, 1955).

and Congo and Angola. Indeed, one of the earliest (1891) observers of the practice in the South drew a direct connection between what he observed and what an 1884 traveler to Congo reported. "The natives mark the final resting-places of their friends," the traveler wrote, "by ornamenting their graves with crockery, empty bottles, old cooking-pots, etc., all of which articles are rendered useless by being cracked." Examining the illustration that accompanied this report, the Southern observer noted that the "engraving of the grave of a Congo chieftain . . . would do very well for the picture of one in the Potters' Field, Columbia, SC."[22] Twenty years earlier, a traveler to Dahomey (present-day Benin) noted that "a small house is built upon the beach, and in it are placed the valuables possessed by the departed—some whole, and others broken—statues, clocks, vases, porcelains, and so forth."[23] In 1904, a missionary to Gabon noted that "over or near the graves of the rich are built little huts, where are laid the common articles used by them in their life—pieces of crockery, knives, sometimes a table, mirrors." Of graves in Nigeria, another traveler reported in 1912 that "all along the edge plates and dishes have been pressed into the mud when soft. These were first broken, as is always done with the property of the dead."[24] This distinct pattern of grave decoration was perpetuated well into the twentieth century: a team of anthropologists working in Gabon in the 1950s found remarkable continuations of the practice.

In the original African context of meaning, decorating graves with personal objects served both to honor and to appease the departed. The dead had entered the realm of spirits, an unseen yet powerful world that exerted influence over the visible, material world of the living. To rightly honor these spirits yet also to secure their favor, since they now had unseen influence over the living, personal objects of the deceased were reserved for their continued commemoration. The breaking of these objects served to highlight this purpose by making them functionally useless for the living; it may also have been imagined as liberating the spirits of these objects for passage into the realm of the dead. In symbolic cosmology, this realm of the dead was underground or underwater. The objects on top of a grave served, then, as a visual signifier of unseen realities, a tangible manifestation of the connection between the realm of the living above and the realm of the spirits below.

Documentation from the New South reveals that only fragments of this African context of meaning were perpetuated. Asked by strangers to explain the meaning of a practice that these very inquisitors viewed as exotic and primitive, practitioners gave a wide variety of answers, many of which display dissimulation rather than candor. Some said they didn't know; some said it was simply an "old-time custom." Others explained that items were broken to keep them from being stolen, while others said that it signified that a member of the family had been broken in death. Some said that possessions were placed on the grave to keep the deceased from coming back again, and others explained that it was done to "ward off evil spirits." Still others stated that it was done "so that the spirit may not find itself in an entirely strange world," while others said it was done "lest the soul be retarded in flight." Elderly African Americans on the Georgia coast came closest to evoking the original African context of meaning. Speaking to folklorists in the late 1930s, Sarah and Ben Washington (b. ca. 1850) said, "I don't guess you be bothered much by the spirits if you give 'em a good funeral and put the things what belongs to them on top of the grave. . . . You puts all the things what they use last, like the dishes and the medicine bottle. The spirits need these same as the man. Then the spirit rest and don't wander about." Jane Lewis (b. ca. 1820) explained that "them dishes and bottles what put on the grave is for the spirit and it ain't for nobody to touch 'em. That's for the spirit to feel at home." She went on to explain that those who died away from home were brought home for burial, and that everyone had two funerals: one as soon as they died, and later a collective funeral—"one big preachin'"—for everyone who died that year. The two-funeral practice and "home bringing" of the deceased were both traditional African rituals, documented by travelers in the eighteenth century.[25]

Yet even among these speakers, interviewed for a folkloric study looking for "African survivals" in a large black-majority area, where the older economy of rice plantations had enabled a greater coherence of Africanized slave culture, a subtle change is evident. The deceased honored with grave decorations no longer exert power over the living from an unseen realm of spirits; rather, if rightly honored in their burial, the deceased seem to be simply at rest. This movement away from the original context of meaning is emblematic of deeper movements: from its African origins, a distinct practice of grave decoration spread to new people and was invested with new meaning in a new context.

Most basically, the practice ceased to be solely African American. In the 1920s, the practice was documented among whites on the coast of North Carolina and in counties in the foothills of the Blue Ridge Mountains. From Alexander County one folklorist wrote, "I have noticed that not only the Negroes in our section put bits of broken dishes, etc., on the graves, but also the whites quite often. On one grave of a white person . . . I noticed last summer pretty bits of china, a broken lamp, broken vases, and a cracked cup or two. Many of the graves in this same graveyard are profusely decorated with all sizes and kinds of stone also."[26] In the 1930s, the practice by whites was documented in Georgia, in central Alabama (the graveyard of Agee's extended description) and the Black Belt, and in central and south Texas; and in the 1960s and 1970s, it was noted in northwest Louisiana and east Texas. Based on the documentation, then, the practice was primarily but not exclusively African American. Considering its geographic scope, what is at work here seems to be the reverse of "Conversation with Death" and its oral patterns of transmission.

Just as "Conversation with Death" was a song crafted out of European tradition and spread from its Appalachian home, remaining especially strong in predominantly white Appalachia but by no means confined to it, so too was grave decoration a practice carried from African tradition and disseminated by African Americans, perpetuated especially in the black-majority Sea Islands and Low Country but by no means limited to those areas or to African Americans. Faulkner's literary evocation that the "profound meaning" of this practice was one "which no white man could have read" (echoed by folklorists and historians in subsequent analysis) needs amending: in appropriating the practice and perpetuating it to honor their own dead, whites joined blacks in conveying meaning through this distinct ritual.[27]

But where the ritual had once held meaning as a common practice in different African societies, in the New South it had become distinctly marginal. This comes through most clearly in the sense of difference conveyed by its middle-class observers. The practice caught their attention because it was exotic and unfamiliar, foreign and mysterious in its meaning. It was "fetishism" inherited from "savage ancestors"; "an old heathen custom"; an instance of "voodooistic behavior" or "black magic"; a survival of "animistic belief" from "primitive man."[28] Less hostilely, the practice was categorized as a "folk belief," as something belonging to "folklore." Insofar as details accompanying its documentation locate the social position of its practitioners, they further suggest its difference from the middle class. It was found in a "Potter's Field" on the edge of Columbia and among "poverty-stricken country folk" in Texas; among black and white tenants in central Alabama, the Black Belt, and the South Carolina Low Country; and in marginal places like the "pine barrens" inland from the Georgia coast and the foothills of the Blue Ridge Mountains.[29] Like songs of personified Death or carefully stylized oral narratives of conversion, grave decoration in the New South had moved from its origins to become a folk practice of the poor.

In this movement, the practice was invested with new meanings. Certainly it retained its basic form as a way of honoring the dead: atop the grave were personal possessions and important items of the deceased. Yet innovative little details suggest significant cultural transformation. Shells, medicine bottles, and lamps were recurrent new features. Shells were observed in places as disparate as the South Carolina Sea Islands; Columbia, South Carolina; counties on the North Carolina coast, in the Piedmont, and in the foothills of the Blue Ridge Mountains; Bibb County, Alabama; and central Texas. Medicine bottles were documented in North Carolina and Georgia; in Columbia,

South Carolina, and Ocilla, Georgia; in Copiah County, Mississippi, and Columbus in the Black Belt; in Barataria, Louisiana, and central Texas. Lamps were spotted in the South Carolina Low Country and Midlands and along the Georgia coast; in Lee County in the Alabama Piedmont and Alexander County in the Blue Ridge Mountain foothills; in Columbia, South Carolina, Copiah County, Mississippi, and central Texas. These items went beyond commemorating the individuality of the deceased. They conjured up imagery of the coast or water's edge, of sickness and healing, of light shining in darkness. Death, such imagery suggested, put one at a boundary—on the edge of transformation.

What that transformation consisted of was indicated by other imagery. The "carved wooden heads of wheat" adorning graves in a Calhoun County, South Carolina, graveyard were beacons of a harvest that had not yet come to pass. Similarly, the clocks placed on graves in the Georgia Sea Islands and the South Carolina Low Country and Midlands emphasized time—time envisioned as an expectant wait. An alarm clock on a Sapelo Island grave made this point explicitly in provoking the question, When would it ring? In Bibb County, Alabama, the rough pine headboards carved in the shape of an hourglass were perhaps most evocative of waiting. When, they asked suggestively, would the sand fill the hourglass—or when would the filled hourglass be turned upside down to record a new time?

Taken together, these symbols displayed hope in resurrection, in the raising up of the dead to new life. With his artistic insight, Faulkner captured this rich symbolism: the object-covered grave mound seemed to be "thrusting visibly upward out of the earth itself," harbinger of a body longing for its resurrection.[30] The orientation of grave decoration, then, had shifted from its original African meaning. Objects placed on graves were no longer honoring the dead who had entered the realm of spirits—a realm that exerted power over the living. Rather, objects now waited with the body of the deceased in hopeful expectation of new life in a transformed world—a new life that was remarkably tangible and material. One's favorite cup and saucer, a beloved pipe, a walking stick, a child's favorite fire engine or doll tea set: these items were not worldly ephemera—merely material objects—but material objects that precisely in their materiality would be useful and meaningful to the resurrected dead. The original African practice had been Christianized, as Julia Peterkin discerned. Evoking newness and transformation in her vivid description of springtime in the "old graveyard," she wrote of how "old graves sunken with waiting so long for Gabriel to blow his trumpet and clothe old bones with living flesh are sprinkled with blue violets," how the wooden heads of wheat were carved by "somebody who believed that some day 'The trumpet shall sound and the dead shall be raised incorruptible.'"[31]

The New South context sharpened this meaning. As in their songs of death and the rich imagery of their conversion narratives, folk Christians were affirming materiality in the face of a dominant culture that denigrated the poor in their very bodies and in their material lack, which appeared as transparent badges of a lack of respectability. They were doing this with objects that, from a purely practical point of view, were costly to "waste" on grave decoration. Water pitchers, oil lamps, crockery, bottles, cups and saucers, chamber pots, spoons, shoes, and other items were all useful on a regular basis, most especially for people living lives defined by lack. Perhaps a few of the items had been broken accidentally before the person's death, but the breaking of items *after* the person's death involved important loss. Surely such breaking was not done lightly or without careful consideration. It was done for the sake of conveying religious meaning deeper than (hardly unimportant) utilitarian purposes.

This is not to say that the practice involved only the sacrifice of the practical for the sake of the religious: some items placed on the graves were certainly uncommon in the lives of the poor. China, glass telegraph-wire insulators, electric light bulbs, shells in areas distant from the coast—not to mention a porcelain Superman and a grandfather clock—were not typical possessions of the poor. Indeed, one determined impoverished man bartered berries for burned-out light globes "with the express purpose of using them in the cemetery."[32] The careful placement of such exotic items, complementing the strange spectacle of the assemblage of household goods and personal items, accentuated a sense of mystery. The dead waited for a transformation, but the nature of that transformation was mysterious and elusive. The assembled goods—common and uncommon—suggested the materiality of that transformation, even as they suggested its strangeness and unfamiliarity.

The broader setting of the graveyard further conveyed this element of mystery. To middle-class observers, nothing had been done to beautify the surroundings. In Lowndes County, Alabama, the hillside graveyard was so "seamed and gashed by rains" that it seemed as if the "poor hills were skinned and bleeding." In two cemeteries in Lee and Pike counties, an observer was struck by how "in neither case were there flowers nor a single decorative plant or flowering shrub in the entire cemetery." A Bibb County graveyard had "almost no trees in it. . . . It is all red clay and very few weeds." In Glynn and McIntosh counties on the Georgia coast, "one never sees shrubbery planted to beautify the area or fresh flowers kept on the grave." Graveyards in the

Piney Woods of East Texas and northwest Louisiana were regularly "scraped" to clear the area of vegetation, and the "subsequent mounding of the graves with fresh dirt, gravel, or sand" gave them "the appearance of a fresh burial."[33] A graveyard in the South Carolina Sea Islands was surrounded by "one of those ragged patches of live-oak and palmetto and brier tangle," while inside the wild enclosure there were "graves scattered without symmetry, and often without head-stones or head-boards, or sticks." Similarly, in a cemetery in Barataria, Louisiana, there were "no headstones, no inscriptions."[34] Graves "seemed to be placed throughout the cemetery with no order" near Charleston, and none were marked.[35] The placement of graves seemed to defy any sense of order, and the ground was often kept in a rough, raw state of bareness amidst unkempt surroundings. It was neither restful lawn nor well-tended field but a place of otherness. Tangible items and the landscape itself were mobilized to express a sense of strange yet hopeful mystery.

With a careful collection of common and curious items, in rough and raw settings, folk graveyards stood in sharp contrast to the cemeteries of the dominant religious culture. Texas folklorist Dorothy Michael noted how the first folk cemetery she saw, with "delightful drugstore decoration" atop graves, differed dramatically from "the smooth lawns and flat, uninteresting markers of sophisticated city cemeteries."[36] These cemeteries were of a type pioneered by Boston's early nineteenth-century Mount Auburn Cemetery. In carefully ordered rows, with a serene expanse of lawn, the garden-like cemetery conveyed a powerful sense of rest and calm. The order, the serenity, and the beauty mirrored the values of domesticity. Together, the elements sent a clear message: the deceased had gone on to their otherworldly home.[37] The dead had been liberated from the merely material. The orientation was toward that "other" world, the spiritual home that was the object of one's religious longing. Just as the cemetery setting expressed the calmness of rest, so too in death the soul found perpetual rest in a heavenly home. Folk graveyards projected a different message: their raw settings and assembled goods pointed to a mysterious yet tangible transformation that would happen to *this* world. The orientation was one of return, not departure—albeit a strange return.

Folk graveyards punctuated the landscape as heralds and beacons of strange, sacred transformation. They used an assemblage of secular items to suggestively embody a hint of this sacred transformation. The goods atop graves in the New South era, both common and uncommon, were almost entirely mass-produced objects brought by the market revolution. With folk creativity, such secular goods were repurposed to express religious meaning.

Using the secular and tangible to convey religious and intangible meaning, folk Christians displayed a strong sacramental impulse.

The same basic impulse—to grasp the sacred in the common material of everyday life—was at work in lore about holidays. Across the New South, a legend was told about what happened at Christmas. In Robeson County, North Carolina, on "Old Christmas" (January 5 or 6: the Julian calendar's date for Christmas before the mid-eighteenth-century change to the Gregorian calendar), everyone rested from their labors, and "that night the domestic animals go down on their knees."[38] In eastern and central North Carolina, it "was believed that at Old Christmas, animals got down on their knees and turned to the East." In Transylvania County, it was told that "exactly at midnight on the night of Old Christmas, all cattle and horses everywhere stand up and then lie down on the other side," while in Buncombe County, the legend said that "cows kneel at midnight on the eve of Old Christmas."[39] Across the mountains in Wise County, Virginia, children watched on Old Christmas as a cow "lay down and was well contented until about a half an hour before midnight." Then "just at the stroke of midnight she fell down on her knees and horning the ground she moaned and groaned for five or ten minutes."[40] In Demopolis, Alabama, and Columbus, Mississippi, in the Black Belt, it was said that cows and sheep "kneel in prayer on Christmas Eve night."[41] In Copiah County in southwest Mississippi, a man stumbled into a stable on Christmas Eve night and came across animals kneeling.[42] In coastal Louisiana, it was told that "cows get down on their knees at midnight on Christmas Eve," while in the Ozarks, the legend said that "the cattle all kneel down and bellow at midnight on January 5th—the eve of 'old Christmas'—in honor of the birth of Jesus."[43] Also in the Ozarks, "some say that the critters have the gift of speech on this night, so that they may pray aloud in English." It was also said that "boys born on Old Christmas are supposed to be very lucky in raising cattle; some say that these 'Old Christmas children' can actually talk the cow brute's language."[44]

One North Carolina man, having forgotten what day it was, left a vivid account of how he stumbled across the truth of the legend in spite of himself: "I was a-crossin' Grandfather [Mountain] one time on the night of Old Christmas. It was bitter cold and the fog had froze on the pines and balsams till every leaf was inch deep in rime. 'Twas a full moon and purt night clear as day at 12 o'clock. I was drivin' two yoke of cattle and a-goin' East. Jest at midnight them steers all stopped. I hollered at 'em, fur I'd forgot the time. They never paid no attention to me. Old Buck, the head steer, dropped on all four of his knees and all the others done the same thing. They stayed right there still on their knees five minutes, and I stood thar a-feeling right plum weak."[45]

Such lore had its origins in early modern England. In his early nineteenth-century *Observations on Popular Antiquities*, folklorist John Brand wrote, "A superstitious notion prevails in the western parts of Devonshire, that at twelve o'clock at night on Christmas-eve, the oxen in their stalls are always found on their knees, as in an attitude of devotion; and that (which is still more singular) since the alteration of the style, they continue to do this only on the eve of Old Christmas-day." How far back in time this "notion" existed is difficult to determine. Certainly it was in existence well before 1752, when England's switch to the Gregorian calendar moved Christmas to December 25 and created, for those who opposed the move, the continued celebration of "Old Christmas" on January 6 or 7. As in many other instances, lore flourished orally in a scope (in time and space) well beyond its written documentation. Had Brand not written it down, this conversation would be lost: "An honest countryman, living on the edge of St Stephen's Down, near Launceston, Cornwall, informed me, October 28, 1790, that he once, with some others, made a trial of the truth of the above, and, watching several oxen in their stalls at the above time—at twelve o'clock at night—they observed the two oldest oxen only, fall upon their knees, and, as he expressed it in the idiom of the country, make 'a cruel moan, like Christian creatures.'" Likewise, in his 1881 *Popular Romances of the West of England*, folklorist Robert Hunt recalled, "I remember, when a child, being told that all the oxen and cows kept at a farm in the parish of St Germans, at which I was visiting with my aunt, would be found on their knees when the clock struck twelve. This is the only case within my own knowledge of this wide-spread superstition existing in Cornwall."[46]

New South documentation suggests that this English folklore was circulated in a reverse pattern to that of African grave decoration. Whereas grave decoration was especially prominent in the black-majority Sea Islands and Black Belt but reached only the foothills of white-majority Appalachia, this Christmas lore was especially prominent in Appalachia even as it spread out from this white-majority area to the Sea Islands and Black Belt. In the New South, it ceased to be solely Anglo-American folklore but became instead the cultural property of whites and blacks—more specifically, impoverished whites and blacks, the same "superstitious" class of people who were active practitioners of the tradition of grave decoration.

In the New South, this lore was perpetuated intact—proof of the durability of knowledge once it gets codified in an oral culture. People who may no longer have even known the history behind Old Christmas continued to celebrate it and to tell of how cows knelt reverently on that day. At the same time, creative new variations appeared in New South lore. In Robeson County, North Carolina, it was told that on Old Christmas, "chickens come down from their roost," and despite winter's frost, "rosemary and poke 'put out.'"[47] "Hop vines spread out on Old Christmas even if there is snow on the ground," it was said in Wake County; and in Buncombe County, it was told that on Old Christmas "horses talk" and "water turns to blood at midnight."[48] In Wise County, Virginia, one legend said that on "dead midnight" of Christmas, a bee hive would leap into frenzied activity, "roaring . . . . just like they do in summer."[49] Likewise, in the Ozarks, it was said that "bees in a hive always buzz very loudly exactly at midnight on the eve of Old Christmas; if several bee gums are set close together, the 'Old Christmas hum' can be heard some distance away."[50] In the South Carolina Low Country, it was told that not only sheep and cattle but "fowls of the air" too knelt at midnight on Christmas, and that on Christmas morning, "the sun shouts."[51] In the Ozarks, it was said that "on the morning of Old Christmas there are two daybreaks instead of one."[52] In Atlanta, the sun shouted and danced—but on Easter morning, not Christmas.[53] In coastal Louisiana, it was believed that "roosters crow all night before Christmas," and "animals talk to each other at twelve o'clock at night on Christmas Eve."[54]

Of "isolated sections of the Blue Ridge," folklorist Jean Thomas composed a vivid account of lore surrounding celebrations of Old Christmas. Every year at midnight, households grew quiet as all members of the household, still very much awake, listened eagerly for intimations of Christ's birth: "in the waiting silence comes the low mooing of the cows and the whinny of nags, and looking outside the cabin door the mountaineer sees his cow brutes and nags kneeling in the snow under the starlit sky. 'It is the sign that this is for truth our Lord's birth night,' Granny whispers softly. Then led by the father of the household, carrying his oldest man child upon his shoulder, the women-folk following behind, they go down to the creek side. Kneeling, the father brushes aside the snow among the elders, and there bursting through the ice-bound earth appears a green shoot bearing a white blossom."[55] Similarly, in the Ozarks, it was said that "elderberry always sprouts on the eve of Old Christmas—even if the ground is frozen hard, you'll find the little green shoots under the snow."[56] A variant on this, in Wise County, told of how on Christmas morning, the buds of elder bush would burst open in a vibrant display of color—even though the night before, the ground might have been frozen hard with not the slightest suggestion of new life.[57]

Creative variations on traditional lore reveal that what was at work was more than the mere survival of an element of the past. Just as in the practice of grave decoration, so too in the telling of Christmas lore were folk Christians actively appropriating inherited cultural material—working within a tradition to convey new meanings for a new context. Newly available commodities disseminated by the market revolution figured prominently in grave decoration; in Christmas lore, it was common fixtures of the natural world: cows and sheep, elder and hops, the morning sun. On a holy day, these ordinary things took on a heightened, sacred meaning. In their actions—quite independent of human agency—they became signifiers of a sacred event. Caught up for a time in the drama of sacred history, they became visible manifestations of unseen, past realities. For a brief but rich moment, they became sacraments. For those who had heard the lore and learned what to expect, these sacred displays punctuated ordinary time with figurative reenactments of holy history. The New South present was a visible participant—through natural things acting strangely and mysteriously—in a sacred story.

This interweaving of "secular" present and sacred past was both fortified by and echoed in folk sermons. Whereas middle-class observers were blind to grave decoration, or simply found it puzzling, and considered Christmas lore a survival of quaint superstition from an archaic world, the ubiquity of the sermon in Protestant worship attracted significant attention to its practice among the poor. The attention was decisively negative. Reporting on a sermon she had heard among white mountaineers in a log schoolhouse in the Smoky Mountains, a Baptist home missionary wrote that "the long sermon, rhythmical throughout, was simply a string of quotations chosen at random from Genesis to Revelation, with the text, 'If thou be the Christ-ah / Tell us plainly-ah,' brought in with the regularity of a refrain."[58] A Mississippi planter found little substance in a sermon he observed in a church of black tenants: the preacher begins, he wrote, "in a loud, singsong manner, keeping time with the singing of the congregation. . . . On and on at great length he hammers his theme out until it is thin as tinfoil."[59] In his field study of black tenants in four representative counties, a Tuskegee chaplain wrote that the sermons he had heard were merely "a heated hodge-podge of emotional shibboleths mixed with bits of common sense" and that "many were crude and some were 'otherworldly.'"[60]

In reality, folk sermons, like conversion narratives, were a highly developed oral form, employing various mnemonic devices, codifying content into familiar tropes and formulas, and allowing imaginative room for individual variation and creativity. A folklorist who, in the late 1960s, studied the perpetuation of this oral form by mid-century migrants from the fading New South to Southern California characterizes folk sermons as distinct American art, worthy of the serious attention bestowed on oral epic poems like those of the Yugoslavian *guslars* studied by Milman Parry and Albert Lord.[61] Rich and creative as this oral form was, its very orality made it—like "Conversation with Death," conversion narratives, and Christmas lore—cultural material whose documentation is but a tiny glimpse of the form in its entirety. Documented folk sermons are overwhelmingly from the mid- to late 1930s, and they are largely concentrated in distinct areas: white-majority counties in the Cumberland Mountains and Appalachian foothills, and black-majority counties in the Alabama Black Belt, Mississippi Delta, and Texas Blackland Prairie. Yet despite the real differences of these areas, the documented sermons display common features, not least of which is an imaginative interweaving of biblical narrative with the New South present.

At Bolton Creek Baptist Church in Travis County, Texas, preacher Chester Hulen imagined Jesus walking the country roads of the New South:

> He goin' to walk around some more. He goin' to see old brother Franklin out working in the field. He goin' to watch brother Franklin, and he goin' to see him when he takes the team out and goes to the barn. He goin' to see him feed his team, and then he goin' to see him go down on his knees out there in the mule lot, and pray. Jesus goin' to see brother Franklin prayin', and he goin' to rejoice. Praise the Lord. . . . He goin' to go down past old brother Ford's place, and he goin' to see brother Ford. He goin' to see brother Ford out in the blacksmith shed, a-hammerin' away on a hot plow point, and a-singin' one of the Lord's church songs. He goin' to see the light of salvation shinin' in old brother Ford's face, and then he goin' to rejoice again.[62]

Jesus was no deity distant in time or space; rather, he was so close as to see the little everyday details of agricultural labor. In narrating Jesus visiting impoverished rural people where they were, Hulen's sermon dignified the poor in the face of a dominant culture that denigrated them. Their "secular" labor was intertwined with their religious devotion—just as the "secular" world was intertwined with the religious.

At Laurel Grove Primitive Baptist Church in Wise County, Virginia, preacher George Dinsmore wove together the Creation story and the story of Jesus's burial to insist on the materiality of God's redeeming work in the world: "Here's the reason Jesus went down in the grave: he went—I'm gonna preach it—for *man*, and you brethren can have it just like you want it. That may be, it may be too strong for you, I don't know. But—I'm gonna preach it—it was a *man* that Jesus went down after, and—I'm gonna preach it—it was a *man* that God created in his image and likeness and formed him up out of the ground and created him in his image and likeness—I'm gonna preach it—it was that *ground* like I walk on and till."[63] From the dusty man of Genesis, to Jesus's descent into Hades to rescue the dead, to a fresh-tilled field in the present, God was working with earthly matter to bring new life. Creation, resurrection, and crops—the raw materials were the same, and each was an analogue of the other. No Docetism here: Jesus had to really die, had to really be buried, to break the bondage of death and redeem human beings in their fleshy materiality.

Tanner Franklin, preaching at a Baptist church in Austin County, Texas, brought the parable of the lost sheep into the pattern of rural life:

> There ain't a road you walk and there ain't a place you pass, that old Satan ain't hidin' round, tryin to catch you. He's watchin' for you on Saturday nights, when you goes in town, and he's watchin' for you when you come out of town. He's always just more than ready to catch one of the Lord's sheeps. Amen. It's so, church. Old Satan catch a sheep out in the wilderness somewhere, then he go to the Lord and try to tell him that there's just one sheep lost, so that ain't so bad. But the Lord don't pay no mind to that sort of talk. No, he don't. The Lord knows that he's got to have all them sheeps in that pen before he can rest right. He's got to go out there and find every last one of his sheeps, before he can say that his sheeps is saved. Amen.[64]

Satan was close and ever-present, a highway robber watching the ritual of going to town on Saturday nights. But Jesus was close and ever-present too, unable to rest until he had gathered every single one of his sheep. In their listening, Franklin's hearers immediately became "the Lord's sheeps," admonished to be vigilant against lurking evil even as they were fortified by a watchful Jesus who had refuted Satan's claim that "one little sheep never mattered."

These sermon narratives blurred the line between the New South present and the biblical past, imaginatively transporting listeners into a strange world where the secular present and the sacred past overlapped. Some preachers accentuated this with their repetitive use of "I can see" or "I see" throughout the sermon. In Travis County, Texas, preacher Giles Cummins told the story of David and Goliath as if he were a firsthand witness: "Well, I can see a paschal lamb with sheeps a-grazin'. And I can see a little boy sitting there playing his harp. He weren't studying no war, he was studying about the Lord. Little David sat there and played on his harp, and he sung to the sheeps. He was a praying child. Yes, good Lord, he was a praying child."[65] In Macon County, Georgia, a preacher witnessed the dispute of Ahab and Naboth: "I saw him.... Ahab went down and tried to find Naboth in the vineyard.... Naboth said, 'No, Lord, I can't labor in the vineyard.' But bye and bye old Ahab got mad and went on home. Ain't dat right, brethren? While Ahab had gone home, his wife—he got in the bed, he wouldn't eat nothin' and he wasn't, wouldn't drink nothin'—his wife said to him, 'What's the matter with you?' He said, 'I went down to trade with Naboth concerning his vineyard and he wouldn't trade.'"[66] The most remarkable instance of this first-person narration (at least in the existing documentation) is in a sermon preached by Sin-Killer Griffin at the state prison farm in Brazoria County, Texas. With vividly arresting imagery, cascading lines that heighten the drama, and poetic license with the text, Griffin's sermon is a striking example of folk sermons as an art form. It is worth quoting at length to convey its masterful narrative impact. Griffin's scene was the hill of Calvary:

> I seen while he was hanging, the mountain began to tremble on which Jesus was hanging on. The blood was dropping on the mountain, holy blood, dropping on the mountain, my dear friends.... I seen then about that time while the blood was dropping down, one drop after another, I seen the sun that Jesus made in creation, the sun rose, my dear friends, and it recognized Jesus hanging on the cross. Just as soon as the sun recognized its maker, why it clothed itself in sack clothing and went down, went down in mourning. "Look at my maker hanging on the cross." And when the sun went down, we seen the moon, that was his maker too, he made the moon. My dear friends, yes, both time and seasons. We seen, my dear friends, when the moon recognized Jesus dying on the cross. I see the moon, yes, took with a judgment hemorrhage and bled away.... I seen the little stars, great God, that was there, they remembered Jesus when he struck on the anvil of time and the little stars began to show their beautiful ray of light. And the stars recognized their maker dying on the cross, each little star leaped out of silver orbit to make the torches of a dark unanointed world. It got so dark until the men who was putting Jesus to death, they said they could feel the darkness in their fingers. Great God almighty, they was close to one another and it was so dark they feel one another and hear one another talk, but they couldn't see each other. I heard one of the centurions say, "surely, surely, this must be the Son of God."[67]

Griffin's "I seen," "We seen," and "I heard" seek to make the listener an engaged witness to the unfolding drama. His striking imagery paints, in the mind's eye, a vivid scene of cosmic catastrophe. It is the antithesis of Christmas lore, with animals and plants celebrating Christ's birth. Here, sun, moon, and stars are the actors, each in its own way mourning Christ's death. They compel even the executioners to confession.

Some middle-class observers, dismissive in certain ways of the religious culture of the poor, were nonetheless captivated by the living drama—the collapsed time between sacred past and New South present—that they heard in folk sermons. "He talks to his congregation about Moses and Daniel at midday as though he had eaten breakfast with them," Arthur Raper wrote of the typical tenant farmer-preacher he encountered in Greene County, Georgia.[68] "The dramatization of incidents of the New Testament constitutes a large part of the sermon," Charles Johnson noted in his study of Macon County, Alabama, "but the experiences are so related as to make it possible for people to identify themselves with the characters in this great struggle."[69]

Raper and Johnson were describing what they heard in black folk sermons, but dramatization of biblical characters—with a sense of immediate familiarity that invited personal identification—was a staple of folk sermons among both blacks and whites. The Samaritan woman who spoke with Jesus at the well appeared in sermons in Walker County, Alabama, and eastern Kentucky. Nicodemus, the educated teacher who could not understand Jesus's elusive statement about being born again, figured in sermons in eastern Kentucky and central Texas. Paul, fervent persecutor of the church turned apostle, was the centerpiece of sermons at Atmore Prison Farm in southern Alabama and Macon County in central Alabama. The prophet John, criminalized and in solitude on the isle of Patmos when he received visions, was the main character in sermons in Anderson County, South Carolina; Baton Rouge Parish, Louisiana; and Austin County, Texas. Many of these sermons feature solitary characters, lonely models of faithfulness to God despite social rejection: Ruth, who forsakes family (Walker County, Alabama); Abraham, commanded to sacrifice his only son (Macon County, Alabama); Daniel, who "kept the old church ship sailing himself" (Travis County, Texas); the prodigal son, who squanders wealth in a foreign country (Travis County, Texas, and Wilcox County, Alabama); Noah, alone with the animals (Sunflower County, Mississippi); Samson, fighting the Philistines with a mule's jawbone (Austin County, Texas); Elijah, a lonely fugitive from persecution (Macon County, Alabama); and Joseph, sold into slavery by his brothers (Macon County, Georgia).

In this close familiarity with biblical characters, preachers took creative license with the text, remaining within the spirit of the overarching biblical narrative but weaving in their own innovations and personalized variations. For Ben Palmer, preaching in Travis County, Texas, Adam became the name of the prodigal son:

> I can see Adam now, stickin' his money in his pocket, takin' his belongings and struttin' off. Oh, but he was the biggest thing that ever happened! And there was his poor old daddy standin' there at the gate, a-shakin' his head and sayin' goodbye. He knowed Adam never had sense enough to come out of the rain. And he knowed couldn't nobody tell Adam nothing. Adam goin' to have to find out for himself. Amen. Yes, I can see him now. Oh, yonder he go—marching along the road calling himself big. . . . Well, it weren't no time 'til the word got around that there was a smart-aleck with money in town, and that's just what old Satan always watchin' for.[70]

Palmer's prodigal son became a negative exemplar of the "mammonism" of the New South, the personal acquisitiveness that the ethos of respectability sanctioned, undergirding and fortifying the expanded consumerism of the market economy. In collapsing the identities of Adam and the prodigal son, was Palmer imagining individual self-aggrandizement as original sin?

At Little St. John Church in Anderson County, South Carolina, a preacher added vivid new details to the story of the prophet John of Revelation:

> How you reckon the Lord let three or four or five wicked men take John and do him like they done him, them lowdown, despicable and disreputable men, what John bound hand and foot with ropes and fetters and chains and bonds, and took him aboard that unfit ship, and fetch him away down to that Lonesome Valley. . . . [God] let 'em take John way over in that Lonesome Valley, where there wasn't a man, nor a house, nor a village, nor a marshal to prevent the imposition of wicked people. . . . Now with John chained there, there come a voice a-callin', "John, O John! Come up here; come up here, John!" "What do you want, Lord? What do you want now?" "Come and see! Come and see!"[71]

The text of Revelation says almost nothing about how and why John got to the penal colony of Patmos—the account of John being bound, shipped, and chained is the preacher's own innovation. The preacher draws explicitly on the folk song "Lonesome Valley" and implicitly on the folk song "He Never Said a Mumblin' Word" to paint vivid imagery of John's mistreatment and

confinement. Yet these innovative details accentuate the basic spirit of Revelation: the persecuted and shunned are nevertheless those who are open to
hearing God's strange, commanding voice. Turned around, the message is
that those who don't walk the lonesome valley are deaf to the divine call.

A remarkable sermon fragment from Sunflower County, Mississippi,
shows how familiarity with biblical characters, creative license with the biblical
text, and the thin line between the biblical past and the New South present
were synthesized to convey a tangible sense of the sacred interwoven with
the secular. The preacher was a tenant farmer, and his subject at this summertime evening meeting was Noah and the great flood. Noah was a "just man"
whom God isolated and singled out for rescue in the midst of colossal
destruction. Everyone around him was caught up in the patterns that sustained and celebrated life—marrying and dancing—but Noah withdrew from
these practices and dedicated himself to heeding God's strange command to
build an ark. Noah worked and worked, and finally the ark was finished. Then
it began to rain furiously, and the waters began to rise. Noah called the "beasties" of the earth to be with him, and then he went into the ark by himself,
even as everyone else took no notice of the rising waters and continued in
their marrying and dancing. When the waters rose to the third story, "God
himself locked the door to the Ark and pinned down the windows. People
began falling off the housetops, mothers with their children in their arms crying out for Noah to save them. The water got so deep that people were hanging on the tree tops and one by one being hurled into the water, all hollering
for help from Noah, as long as they could holler at all. But Noah could not
help them because God had locked the door and taken the key and pinned
down the windows."[72]

This preacher wanted to depict a stark, terrifying scene of awful violence.
In the Genesis text, Noah is safely secure in the ark while the floodwaters
engulf the world, but in this sermon, God takes an aggressively active role,
locking the ark's door and pinning down its windows (repeated twice in close
proximity for emphasis). The disturbingly vivid details of people falling off
housetops, mothers with children crying out, and people hanging in the treetops are all likewise original to the sermon. They heighten the drama and the
pathos while staying, like other folk sermons, within the spirit of the biblical
story. Perhaps the most significant textual deviation is a drastic edit: in the
biblical text, he is accompanied by his wife, his sons, and his daughters-in-
law; in the sermon, Noah is utterly alone, with only the "beasties" as company, and because God has locked him in the ark, he cannot reach out to
other humans even if he wanted to. The mixture of imagery powerfully

conveys Noah's utter alienation, deviating from linear logic (How will the world be repopulated if Noah is utterly alone?) to express an anguished mood and create a vivid portrait of solitary faithfulness amidst wholesale catastrophe.

The sermon's meaning was heightened because its 1935 hearers surely had strong personal memories of the great 1927 Mississippi River flood. Sunflower County native and sometime resident Charley Patton had evoked the terror of the flood in his 1929 masterpiece "High Water Everywhere," using phrases that resembled the preacher's and, like the sermon, deviating from linear logic to compile imagery and create a mood of doom. Patton took his listeners through the ravaged towns and countryside of the Delta, and the sermon with its housetops and treetops could easily have been the contemporary Delta rather than the ancient Near East. The sermon's blurry line between past and present imbued the Mississippi River flood with sacred meaning: like the primordial flood, it was God's terrible act of destruction. And like the primordial flood, it forced the uncomfortable question of whether people could withdraw into lonely isolation to hear God's message or whether, caught up in the routine cycles of social life, they might become deaf to God's summons until it was too late.

In this style of biblical interpretation, folk Christians differed significantly from a contemporary movement with which they are often associated: fundamentalism. Even astute, careful observers like Flannery O'Connor and Robert Coles employed this category as shorthand for the religious culture of impoverished Christians of the twentieth-century South. O'Connor declared her "kinship with backwoods prophets and shouting fundamentalists," and Coles wrote of "a backwoods fundamentalism that can be passionately idiosyncratic."[73]

The fundamentalist movement that originated in the early twentieth-century urban West and North did not become widespread in the South until after World War II.[74] Even then, the fundamentalist understanding of the Bible as an inerrant, inalterable fixed text, to be interpreted through the lens of common-sense realism (with words corresponding unerringly to actual real-world past or future events, like a newspaper or history book), was far removed from the folk Christian vision of the Bible.[75] As folk sermons and Christmas lore suggest, folk Christians took creative license with the Bible, altering stories to capture and express their truthfulness for the present. The stories and, more basically, the grand narrative of the Bible were the focus, not the mere text itself. Those stories were strange and mysterious, yet also tangible. Creative engagement with the world of these stories—a world in which the sacred past was interwoven with the living, everyday present—was the way to get their point and realize their meaning. When the Bible was opened up in this manner, the sacred spilled over into the secular, transforming it. Teacher Rossa Cooley memorably evoked this effect in her description of the imaginative world of impoverished blacks on St. Helena Island, South Carolina. "A religious imagery overlays fields and roads and tidal rivers," she recalled. "Abraham and the prophets are more real to them than the old slave owners who gave their names to the plantations. The Bible heroes live in the imagination of the people like the great oak on the road to Coffins Point."[76]

This religious overlay was also on dramatic display in the folk ritual of baptism. Two scenes in different corners of the region reveal that the folk practice of baptism—like grave decoration, Christmas lore, and narrative sermons—was another instance of the sacramental impulse, the longing to encounter the sacred in the tangible, earthly phenomena of everyday "secular" life.

On the edge of a pond on the outskirts of Natchez, Mississippi, a crowd of several hundred had gathered, waiting in anticipation. Then, from a house some distance away, the candidates began to proceed. They were all—men, women, and children—wearing white robes, and their heads were bound in white cloths. They came slowly and solemnly, singing a "dirge-like song" as they walked two-by-two to the edge of the pond. The preacher was waiting, standing in the water, with three helpers on either side. The preacher's lively exhortations met with great excitement from the gathered crowd. "Shouts and groans came up," and periodically people broke into song:

*I'm goin' down to Jordan—Hallelu!*
*I'm goin' down to Jordan—Hallelu!*
*With the elders in the lead.*

The helpers then led the candidates into the water, one by one, where the preacher lifted his hand, pronounced the words of baptism, and plunged the candidate into the water. The immersed candidates struggled and "thrashed about"—a dramatic change from their earlier funereal solemnity. Each immersion brought an increasingly passionate response from the gathered crowd: "The shouting became more wild and unrestrained, the struggles of the candidates more violent. . . . The crowd surged back and forth, and as one bystander would rush to greet a candidate coming out of the water, shrieking forth joy and thanksgiving, the crowd would join in vehement song."[77]

On the edge of a small river in Wise County, Virginia, on a bright July morning, a crowd was gathering. It was a festive day: "sacrament meeting" at

Little Stone Gap Church. But before this meeting, the joiners had to be initiated, and so everyone was meeting an hour early at the river. As people gathered, they shook hands and exchanged greetings. Then a solemn hush fell over the crowd as the preacher began to talk—quietly at first, then with rising volume to encompass the entire gathering. The preacher called out a familiar tune, and the group broke into song:

> *On Jordan's stormy bank I stand*
> *And cast a wishful eye.*

Everyone fell to the ground on their knees in prayer after the song, with the preacher praying passionately as "smothered sobs" and "fervent amens" came up from the crowd. The preacher then waded into the water, and as the crowd began another song, initiates waded into the water to be immersed, one by one:

> *Down to the sacred wave*
> *The Lord of life was led*
> *And he who came our souls to save*
> *In Jordan bowed his head.*

From the water the baptized came shouting, and their shouts set off echoes through the gathered crowd: "A shouting sister is led from the water. She clasps a sister standing on the bank. It is too much. The clasped sister starts shouting the praises and several more break out in the crowd. . . . As another sister is led into the water, the tear stained face of an old lady breaks into a smile, she shifts the feeble weight of her aged body to the one crutch under her right arm, and talks of the wondrous love of God in a trembling voice." Finally, when all the initiates were baptized and the last snatches of shouting and praises fell silent, the crowd proceeded en masse to the distant church house.[78]

Scenes like this recurred throughout the New South, in black-majority areas like humid, Spanish-moss-covered Natchez, and in white-majority areas like rugged, mountainous Wise County. They were a regular religious performance—a stylized ritual—with both common defining features and localized variations. These rituals were the most visible instance of the sacramental imagination of folk Christians. Numerous outside observers—from studious folklorists, to passing FSA photographers, to critical home missionaries—documented such rituals and their stylized features. As the preceding scenes suggest, outside observers couldn't help but notice how these religious performances involved intimate acquaintance with parts of the natural landscape. In these moments, seemingly ordinary phenomena—a pond, a river, the waters that enclosed an immersed body, the edge of the shore where the crowd gathered—were suffused with sacred meaning. Such places became material sites where the presence of God was experienced.

Baptism itself was hardly the unique cultural property of folk Christians in the New South. From earliest Christianity through the development of Catholicism, perpetuated by Protestants even amidst their wholesale reforms, baptism was an essential ritual marking initiation into membership in the church. When it first appeared in the eighteenth-century South, the Baptist movement brought heightened meaning to this universal Christian ritual. Baptists insisted that the genuine church was composed only of consciously willful, voluntary members. Every individual had to choose to join the church on his or her own; any other ties—family, kin, class, nation—could not carry the individual into the Christian community. Baptists thus rejected the time-honored practice of infant baptism; only when a child had reached a certain maturity could she or he make the conscious, voluntary decision that gave initiation its genuine meaning. Dramatizing this radical theological insistence was the Baptists' practice of fully submerging the initiate in a body of water—a sharp contrast to the light sprinkling of water from a stylized font in the front of a church. Bodies of water necessarily took the Baptists' practice of baptism away from a church building and into the natural, secular world. This inherently had the effect of further signifying the Baptists' claim about the genuine church: it was no pillar of society, no bulwark of social order in parallel function to the state, but rather a strange, voluntary community summoned out of the familiar social matrix. The wildness of baptismal sites (rivers, creeks, ponds, lakes) carried this sense of initiation into a community different from all others that regularly sustained the social order.

As the society of the New South coalesced, Baptists led the way as the single largest religious group. Their distinctive ritual in no way disappeared—they continued to practice adult baptism by immersion, and it continued to mark initiation into the church. But the frame surrounding the ritual was changing dramatically. As "First" churches were constructed on the main streets of New South towns and cities, they took advantage of urban water systems and built indoor baptismal pools. This movement of baptism from a body of water on the edge of society to the very heart of a church building paralleled the Baptists' changing sense of themselves.[79] They were no longer isolated communities of the faithful; in the New South, they were pillars of the social order. Baptism was not about entrance into an unusual alternative community but (like the larger understanding of conversion explored in

chapter 3) rather about self-appropriation of the moral habits of respectability. In rural areas where indoor baptismal pools were simply not an option,
the older practice remained. Yet even here, the rural middle class was coming
to see baptism as did their urban peers. Like the incipient banker whose financial trustworthiness was displayed in the rural baptism Max Weber witnessed, the ritual (even if in the chilly waters of a creek-fed pond) signified the
conscious adoption of bourgeois respectability, of the morality that would
fortify social order in the New South.

In their own practice of baptism, folk Christians were engaging in classic
folk techniques: they were drawing on inherited cultural materials—materials
that were not their sole property but in fact widely shared—and weaving
them together with what was locally at hand to craft new rituals of meaning. They could have sought to (literally) join the middle class in an initiation
ritual signifying incorporation into the social order, but instead they proceeded out from town or church building to remote sites—sites on the edge
of human reshaping of the landscape. As songs surrounding baptism suggested, remote bodies of water became, imaginatively, something mysterious
and other: "I'm goin' down to Jordan," "on Jordan's stormy bank I stand," "in
Jordan bowed his head." Such songs invoked the sacred story of the Bible and
cast the shadow of the New Testament across the New South landscape. Just
as the original baptizer, John, had beckoned people out to the wilderness of
the Jordan River, so too in the New South baptism was a summoning out
from society to be incorporated into the people of God, people with a long
and unusual history. The central moment of that incorporation—immersion
in the body of water—signified a dramatic transformation. The initiates
thrashed about in the water and emerged with wild shouts and shrieks,
waves of ecstasy that had an explosive, igniting effect on the gathered witnesses. The wild self-abandon, the loss of self-control—so different from the
bourgeois ideal of upright respectability—displayed the belief that what was
happening in the ritual was nothing less than the birth pangs of a new life.
The initiate had been lowered into a watery grave, shedding all the various
identifications that society conferred through immersion in a site of wilderness. The initiate's rising up and emerging from the water to rejoin the people
on the shore was a birthing, the beginning of a new life and new identity as a
member of the people of God.

Like the conversion narratives with which it was closely intertwined, the
initiation ritual of baptism moved out of a "religious" site and into places in
the "secular" world. In vivid, visible ways, preacher, congregation, and initiates went to a river, a pond, a creek, or a lake with sacred stories and songs to

FIGURE 21 *Baptism in River, South Carolina* (photograph by Doris Ulmann; Doris Ulmann Photograph Collections, PH038_28_3423, Special Collections and University Archives, University of Oregon Libraries, Eugene, Oregon).

frame their actions. This had a sacralizing effect: seemingly ordinary, mundane sites became spaces with sacred meaning, where the initiate was truly incorporated into the people of God. The thrashing, shouts, and shrieks heralded birth, but the uncontrolled ecstasy also signified that the ordinary and common had been transformed into the holy and other. Ordinary behavior could not contain such a mystery. The gathered people were in the presence of God—precisely in the tangible, earthly phenomena of a river, cool water, and a muddy shore.

For a rich moment, baptism sacralized specific places in the landscape in its celebration of new life, of a new identity as a member of God's people. It was a highly visible and communal public ritual. On the other end of visibility, folk Christians attached sacred, ritualized meaning to highly individualized, intentionally hidden places in the landscape. For Tom Bronner in Bolivar County, Mississippi, his personalized "praying ground" was a secluded spot "under a pecan bush on the bogue bank." He "had been there so many times," he recalled as an elderly man, that "it was clean where I had been praying."[80] In neighboring Sunflower County, "people had a private 'praying ground' to which they went at night to pray."[81] A woman in Florida's Midway community recalled that her own special "praying place" was near the swamp.[82] "My regular praying place" was "behind a big beech tree a little distance from the house," a man in central Tennessee remembered. "Often during the night, when I would feel to pray, I would get out of bed and go to this tree."[83] In Wise County, Virginia, G. W. Blevins's praying place was a large rock beside the muddy Norton Road. A Wise County neighbor "went down under a pine tree every day to pray." Lloyd Chandler in Madison County, North Carolina (as noted in the introduction) regularly hobbled two miles into the woods to his special praying spot beneath a large dogwood tree. A sociologist noted that a group of millworkers at a church in Gaston County, North Carolina, "believe that prayer at 'the white spot'—a bare place in an old field—has special efficacy, and go there frequently to pray."[84]

The highly personalized, carefully secluded nature of "praying spots" made them spaces that—quite unlike outdoor mass baptisms or grave decorations—were extremely difficult for outside observers to see. Because they were so individualized, they were not imbued with the status of "lore" and thus not documented with rigorous care, like the Old Christmas legends. But seen in the context of the other, better-documented phenomena, their significance is clear. They display the same basic impulse: to grasp the sacred in the seemingly ordinary, natural surroundings of everyday life. Functionally, a place to pray in solitude could have been a room (even in the small dwellings that the poor occupied, like the kitchen before or after mealtime) or one of the various outbuildings that surrounded the dwellings of the rural poor. But praying spots were all vividly natural, with specific, concrete elements taking on a heightened meaning. A pecan bush, a beech tree, a dogwood tree, a bare place in an old field—these natural spaces became sites of communion with God. Reiterating and reenacting a dominant theme in the conversion narratives—that true religion is found in liminal spaces on the edge of human society—praying spots in undomesticated nature beckoned individuals away from family and neighbors into solitary openness with God.

In this movement, in innumerable variations based on individual setting, they did what grave decoration, Christmas lore, folk sermons, and outdoor baptisms did: they sacralized the landscape. Secluded and distant spaces, at a remove from human artifice and reshaping, were imagined as places to ritually and routinely seek and encounter God. They were transformed from the natural and mundane to the special and sacred.

In his 1918 essay "Science as a Vocation," Max Weber famously argued that modern Western rationality had wrought a "disenchantment of the world." Whereas the world had once been imagined as an arena of the ordinary and common, infused or punctuated by the presence of the sacred, in the modern West, the sacred had either been removed into an utterly transcendent, mystical other (or inner) world or been collapsed into a thoroughly immanent "brotherliness" of "human relations" in the social world. The sacred had vanished from living experience in the world. Spaces and places were no longer tangible, visible manifestations of the sacred—they were no longer "enchanted."

This hardly meant that modern Westerners had ceased to be religious. Their Christianity went in one of two directions, Weber argued: utter transcendence or thorough immanence. The dominant evangelical culture of the New South moved in the first direction. As the ideal of domesticity spread, the valorization of the home as sacred refuge went hand in hand with the extension of market logic to every corner of the region. The sacred retreated into the domestic haven, while the secular world became a bundle of resources to be exploited for profit. Older enchantments of the world—mystical conversion narratives with rich worldly imagery, lore about the sacred meaning of cosmic events, the dramatic and messy practice of baptismal immersion in a river or creek—came to be seen as primitive, as belonging to an outdated mentality.[85]

The folk Christian imagination moved in a very different direction. It perpetuated an older sense of an enchanted world but imagined such enchantments anew. To those within this imagination, the landscape of the New South was not secular but rather marked with manifestations of the sacred. Personal possessions arranged in enigmatic display atop graves; cattle kneeling, a beehive buzzing, an elder bush bursting into color on Old Christmas; narrative sermons imagining biblical characters and events in the New

South present; the waters of a river or pond becoming the Jordan for a ripe moment; the bogue bank under a pecan bush or the rocks under intertwined dogwood trees serving as one's solitary praying place—in these various ways, intimations of the sacred were all around. Ordinary, secular things and places—household goods disseminated by the market revolution, livestock and shrubs, a dusty road or a raging flood, a spot in a river or deep in the forest—became tangible, earthy manifestations of sacred realities. The sacred was not otherworldly or utterly transcendent but, for those with eyes to see, enchanting the present landscape in a variety of ways.

An "outward and visible sign of inward and spiritual grace"—such was the Protestant definition of sacrament in the wake of the sweeping transformations of the Reformation. But the Reformation did not change the church's critical role as sole agent of the sacraments. Nor did the evangelical movements of the eighteenth century. Though the Baptists and Methodists brought innovations like adult baptism by immersion, foot washing, and love feasts, the church as a gathered community of Christians (typically in a regular place) remained the unique practitioner of the sacraments.

Folk Christians moved out from the church and into the secular world to seek outward, visible manifestations of the sacred. They imagined ordinary elements of everyday life taking on heightened religious meaning. Outside the physical space of the church and the finite gathering of the Christian community, in such secular spaces as a rugged hillside, a cattle stall, or the edge of a swamp, they sought tangible contact with the sacred. This was an earthy transformation of sacramental theology. Pushing sacraments out into the world, fostering local variations and personalized adaptations, folk Christians opened up the sacraments to grassroots experimentation. Sacred realities were not distant and removed but seen and felt in a variety of rich symbols. To those who understood the symbolism, the New South landscape was enchanted, pregnant with sacred meaning.

## CHAPTER FIVE

# The Ethics of Neighborliness

Willie Johnson was born in 1897 on the western edge of the New South, in Bell County, Texas. This Blackland Prairie area of central Texas, like the Mississippi and Arkansas Deltas, was a relatively new frontier of the South. The land had been slimly populated in the antebellum decades, and the fertile, black soil promised bounteous yields as cotton cultivation expanded dramatically in the postbellum decades. For landless freed people and their sons and daughters, such new frontiers were places of exciting opportunity and fresh beginnings, where renting could be a step on the path to landownership.

Yet Johnson's family was unable to realize the hope of ownership. In the 1910 census, his father was noted as a laborer at odd jobs and a home renter; ten years later, his father was working as the driver of a dray wagon, his stepmother as a washerwoman, and they were still renters. Though Bell County was one of the more productive counties in Texas—generating over $5.7 million worth of crops in 1910—tenant farms outnumbered owner farms by a ratio of three to two. The shrinking basis for economic optimism took a toll, and Johnson's young family began to fall apart. His mother died when he was a boy, and his father remarried. But the marriage was not a happy one, and young Willie became the scapegoat. Not long into the marriage, Willie's father learned that his new wife was cheating on him, and he confronted her in a tense altercation. But she subsequently enacted a dark revenge: she threw lye water in young Willie's face, blinding him for life at age thirteen. Hemmed in by poverty and the bitter frustration of disappointed hopes, the raw facts of life took a toll, on families, relationships, and children.[1]

As he came of age in the 1910s, Johnson took the violence, the loss, and the insecurity and social breakdown of his world and fashioned them into an oeuvre of austere, haunting music. With carefully plucked high notes and masterful use of a slide, Johnson used his guitar to create a mood of tension and anxiety. There were no comforting melodies or soothing rhythms but rather a spare, punctuated sound that evoked impending breakdown and dissolution. Johnson's singing style heightened the tension: he sang in a rough, distorted growl, only occasionally interrupting it to sing in his naturally soft tenor. Unlike his natural voice, the growl was not pretty. It was a disturbing sound that disrupted the listener to convey suffering and struggle.

"I was sick and I couldn't get well," he sang, sounding indeed like a suffering, dying man. "I'm dead and buried, somebody said I was lost," he growled, grimly narrating his own death and abandonment. Sometimes the pain of life was too much: "Lord, I just can't keep from crying sometimes / When my heart is full of sorrow / And my eyes are filled with tears / Lord, I just can't keep from crying sometimes." In "Motherless Children Have a Hard Time," he painted scenes of painful alienation and callous disregard: "Motherless children have a hard time when mother is dead (3x) / They'll not have anywhere to go / Wandering around from door to door / Motherless children have a hard time." The orphan was thrown into the care of others, but no one else—father, brother, sister—offered genuine care. "Sister will do the best she can when mother is dead (3x) / But soon as she's married she'll turn her back on you / Nobody treat you like mother will when mother is dead." Johnson was clearly drawing on his own autobiography, but he was doing more than that. The song painted a stark picture of social alienation. It turned motherly love—an essential element in the trope of domesticity—on its head, stripping away the mother to evoke a harsh, unforgiving world. Everyone was a motherless child, a lonely orphan in a world that offered no safe haven. In the void left by the mother's death, by the absence of self-giving love, everything was falling apart.

Johnson's musical evocations of breakdown were not simple artifice. They sprang from a world where chaos and dissolution were ever-present possibilities. In Macon County, Alabama, a woman told of what happened when the family "lost all that we had"—when their tenuous hold on landowning came undone and they fell back into the ranks of landless tenants. Her husband was especially broken by the humiliating change: "On his fiftieth birthday, the twenty-fourth of November, we worked in the field all day and he kept saying he wouldn't be here long, and he wanted us to hurry up and get the cotton picked. It made me nervous. Every time he'd come home I'd send the boy behind him 'cause I didn't know what he might do. We took some potash from him one night. He wouldn't eat no supper . . . he got outta bed and wandered out dere in the field. Then he got hold of some more potash and et it, and died and never said what he lost hisself fer. He just suicided and killed hisself."[2] Though he left no suicide note or verbal explanation, the man's use of potash to kill himself presented a dark irony: this newer commercial fertilizer, intended to enrich the soil and produce bountiful crop life, became the means of his own self-destruction.

In Bacon County, Georgia, the violence was grimly interpersonal. Jay Scott and Junior Carter had been at odds for some time. Scott ridiculed Carter's disfigured appearance—he had lost his right eye in a farm accident, and Scott and others poked fun at him, calling him "Bad Eye" and other nicknames. Tensions had been simmering since they had had a disagreement about some hogs. So one winter day, when Scott sauntered up the road past Carter's farm, Bad Eye was in no mood for banter as he chopped wood in the yard. For a long time Scott simply stood there and watched Bad Eye work, but he couldn't hold back the taunts. " 'Watch out, old man, a splinter don't fly up there and put out that other eye.' Bad Eye kept on chopping, the strokes of the ax regular as clock ticking. He never even looked up. 'Splinter in that other eye, we'd have to call you Bad *Face*.' " Scott then noticed Ruby, Bad Eye's wife, on the porch, and brought her into the taunting: "Why don't you git your old woman out here? They tell me she does most of the ax work for you anyhow." Bad Eye kept working, but he warned Scott not to leave the road and come into his yard. Scott took this as a challenge, and he "came across the ditch, put one foot in the wire and one hand on top of the fence post, getting ready to climb up and swing over. But he never did. That was as far as he got. Bad Eye, who had started chopping again, never missed a stroke, but drove the blade of the ax through Jay's wrist and two inches deep into the top of the post. Ruby said she bet you could hear him scream for five miles. Said she bet somebody thought they was slaughtering hogs, late in the year as it was." Scott tied his arm off with his belt as a tourniquet, then fainted in the ditch. Later, he tried to get his hand back, to bury it, and two of Carter's kinsmen were killed in the ensuing feud. But Scott failed to get back his severed hand. Scott's forces had the final word, however: "Bad Eye went fishing one day and didn't come back. They finally found him floating in Little Satilla River. His blue and wrinkled body had raised the fifty pounds of rusty plow points tied about his ankles."[3]

In Wise County in southwest Virginia, Moran "Dock" Boggs was brooding over a raw violence that he intended to carry out. His father had owned land in Harlan County in eastern Kentucky, but after selling off portion after portion to coal speculators, he moved to the developing town of Prince's Flat to make a living as a blacksmith and gunsmith. In 1894, Prince's Flat was renamed Norton in honor of Eckstein Norton, president of the Louisville and Norton Railroad, whose newly laid tracks now came through the town.[4] Boggs's father's saga was emblematic of changes sweeping over the South in the late nineteenth century. A remote marginal area of subsistence farmers in the antebellum era, eastern Kentucky/southwest Virginia became quickly transformed by the advancing logic of the market. Once-neglected land was now seen as valuable because of the untapped resource it contained—coal—and hundreds of miles of new railroad track were built to get the extracted resources to market. Concentrations of capital, in the form of railroad and coal companies, came to exert new power over everyday life.

This was the world into which Boggs was born in 1898, but the relative independence of his father's artisanal labor would not be his own: at the age of twelve, he started working a ten-hour day in the mines. By the age of twenty, though, he seemed to be finding a way out. He got married and, with the money he had saved, rented a farm and subcontracted part of a mine. "I was making as much as any foreman," he recalled. "Had a whole section of the mine under me, and me just twenty years old." But that sense of security, of control, quickly proved to be all too fragile. Boggs's wife got sick, and he fell badly into debt. Ultimately, they were forced to move in with her parents, in eastern Kentucky, and Boggs lost his good-paying job. He came to feel "run over" by his in-laws, and they became in his mind a tangible sign of his own economic failure, a symbol of his confinement and humiliation. He began to brood on a dark revenge: "I done made up my mind," he said many years later, "that I was gonna kill all's in the house. The old man, the old lady, the boys, everyone's there, I swear, I gonna kill everyone of 'em." At forty years' distance, Boggs was still deeply disturbed by what he had planned: "It's a bad thing, a man to have it figured out in his mind—I'm talking about being set on it, I was set on it."[5]

But he never carried it out. Instead, he poured the darkness within him into music, giving voice to his grimly confined world in an oeuvre of stark, haunting songs—just as Willie Johnson was doing in the same years, on the other corner of the New South. In "Country Blues," he painted a frightful scene of a social world falling apart at the seams.[6] Violence, deception, betrayal, and dissolution were the defining features of this grim country. As his banjo set an anxious, foreboding tone, with its fast-plucked, high staccato notes, Boggs's shrill twang and strange intonations extended an invitation that verged on the sinister:

> Come all you good time pee-eee-eee-aa-ple
> While I've got money to spend ...

This was a fragile world: spending money was no guarantee, and the singer sought to grab some "good-timing" while he could. He was haunted, though, by the memory of what had happened the last time he had cash to spend:

> When I had plenty of money good people
> My friends were all standing around
> Just as soon as my pocketbook was empty

Not a friend on earth to be found . . .
Last time I see my woman good people
She had a wine glass in her hand
She was drinking down her troubles
With a low-down, sorry man . . .

Not only was the world fragile, but the bonds that typically hold a society together—family, friends, kin, neighbors, local community—were scarcely existent. The singer's friends quickly turned out to be pseudo-companions, abandoning him as soon as his cash ran out. The singer barely knew where his girlfriend (or wife?) was, though he was sure that she was engaged in the same kind of dissolute, decadent behaviors that he was. The society seemed to rest on a raw materialism. Money brought people together—but evanescently, fleetingly, only as long as it was around. Its absence led people to abandon each other, to seek to drown their troubles in the oblivion of drunkenness.

The song took a fast, downward turn, and the singer was now in jail. From his cell he watched the callous world go by, and in himself, he felt a dangerous slide into breakdown:

All around this jailhouse is plenty good people
Forty dollars won't pay my fine
Corn whiskey has surrounded my body poor boy
Pretty women is a-troublin' my mind
If I'd a-listened to my mama good people
I wouldn't a-been here today
But a-drinking and a-shooting and a-gambling
At home I cannot stay . . .

The singer knew there was a different way to live, but he seemed fatally driven to self-destruction, to patterns of rough competitiveness and violent contest. Ultimately, these patterns had come to consume him, and the jail cell stood as an apt metaphor for his personal confinement. But it could also be understood as a metaphor for the larger confinement of his social world. It was not a landscape of open possibility and far horizons but rather a tightly circumscribed world of minimal options.

The song took a final turn, a dark and morbid one. Boggs had opened by beckoning his listeners to join him in fleeting pleasures; now he told them to dig his grave.

Go dig a hole in the meadow good people
Go dig a hole in the ground

Come around all you good people
And see this poor rounder go down

A starkly sketched mortality mirrored the confining jail cell with its ever-present sense of limit and finitude. And the pseudo-friends who'd gathered for "good-timing" could be counted on again only to dig a grave. The sense of social isolation was severe, and Boggs accentuated it by darkly taunting his estranged girlfriend to come visit his grave:

When I am dead and buried
My pale face turned to the sun
You can come around and mourn little woman
And think the way you have done

Even in death, there was no restoration of human community, no coming together to mourn and lament. Boggs ended the song with an austere image of his pale face gazing past the world while his woman presumably stood by the grave, alone and ruminating. The patterns of life continued with ripple effects after individual death, and Boggs hoped for some kind of strange postmortem revenge. Was it her fault that this "poor rounder" had ended up where he did? Surely not, but Boggs wanted to haunt the memory of his girlfriend with something like survivor's guilt. The breakdown that Boggs had sketched—the rough lines that never came together in unity—would persist.

The "country" of "Country Blues"—a world of dissolution and alienation—was of a piece with the stark scene evoked by Willie Johnson, and though Boggs and Johnson were crafting art and not documentary work, it was also of a piece with the grim real-life scenes in Macon and Bacon counties. Boggs and Johnson lived on opposite corners of the New South, and their family sagas were certainly different: Johnson's family embodied the black quest for landownership in the post-Reconstruction decades, while Boggs's family displayed the demise of subsistence agriculture and the loss of white yeoman independence. Yet both families lived in places rapidly transformed by the New South's market revolution. They lived in New South frontiers of cotton and coal. They lived in places that, for many, became scenes of frustration and confinement, of grim interpersonal violence and social breakdown.

In his fieldwork with the Mexican poor in the 1940s and 1950s, American anthropologist Oscar Lewis found similar phenomena at work, a "world of violence and death, of suffering and deprivation, of infidelity and broken homes . . . of the cruelty of the poor to the poor." From this fieldwork, Lewis developed the idea of a "culture of poverty"—"a way of life, remarkably stable and persistent, passed down from generation to generation along family lines," with "its own modalities and distinctive social and psychological consequences for its members."[7] Lewis's concept became part of American policy discourse during the Great Society's War on Poverty and afterwards as emergent forces attacked such programs as wasteful failures. The concept was reworked to argue that there was something wrong with poor people, some distinct pathology, and that the real barrier to substantive change lay in the culture of the poor themselves. Until the poor changed their self-defeating, self-imprisoning, decadent culture, the critics said, no social program could rescue them from poverty.

That the poor had a distinct pathology, that the core problem was their own culture, were ideas woven into the fabric of the dominant religious culture of the New South well before Lewis's work. A black denominational official saw "illicit living" and "heathenism and immorality" in communities of poor blacks, even as a white denominational newspaper characterized poor whites as "ignorant, selfish, profane, intemperate, and improvident." Agricultural tenancy had created a "class of mentally and spiritually undeveloped people," a black educator wrote, a class who, "whether whites or blacks, necessarily show evidences of evil habits, irreligion, and lawlessness." "What is the chance to socialize, civilize, or Christianize a landless, homeless people?" a white extension agent pessimistically asked. "What can be done for people who move from pillar to post . . . who lack identity with the community in which they live, who feel little or no responsibility for law and order?" Such people, a white Baptist official claimed, were "undrilled, undeveloped, uninstructed, raw recruits of civilization." But an Episcopal priest in Memphis challenged such thinking, even as his challenge revealed the logic of the dominant culture. "It is stupid to condemn [tenants] as idle, shiftless, and immoral," he wrote in an open letter to President Roosevelt. The poor were not immoral agents deserving critique; rather, they were victims who should be pitied: "the tenant farmer is today the product of a vicious, stifling environment into which he was born."[8]

The dominant evangelical ethos came to imagine poverty as a moral problem, with its root in the poor's own willful rejection of proper ethics. With their poverty as a transparent badge of their moral failure, it was no wonder that bad choices led to other bad choices, with a cascading effect of dissolution and decadence. From this point of view, the breakdown displayed in the early life of Willie Johnson, in the feud between Junior "Bad Eye" Carter and Jay Scott, and in other anecdotes, was clear proof of the fatal fruits of an immoral culture.

Lewis's "culture of poverty" can be read in a different way, though, closer to its original meaning and without the politicized, status-quo-absolving meaning it later acquired. When lack, insecurity, marginality, and confinement are the defining features of life—that is, when poverty is the overarching economic reality—the appearance of attendant phenomena like violence, deception, and dissolution should come as no surprise. These are authentic human responses to a world of minimal options. Born into a world that they did not create and experiencing an abiding and painful feeling of being stuck—and suffering ridicule precisely for being stuck—poor people are displaying their humanity in acts of violence, deception, and dissolution. They are lashing out, albeit destructively, at the confinements that define their lives. Frustrations reach a boiling point and violence erupts, lying seems like the only way to experience a little freedom, despair becomes ascendant, and a downward spiral of self-destructive behavior becomes consuming. There is no unique pathology afflicting the poor—just human beings caught in a world of minimal options.

This was a key point in Howard Thurman's 1949 *Jesus and the Disinherited.* Thurman argued that fear, deception, and hatred were the defining features in the inner lives of the poor. Fear, along with its "twin sons . . . . anxiety and despair"; deception, which was "perhaps the oldest of all the techniques by which the weak have protected themselves against the strong"; and hatred, which "destroys finally the core of the life of the hater," were legitimate behaviors in the face of poverty and marginalization. Those born into poverty especially displayed its pathos: "The doom of the children is the greatest tragedy of the disinherited. They are robbed of much of the careless rapture and spontaneous joy of merely being alive. . . . So many tender, joyous things in them are nipped and killed without their even knowing the true nature of their loss. The normal for them is the abnormal. . . . The child of the disinherited is likely to live a heavy life."[9] But as noted in the introduction, Thurman did not conclude his assessment there. He argued that Christianity was a force of liberation, that it carried special meaning for the poor. With its message of inner transformation, Christianity showed how the poor could triumph over fear, deception, and hatred and be freed to live lives not defined by their severe external constraints.

Ruminating on her life, a sharecropper in Alabama described how everyday life often involved a tense struggle:

I'll wake up sometimes and I'll ask myself whether it's going to be today that something real bad will happen. Some days just go fast and nothing real bad happens, but all of a sudden we'll get a lots of troubles come our way, and it makes you wonder if you can last. It's then that you stop and remind yourself the Lord is up there, and He doesn't miss a single trick. I mean, how could He? . . . I admit that every once in a while I catch myself getting worried. That's when I'll say to myself that maybe *this* is Hell, right where we are, right here. And it's not a good thought to have. It's a bad one! But sometimes you can't help yourself.[10]

A Kentucky coal miner echoed her in his description of the struggles, inward and outward, that marked his life:

Sometimes over there in that little church of ours I feel there's forgiveness in this world, and the good Lord, He's near us, and He isn't going to let us get completely taken over by the bad in the world, the bad that's in yourself and the bad that's in others. But like the Bible will tell you, it's a big struggle, and no matter if you're high or low, you're going to be fighting the struggle all your life, and a lot of the time you'll be near to losing, with the Devil just about to claim you his property, but then you'll be singing a hymn or like that, and you'll turn around and realize you're in danger and get saved in the nick of time, yes sir, right in the nick.[11]

These remarkable statements come from the same harsh, circumscribed world of the opening anecdotes. The sharecropper and the coal miner were intimately acquainted with the forces of potential destruction, with the fear (the sharecropper) and the hatred (the coal miner) that threatened to consume their lives. Surely they had seen others fall into a downward spiral, and they knew how easily they themselves could fall. But interrupting this consuming culture of poverty was the challenging presence of Christianity. It presented a vision of hope and forgiveness in the face of fear and hatred. For the sharecropper, it was the hope of God not missing a single trick; for the coal miner, it was "that little church" as a beacon of forgiveness in a harsh, unforgiving world. But there was no easy consolation or triumph. The struggle to believe Christianity and not be swallowed by the forces of destruction was vivid and perpetual.

This struggle is audible in Blind Willie Johnson's music. Johnson evoked a world of impending chaos and breakdown, but in the midst of that world he imagined the disruptive presence of Christianity. Like the prophet John of Revelation—an enigmatic figure that Johnson memorialized in his "John the Revelator"—Christianity interrupted established patterns with a strange, subversive summons.

FIGURE 22 Blind Willie Johnson, in a 1927 promotional photograph for Columbia Records (Michael Ochs Archives/Getty Images).

In "You'll Need Somebody on Your Bond," Johnson sang, "I heard the voice of Jesus saying / Come unto me and rest / Do you want to lie down? / Lay down upon my breast / I came to Jesus as I was / Weary, poor, and sad / Found in him a resting place / He has made me glad." He echoed this in "Praise God I'm Satisfied": "Upon the mountain dreary / I wandered sad and alone / How well my savior found me / He claimed me for his own / Placed his arms about me / And he drew me to his side." "Trouble soon be over," he sang in an eponymous song, "Sorrow will have an end / Well Christ is my burden-bearer / He's my only friend / Saying to me end all my sorrow / And telling me to lean on him." In the rousing song "I'm Gonna Run to the City of Refuge," Jesus was like the ancient Hebrews' special cities in which fugitives could find safe haven. In "Church I'm Fully Saved Today," Johnson echoed the title of the first song he ever recorded: "I know his blood can make me whole / Church, I'm fully saved today."

These Christian claims all gained meaning when people, made aware of their own essential insecurity, humbly confessed the need for divine help. They were not whole but fugitives on the run, plagued by trouble, wandering on a dreary mountain, weary and longing for rest, in need of a bondsman to get them out of prison. Johnson sought to elicit this confession from his listeners. Stark awareness of weakness was the door to understanding Christian hope.

These beliefs about the nature of human life were joined with a summons to practice. But Johnson's way of voicing this summons was indirect and imaginative. He sought to inspire specific practice by working people into stories from the Bible, fleshing out an idealized way of life through allusion and example. Some songs told of how righteous figures had suffered and yet did not retaliate in kind. In the rousing mystical ode "John the Revelator," Johnson lionized the prophet John of Revelation, who was condemned to a penal colony yet still faithfully wrote down his visions of God. In "Jesus Make Up My Dying Bed," as noted in chapter 2, he meditated on the scene of Jesus's crucifixion. As Jesus hung there in misery, dying, he was concerned with the care and well-being of others: "Late this Friday evening / Before that dyin' moan / Jesus said to his disciples / Come and carry my mother home." Johnson's most haunting reflection on suffering was the wordless dirge "Dark Was the Night, Cold Was the Ground," in which he relied on cultural familiarity with the story of the Crucifixion. He withheld any lyrics, instead uttering disturbing moans and sighs, suggesting a suffering so cosmically intense that it was ineffable.

On the other side of these reflections on suffering without retaliation were anecdotes of healing. "Trod in old Judea / Pathway long ago / People thronged about him / Saving grace to know"—he sang of Jesus in "Sweeter as the Years Go By"—"Healed the broken hearted / Caused the blind to see." In "The Soul of a Man," he recalled how "when Christ had entered the temple / The people all stood amazed / He was teaching the lawyers and the doctors / How to raise a man from the grave." In "I Know His Blood Can Make Me Whole," he emphasized the phrase "hem of his garment," indicating the story in which a sick woman touches merely a piece of Jesus's clothes in hopes of healing and restoration. "Trouble Will Soon Be Over" recalled the young would-be king David, a fugitive on the run, whom God had protected from his adversaries: "God is my strong protection / He is my bosom friend / If trouble rose all around me / I know who will take me in / He proved a friend to David / I'll heed him every day / That same God that David served / Will give me rest someday."

Taken together, these meditations on suffering and healing said this: there was intense suffering in the world, and yet the way to respond was not with retaliation. Rather, the God of the Bible worked for healing and restoration. Suffering should be met with compassionate care and reaching out to others. Several of Johnson's songs beckoned people to empathetic community. "Come and go with me / To that land / Come and go with me / To that land," he invited in an eponymous song, "There'll be no dying / In that land / There'll be no dying / In that land / We'll all be holy / In that land / We'll all be holy / In that land / Don't you want to go? / To that land / Don't you want to go? / To that land / Where I'm bound." In another song he implored, "Take a stand, take a stand / Take a stand / If I never ever see you anymore / Take a stand take a stand take a stand / I'll meet you on that kingdom shore / Pray for me pray for me pray for me / If I never ever see you anymore / Shake my hand shake my hand shake my hand / Keep the faith keep the faith keep the faith / I'll meet you on that kingdom shore." The first theme noted—the essential fragility and instability of life—is transparent here, but now it is fused with a message of reaching out to one's neighbor in this fragile world.

In "Everybody Ought to Treat a Stranger Right," he brought his vision of practice and belief together into one succinct song. "Everybody ought to treat a stranger right / Long ways from home," he urged in the chorus, "Well be mindful if you're speaking / Be careful how you go along / You must always treat a stranger right / Don't insult him in your home." The call here was to communal compassion and warm hospitality. He then expanded the scope of this practice by grounding it in the idea of an essential human homelessness: "Well all of us down here are strangers / None of us have no home / Don't never hurt your brother / And cause him to live all alone." In this fragile world, no one ever had a sure footing; everyone needed the help and compassion of his or her neighbors. This was what the Christian story was basically about: "Well Christ came down as a stranger / He didn't have no home / He was cradled in the manger / And oxen kept him warm." Into this insecure world the Christian God had come humbly and without fanfare. Jesus was a stranger and sufferer too, and yet he responded not with revenge or power but with the compassionate work of healing and restoration.[12]

From eastern Kentucky and southwest Virginia, from people who were Dock Boggs's neighbors and contemporaries, uncanny echoes of Johnson's core themes were being articulated in song and sermon. Sarah Gunning sang: "Christ was a wayworn traveler / He traveled from door to door / His occupation chiefly was / Administering to the poor." Here was the Son of Man with nowhere to lay his head. Rejected by the world, homeless in his wanderings, he found kindred spirits in the poor. And his contemporary followers could expect similar mistreatment: "They called my Lord the devil / They called his saints the same / But I ain't expecting any more down here / Than burden, abuse, and shame."[13] "I long to see my Savior first of all," Tilman Cadle intoned. But this was not the gentle savior of evangelical piety; it was the crucified Jesus who had suffered the world's scorn and punishment. Cadle continued, "I shall know him, I shall know him / And redeemed by his side I shall stand / I shall know him, I shall know him / By the prints of the nails in his hand."[14] Likewise, Findlay Donaldson meditated in song on the image of the Crucifixion: "Led him forth as a captive / On him the multitude scorn / They arrayed him in purple / They cruelly crowned him with thorns / Look at him dying." But the Man of Sorrows suffered purposively: "I know it was the blood / I know it was the blood / I know it was the blood for me / One day when I was lost / He died upon a cross / And there he shed his blood for me."[15] In a sermon on what he called "the blood route," with the poetic cadence of his songs but with the explanatory power of prose, Donaldson explored the leveling meaning of Jesus's suffering:

> Because the Bible plainly tells us that Jesus Christ died on Calvary's cross and shed the last drop of his blood that through him—not through some church—not though some big fine house—not through some big fine school—not through some great big preacher—not through some other way but the way that the Lord has laid down. . . . The plan of salvation has always been the blood route. . . . There's no man can stand between you and your sins. He may be great in this world, he may have a great influence, he may come from some great family and the citizens of the community they might speak well of him, they might say, "O, look at him, he's great, he's wonderful"—but did you know in the plan of God there's no man greater than his precious Son.[16]

As Johnson did in "Everybody Ought to Treat a Stranger Right," G. W. Blevins succinctly expressed a host of themes in a song he crafted about the Tree of Life. A miner and farmer in Wise County, Virginia, Blevins suffered for much of his life. Yet he ultimately experienced healing, became a preacher, and sang a new song—a vision of life, beauty, and community:

> There's a straight and narrow way into life
> It leads to the city of God we're told
> Where the walls of that city's pure jasper
> And the streets of that city's pure gold
> There stands the tree of life it's always blooming
> On either side at the river of life

Its leaves is for the healing of the nations
It'll cure all division and strife

*good ideas, heard / they get lived out?*

Inspired by and imitating the prophet John of Revelation, Blevins's song portrays eschatological realities to imagine how things in this world should be but are not. The song is about life—"way into life," "tree of life," "river of life"—as it should be ideally lived. That ideal is one of community and reconciliation: an ideal city, a bountiful tree that offers medicine for the world. To these images of communal participation in reconciled life, Blevins's song contrasts callous disregard of neighbor—a "way of death" that leads to ultimate destruction:

There's a way that seems right unto man
The end of the way of death . . .
Then I turned and looked in that place of destruction
I see the rich man as he lifts up his eyes
Sees Lazarus afar off in Abraham's bosom
In the city of sweet paradise[17]

The rich man who was so preoccupied with his own wealth that he never noticed Lazarus, the sore-infested beggar at his gate, is imagined in his eschatological extension—in a place of destructive abandon. While Lazarus dwells in eschatological community, the rich man suffers the pain of ultimate lonely isolation. With its vision of alternative ways of life and death, the song is a summons to self-giving and care for one's neighbors.

The ethic idealized in these songs and sermon from eastern Kentucky/southwest Virginia echoes Johnson's oeuvre in imagining non-retaliation as the way to break the cycle of injustice. Suffering limitation and lack, and the painful awareness of not seeing the fruits of one's labors while hearing the dismissive scorn of the dominant culture, it was sensible and rational that poor people would lash out in retaliation, even if that lashing out was directed at fellow sufferers in their own communities. There was no pathology here but an assertion of humanity, of symbolic repudiation of the forces of confinement. *But*, the ethic said, this was the way of death. It perpetuated the consuming forces of destruction. As long as the poor sought retaliation for injustice—albeit a symbolic retaliation that sought scapegoats in neighbors, kin, and even one's self—they would be contributing to their own dissolution. Self-giving in expansive charity was the way to breathe new life into lives of confinement and injustice; it would break the cycle of destruction and set individuals and communities on a new path. By not responding in kind to injustice, a new way was opened up. The poor could overcome the imprisonment of perpetuation with an alternative vision. Instead of a responsive role, self-giving charity imagined proactive behavior. It envisioned a triumph over circumstance and an assertion of a deeper humanity. Human beings had the inner strength and internal depth to be more than simply products of their circumstances. The "culture of poverty" would be overcome by the ethic of non-retaliation and self-giving. Rather than making other poor people scapegoats for their frustration, the poor could learn to see each other as fellow sufferers, as wayworn travelers and "strangers." Reaching out to each other in charity, they would overcome internal dissolution with an ethic of neighborliness.

This ethic of neighborliness differed substantively from the dominant culture's idealized ethic—that of respectability. At the heart of respectability was self-control as exemplary behavior. Respectable individuals controlled their appetites and their time, shunning frivolous recreations like drinking alcohol or playing cards, not frittering away time but using it purposefully. They displayed the fruits of their self-control in their personal appearance and in the property they accumulated. These were badges of productive use of one's time, of hard work and efficient self-management.

An ethic of respectability, with the valorization of self-control and accumulation; an ethic of neighborliness, with the valorization of self-giving and non-retaliation: these were more than variations on a theme; they were substantially different ethical visions for life in the New South. Both possessed their own internal logic, and both presented a clear model of idealized behavior for a specific context. The two ethics are testament to the fact that Christian ethics is no simple thing—the religion contains within itself the material for a diverse variety of ethical visions.

The difference between the folk ethic of neighborliness and the dominant ethic of respectability is especially pronounced in their different visions of bad/evil. From early Christianity to the seventeenth century, the devil and hell were staple themes in religious culture, appearing in sermons, paintings, songs, lore, theological treatises, and moral instruction. Over the course of the eighteenth and nineteenth centuries, with the Enlightenment's rationalist critique and a new optimism about human capability, Protestants in the West led the way in pushing the devil and hell to the shadowy background. This went hand in hand, Philippe Aries noted, with the new vision of death: death's traditional association with evil and with the possibility of hell was broken as belief in the devil and hell declined, opening the way for the emergent view of death as a longed-for, welcome liberation and reunion. In this epochal shift, a sense of evil as inherent and intractable was being replaced by a newly optimistic, triumphal vision that evil did not exist within fallen humanity but outside—in actions, in places, in deviant social groups, in "certain marginal spaces that morality and politics had not yet colonized."[18] Evil was reimagined into "bad." By the late nineteenth century, prominent American periodicals were reflecting on these transformations. "What Has Become of Hell?" the *North American Review* wondered in 1900, while a year earlier *Scribner's* noted "The Passing of the Devil."[19]

The evangelicals who came to dominate religious life in the New South were very much part of this transformation. In their early insurgent days in the region, they were social disturbers who "raised the Devil" in the face of a rationalist, optimistic culture that had pushed the devil into the background.[20] But as they sought to chart a new course for the South after the Civil War, they became active proponents of a moralizing vision that denied radical evil. The taxonomy of "good" and "evil" as superhuman forces in the world, inspiring fear and awe, shifted to an optimistic taxonomy of "good" and "bad" as behaviors and places that the willful human agent could control. Rather than evil being an insidious, perpetual force embodied in the devil and always assailing fragile humanity, bad was contained in actions and spaces that the triumphal Christian could choose to avoid. New South evangelicals "subdued" Satan, to use Ted Ownby's phrase, not just in circumscribing wild, fun recreations but even more basically in reimagining "Satan" as simply a metaphorical name for wild fun.[21]

Those who avoided these bad behaviors and spaces and thereby displayed the virtues of self-control and self-discipline deserved respect: they were "respectable." As chapter 1 argues, the articulation of this new ethic was critical to the New South's capitalist transformation. Just as the logic of the market revolution spread to every corner of the region in search of resources and commodities, so too the new ethic imagined the Christian's potential mastery of all moral phenomena in the social scene. The new ethic also fostered the spatial divisions of Jim Crow: just as "bad" could be codified and contained, so too the "race problem" could be imaginatively solved by removing African Americans from the spaces that whites occupied. African Americans could appropriate the class ethos of the evangelical vision and seek to demonstrate respectability, as chapter 1 also argues, but the racialized extensions of "good" and "bad" sent powerful messages that suffocated the evangelical vision's class openness. Still, paradoxically but in parallel fashion, middle-class white and black evangelicals embraced the new moral logic of good and bad, of behaviors and spaces, of the possibility of Christian triumph. Though she was reflecting specifically on the racial logic of Jim Crow as it intertwined with

*[handwritten margin note: whiteness as respectable morality?]*

religion, Lillian Smith's ruminations on the message of her Methodist upbringing captured the new evangelical culture's disposition: "Everything dark, dangerous, evil must be pushed to the rim of one's life."[22]

In their own ethical vision, as in their vision of Death, folk Christians were drawing on traditional material. Indeed, in his four-volume history of the devil, Jeffrey Burton Russell traced changing conceptions of radical, personified evil from second Temple Judaism, through early Christianity and the Middle Ages, into the Enlightenment, and on into the mid-twentieth century. Educated Westerners were ceasing to believe in the devil—that is, in radical evil—by the late eighteenth century, Russell argues, but the colossal violence that consumed Western nations after 1914 and 1939 prompted some philosophers and theologians to revisit what had come to seem like an antiquated concept. Russell concludes his sweeping, monumental work with a close reading of the fiction of Flannery O'Connor, in which he finds a profound grappling with radical evil among the people who populate her stories—the arresting fictional characters she based on the real-world folk Christians she observed.[23]

Speaking on the lecture circuit, O'Connor argued that "since the eighteenth century, the popular spirit of each succeeding age has tended more and more to the view that the ills and mysteries of life will eventually fall before the scientific advances of man," but that her Catholic theology and the folk Christianity of her native region believed instead that "evil is not simply a problem to be solved, but a mystery to be endured."[24] Her stories sought to depict the struggle between "evil and grace," and in her second novel, *The Violent Bear It Away*, this struggle became fully embodied: the devil is a character (albeit a shape-changing one) who seeks to drag the young prophet Francis Marion Tarwater into destruction.

Folk Christians engaged in real-world struggles with personified, radical evil—with the devil. In his 1909 study of "the representative average songs that are current among the common mass of negroes," Howard Odum concluded that "the devil is prominent in the religious songs of the Negroes. He is the constant terror and proverbial enemy of the race. He is alive, alert, and concrete. . . . He is the enemy against whom the battle is always on."[25] From the Smoky Mountains in 1914, a home missionary sent in a bemused report about an old mountaineer she called "Uncle Bob." He lived in a one-room cabin, led the singing at his local church, and stored his coffin under his bed. "Uncle Bob was no stranger to the wiles of Satan," the missionary wrote with condescension. " 'I fit with him last night,' he said. 'He come to my bed and axed me to do jest one lettls thing fur him. I tole him I wouldn't, for I knowed when I done that he would make me do sumthin' bigger.' "[26] In the late 1930s at a church in Austin County, Texas, preacher Tanner Franklin warned his hearers that Satan was "forever meddling with the Lord's sheep.... He worries at their souls and aggravates them, 'til it just look like there ain't nothin' to do but to give in to him." Thus, the life of the Christian was a "battle-field," where one was "fightin' it out with old Satan every day."[27] In the same years on the other side of the region, in the coal country of eastern Kentucky, Findlay Donaldson voiced similar admonitions: "That old devil that was cast out of heaven, that old serpent that's been after the human race ever since he was cast out upon the earth, we find him today. He's a traveling through the world, he's after our souls, of our children, he's after you and me.... It's hard to live. Why? Because the power of the devil is so great, the power of Satan and sin is so great over the human race today that you've got to have the keeping power of God."[28]

Of his father Lloyd, Garrett Chandler insisted, "My Daddy saw the Devil every day. You know you're saved when the Devil's right behind you, walking on your heels. If you're not saved, he doesn't have to mess with you."[29] In the same vicinity and in the same years as Chandler's vision of Death, a home missionary listened to a "brother of great repute" preach "one of his notable sermons," a sermon about the power of the devil. Tuskegee student Nathaniel Colley found strong belief in the devil in his close study of the black tenant community of Gee's Bend in Wilcox County, Alabama, in the late 1930s, and writer Richard Wright depicted the devil as a staple theme of folk sermons in his 1941 "folk history" of poor blacks.[30] In a predominantly white rural community in western Tennessee, a small farmer told a sociologist in the late 1930s that the "Devil gets me when I get mad."[31] Speaking to Alan Lomax in the late 1930s, the elderly preacher Floyd Roe said, "I don't think he's visible. He's a spirit. There's no man, I don't believe, has ever seen the Devil with his own two eyes and they never have seen God. God have been revealed to us through Jesus Christ; but the Devil have never been, because he'd have scared us all to death. The Devil gets in you, and when he possesses you, you just as bad as you can be. It's nothing but the Devil makes men do evil."[32]

A white Georgia sharecropper described her sexual seduction by a deceitful preacher: "You see, there's God Almighty, and there's Satan, and I swear it can be hard to know between the two, sometimes, because the Scripture tells us that the Lord was wonderful and smart and He knew how to do anything He wanted, and He could beat the doctors, and beat the priests of the temple and beat the kings and emperors, if He wanted to. But we're told that the Devil is a smart one, too; and he can pull all of the tricks you can imagine, and then some. If you ask me: it's very few on this earth who can tell the difference between Jesus Christ and the Devil. People can turn on you. That preacher turned on me, I believe."[33]

Alone in his room at the end of a work week, a black day laborer in the north Florida community of Midway fought with the devil. "His experience with the Devil is closely tied to his drinking problem" folklorist Bruce Grindal found. "Most often this experience would occur on a Friday evening after work, and begin with feelings of nervous agitation, bad temper, and withdrawal. These feelings then would focus upon an obsessive compulsion for alcohol. There was nothing that could restrain him. . . . That night in bed he would lie awake and toss in a kind of impotent rage. It was then he knew the Devil had him, and the more he struggled, the more he saw the Devil cruelly laughing at his misery. The next morning he would awaken in depression and disgust, and to relieve the pain, he would begin drinking again." He told Grindal, "All the Devil wants to do is kill you, and you are a fool because you let him do it." "Finally," Grindal summarized, "with fear and trembling, [he] would put down the bottle and take to bed; after hours of inner struggle, he would 'cast the Devil off his back,' whereupon he would feel a renewed vigor and sense of life."[34]

Jesse Hatcher, a black small farmer in Patrick County, Virginia, told a symbolic story to depict the Christian's perpetual struggle with evil, which could strike unawares. "We all suffer one way or another," he began, "one way or another, sooner or later. And then lastly, that zone in the flesh will strike us. Did you ever think of that? That zone will strike us. And it's a stumbling block to you if you let it." Hatcher then described his typical late-summer task of pulling fodder from corn, then cutting the tops and tying them together. One time he was working in the cool of the evening, alone, tying the tops together, when he felt "something real cold moving" on his arm, and as he shook it a rattlesnake dropped to the ground. Hatcher ran to his neighbor's house, borrowed his shotgun, and killed the rattlesnake in the corn patch. To him it represented the snares of evil: "Anyway in the world you look at a rattlesnake, he's looking at you. . . . He always sees you first."[35]

There are some tangible behaviors here that one could interpret through the lens of morality—alcoholism and adultery—but the manner in which they and the other anecdotes and glimpses are framed indicates something other than a clear moral calculus of good and bad. Evil is a real force, not simply the sum total of willful human agency, and it is an active force that assails and seeks to conquer. It particularly strikes when the supports of family, kin, neighbors, and church are not around, in the depth of sleep or alone in a field. These attacks by the devil, though, are not a sign of the person's lack of faith. The Christian enjoys no security of distance from the forces of darkness. The devil is "forever meddling with the Lord's sheep," always seeking opportune moments to catch the faithful unawares and pull them into irredeemable destruction.

The struggle against the devil is less tangible but no less real than the dominant ethic that demanded willful refraining from bad behaviors. Despair, violent anger, doubting the possibility of forgiveness, deceitful seduction, tearing others down through gossip, abandonment to the oblivion of addiction—the struggle against these is a difficult one, and if one entertains them for more than a moment, like the rattlesnake on the arm, they threaten to kill. What the Midway man said—"all the Devil wants to do is kill you"—is true for all the struggles, for these forces threaten to tear apart not only the individual soul but the bonds that sustain everyday life. Put simply, the devil destroys *life*; the struggle is right now, in everyday existence.

Seen from the outside and from the perspective of linear prose, like the home missionary who wrote of "Uncle Bob," it appears that well into the twentieth century, primitive, superstitious folk still believed in the existence of an evil being. So real was this being that they could both see and feel him, and so powerful was this being that he was effectively coequal with God. But seen from the inside, from within the imaginative parameters of folk Christians, a very different account emerges: folk Christians used traditional imagery to articulate contemporary phenomena. They used the traditional language and imagery of the devil to articulate destructive, pernicious forces that threatened their lives at every turn. In their songs of death, in their conversion narratives, and in their sermons, they displayed a richly symbolic imagination that was simply different from linear, rationalist prose. The question is not whether they really believed that there was a being called "the devil" (or "Death") in the world. Rather, in this personification, they imagined a force that transcended human moral choice. This force was at work in the world, ever-present and dangerous. Christians had to vigilantly resist it, but there could never be the calm assurance of triumph. Put differently, "everything dark, dangerous, [and] evil" was absolutely not at "the rim of one's life." It was frightfully close, in the midst of the lives of individuals and communities.

In naming the deception, violence, dissolution, and despair that threatened to destructively consume their lives as "the Devil," folk Christians called themselves to wage a persistent struggle against these forces. The ethic of neighborliness envisioned the way forward; the imagery of the devil named that from which one had to flee. Together, the ethic and the account of evil were folk Christians' fight against the "culture of poverty." They sought to

*how diff from respectability?*

name the dangerous forces at play in their impoverished lives, and they ideal-ized a clear code of behavior that called them to rise above responding to their hardships in kind. This vision was not one of structural change, of seek-ing transformation of the very structures that caused poverty in the first place. Rather, it was a vision of personal liberation from a destructive downward spiral—but a personal liberation that necessarily involved a transformed so-cial behavior. Folk Christians sought to fight the devil with an ethic of com-munal neighborliness.

The principal way in which they articulated this—as with their grappling with life and death, with Christian identity, and with experiencing the sacred—was symbolic and metaphorical. Leaves from the tree of life—the bloody tree that held that exemplar of non-retaliation and self-giving—were the only sure safeguard against the wily devil who sought to drag people down into chaos. Its healing leaves of neighborliness pushed people into expansive acts of charity and communal care.

Whether because of its symbolic articulation or because of their abiding sense of the pathology of the poor, various middle-class observers saw no ethic at all in the religious life of the poor. In the estimation of these critics, the religion of the poor was little more than an episodic emotional outpour-ing, a release of frustrations that yielded no ethical fruit that might transform the social lives of the poor. "When the rural church assembles," educator Carter Woodson wrote of the churches of poor blacks, "it is more of a séance. Per-sons have come together to wait upon the Lord. He promised to meet them there. They have no time for the problems of this life except to extricate themselves from the difficulties which will ever beset them here until that final day."[36] "Worship and its major feature, the sermon, seek to 'make men right with God,' to save their souls," sociologist Frank Alexander wrote of a pre-dominantly white tenant community in southwest Tennessee. "'Men must become religious and give up the things of the world; it was to this end that Jesus suffered and died on Calvary's cross.' Words similar to these are reiter-ated Sunday after Sunday.... With one exception, the preachers have no in-terest in a religion which emphasizes social ethics. Their congregations are likeminded. Religion is one's personal relation to a Supreme Being; one's goodness is only incidental to this relationship."[37]

"The real rub is the persisting rural idea of religion," Baptist seminary pro-fessor J. W. Jent argued, "the conscious or unconscious conception of religion as mere emotionalism, hence, having nothing to do with social phenomena or community life."[38] "They attend church, go to revivals, 'get religion,' and pay the preacher," Ralph Felton summarized in his extensive study of the churches of poor blacks, "but their pastoral leadership is not trained to inter-pret religion in terms of daily living."[39] A seminary-educated minister might engage in home missionary work in the "decadent churches" of the poor, leading them to a moral vision: "We must deliver these deluded souls from their bondage to some of the old, outworn traditions and inefficient habits," the Baptist periodical *Our Home Field* insisted.[40] But in the absence of such a minister, churches of the poor were floundering in moral confusion. "It is unique to find a rural Negro preacher who understands and talks about present day community and social needs," Arthur Raper concluded from his fieldwork with poor blacks in the Georgia Piedmont.[41] Erskine Caldwell re-membered his father, a Presbyterian official, voicing a persistent lament: "It was a pity religion had been perverted by certain sects until it had little ethi-cal value left, and was being used by misguided people for the purpose of indulging in emotional and physical orgies. . . . Exultant Protestants in the South had degenerated into excessive emotionalism."[42] The Southern Rural Life Council, an interracial group of academics and denominational leaders, concluded that churches of the poor were "blind to the social nature of man and to the social implications of the Gospel. Too often religion, especially in the rural areas, is too other-worldly, having little relation to daily life."[43]

The verdict was clear: the religion of impoverished Christians contained no ethical vision. Little wonder, then, that what ought to have been a trans-formative force (the church and its message) had no tangible effect in the lives of the poor. Yet this ready critique was badly mistaken. In a host of ways—many seemingly mundane and others quite dramatic—the folk ethic of neighborliness had real, tangible meaning in the everyday lives of the poor. A discrete sample of oral histories from the Blackland Prairie of central Texas—the very area of Willie Johnson's musical creativity—suggests the powerful meaning of the folk ethic. William Ellis, white preacher at the Union (joint Baptist and Methodist) church in the village of Birome, recalled of the 1940s and 1950s, "The part about the country church that was so good was the fact that people were so poor, so poor. The church was the only place they had to go." Edith McKee, in the neighboring white-majority community of Cego, reminisced of the 1910s and 1920s: "It was hard times then. But some-how, it seemed like people maybe appreciated church more than they do today." Roosevelt Fields, who grew up in the black-majority community of Downsville in the 1950s, said, "I come up under the old-timey religion. I come up under the mourners bench. . . . The old folks didn't have—they didn't get no education, but they knew the Lord." He went on to talk about the rural exodus from the countryside and the breakdown of old patterns. The interviewer asked, "So, prosperity in a sense . . ." and Fields broke in, "Hurt. Yes, it does. . . . Not only the church, but it affected families and communities, you know—in our community, where we grew up, no one went hungry. If we killed hogs, everybody got some parts of it. Like somebody down the road kill a hog—we got some parts. . . . But, you know, we got away from that and we just got to a point that—we kind of isolated ourselves. You said, I got mine and I'm satisfied, so you get yours." Carl Neal, who grew up in a white share-cropping family in the South Bosque community in the 1920s, reflected, "Everything was at a much lower level as far as economics is concerned. And I'm not sure if that's not what this country needs. I sure don't want to see it, but . . . because we lose our priorities." Neal described the sharing of food in the old world of poverty and rendered a complicated judgment. "It was harder," he said, "but it was kinder in a lot of ways, too."[44]

These speakers were all looking back, and the distance from that faded world of poverty sharpened their analysis. They were not nostalgic for "the good old days when times were bad."[45] Rather, in the clarity of hindsight, they were able to evoke the critical presence of the church in hard times and the ethic of neighborliness that shaped families and communities. In uncanny echo, elderly African Americans on the Sea Islands drew sharp contrasts between the present and the impoverished past. "Too much love has gone out of the world," one man said emphatically. "We didn't have nothing and we helped one another. Now it seems like all everybody is interested in is making the dollar."[46]

From different parts of the New South—Overton County in Tennessee's Cumberland Plateau and Hale County in western Alabama—there were other echoes of these oral histories. Though her interest was in song collection, a folklorist penned a long description of the ethic of neighborliness in Overton County in the 1930s:

> If there is illness in some family, the people help take care of the sick person, help with the work, and in general, just go in and make themselves at home, so far as running the household is concerned. . . . The author has known people to save special things, for example, cherries, if they were scarce, so that if someone were sick and could not eat something else, the cherries would be available. A person who may be at "outs" with someone else, if his enemy is sick, will quite often provide what is desired, if someone else does not have it. This custom sometimes effects a reconciliation. Arrangements for funerals and burials are taken out of the hands of the family, but carried out strictly according to the wishes of the family

and the deceased. Neighbors handle all the details. There is always some-one to do whatever needs to be done.[47]

In Hale County, Alabama, in those same years, James Agee noted that white tenant "Mrs. Tingle knows a great deal about home and woods remedies and exchanges knowledge and the roots of herbs with the Negroes. . . . She keeps a big assortment of roots and leaves on hand ready for immediate use and turns up with advice and offers all over the neighborhood the minute anybody is sick."[48] He also learned that the Burroughses' black neighbors had given them corn and peas during a severe drought. "There was no saying what they'd be doing by now" without those gifts, Burroughs said, even as he acknowledged that the givers "hadn't had a bit too much for themselves in the first place."[49]

Health care and sharing food—these were seemingly mundane, seemingly ordinary acts of neighborliness, yet they had powerful effects among families and communities. In these acts, people were moving out from care of self into concern for neighbor; and in concrete, demonstrable ways, they were seeking to foster life—the life of others in need. In small but substantive ways, individuals and communities looked different because of this reaching out. It was an expansive sense of neighbor grounded in an expansive ideal of charity.

In a variety of ways, many of the people encountered in the preceding pages displayed the real-world power of the folk ethic. Lloyd Chandler, as noted in chapter 2, displayed a dramatic change from nihilistic violence to egregious charity, giving away what he had, looking out for the suffering, and—as explored in the introduction—enacting richly symbolic displays of community with the lowliest of creatures. Vera Hall, despite all she had suffered in her hard life, responded not in kind but with an inner strength that allowed her to triumph over her circumstances. "Religion," she insisted, "will make you pure and honest in your heart and you'll have the heart and mind to love everybody."[50] Walter Evans, after religious struggles closely intertwined with his struggles as a tenant farmer, felt transformed by God's power and accepted a clear summons to "speak of the wonders of his grace and love toward the children of men."[51] Floyd Roe had witnessed racial terrorism in his youth in Louisiana and Texas, raw violence that left him with a deep and abiding anger. Yet as an older man, he came to firmly believe that "your heart can't be pure as long as malice and hatred is in it. It takes a heart full of love for humanity." Like Chandler with the moles, Hall in her Christmas story, and Old Christmas lore, Roe saw intimations of God's vision of neighborliness in animals and plants:

When I look out on His creation, I see white deers, black deers, and all different colors. I see the same in cows. I see the same in hogs. Then I look out on the earth and I see the earth that He made and I see flowers comin—some red, some blue, some white—all comin up on the same ground. It's a mystery to me, but it's God. And He must mean for us to live together. He must have meant so. . . . If you want a beautiful bouquet, you must get flowers of all colors and bring them together, and that makes a beautiful bouquet. We can't gather all white flowers or all red or blue; but we'll gather flowers of all different colors and blend them all together, and then we'll have a beautiful bouquet.[52]

*[handwritten marginalia: "try to mean'd"; "a symbol of"; "he use a symbol of"; "racial integration & harmony?"]*

Blind Willie Johnson, of course, did not perpetuate the violence he had suffered as a child but found his vocation in the crafting of stark, mysterious songs that evoked the strange power of Christianity. Human beings were more than their circumstances and their social identity; they also contained elusive inner depths, as he provocatively emphasized in "The Soul of a Man." Only in identification with the suffering Jesus would they find true wholeness and healing, he insisted in "I Know His Blood Can Make Me Whole."

For G. W. Blevins, his song about the Tree of Life heralded a new beginning. Blevins suffered for much of his life: he was orphaned at a young age, and as an adult he struggled with tuberculosis, which debilitated him until he was a mere "skeleton nightmare." Meanwhile, he and his wife, who was crippled, eked out a bare subsistence. He was an angry man, and he vented his spleen by engaging in bouts of violence and cheating on his wife. "Something just infest my mind, I was greatly afflicted," he said. But he felt himself pushed into prayer and, ultimately, repentance. On the muddy Norton Road, he sank to his knees, felt for the first time that his prayers went higher than his head, and headed home, "muddy to my pockets."

> When I got in the house my wife raised the conversation. She called me Pappy, said, Pappy, you're not going to be with me many days, said, if you was dead and laid out you wouldn't look any worse. I said, that's all right, I said, I sort of feel that way myself about it. Says, well, I haven't treated you like I promised you when I married you . . . says, will you forgive me? She says, yes, I'll gladly forgive you. And was a little old log house, we had nothing, in fact nothing to eat, no clothes 'cause I wasn't able to work and I hadn't been—and she said that I fell on my knees in the center of the floor and my prayers broke through and the first thing I knowed I was on my feet with my hands above my head.[53]

And Dock Boggs—who had poured his violence into songs that painted a stark, grim vision of the world as a nihilistic arena devoid of meaning or purpose—underwent a dramatic change. He experienced conversion and joined the Baptist church, to which his wife belonged, and became fervent in self-giving. In the worst of weather, in the roughest of conditions, he traveled to carry food to the hungry and clothes to the needy. Years later, speaking to a folklorist as an elderly man, he broke down weeping as he recalled the misery he had seen among his impoverished neighbors.[54]

These anecdotes suggest the power of the ethic to transform lives by calling people away from reactively perpetuating cycles of destruction and into proactive service to others. The anecdotes also reveal what is arguably the deepest meaning of the ethic: in valorizing self-giving and expansive charity, it played a critical role in sustaining life in community. A host of forces, external and internal, besieged the lives of the poor, threatening to undo the sinews of life and plunge individuals and communities into chaos. The ethic named the forces of chaos as evil and lionized the non-retaliatory, self-giving example of Jesus as the way of life. It showed people how not to be passive victims of injustice or perpetrators of patterns of dissolution but rather active agents of neighborliness. The lives of the poor looked different as a result.

A sociologist doing fieldwork in a rural community in southwest Tennessee heard a strong sense of this difference in the responses tenants and small farmers gave to his question, "What difference would it make in your daily life if you became convinced that there is no loving God to care for you?" He was asking about the presence or absence of God, yet the answers he received provide rare prosaic reflection on the meaning of the folk ethic:

MALE OWNER: Be a perfect wreck.

MALE TENANT: Would. Don't know what I might do. Might slip around and shoot some fellow in the dark.

FEMALE TENANT: I'd feel like I was lost.

FEMALE TENANT: Wouldn't have any encouragement then sure enough. Would just end it up sometime.

FEMALE OWNER: I'd be like Paul. I would be of all people most miserable.[55]

In fieldwork with poor blacks in four representative black-majority counties throughout the region, Tuskegee chaplain Harry Richardson heard echoes of such statements in response to his question, "What benefits do you derive from church membership?"

It helps my soul.
It feeds my soul.
It keeps me straight.
It gives me a chance to work with my brethren.
It gives me spiritual strength.[56]

And yet there was a tiny grain of truth in the middle-class critique: the folk ethic did not fundamentally alter the structures in which the poor lived. It showed people how to live as neighbors in poverty and how to avoid falling into chaos, not how to escape out of poverty. It focused on sustaining life amidst hardship, not getting out of it. Indeed, non-retaliation as exemplary behavior posed no direct challenge to the status quo. The folk ethic taught how not to perpetuate patterns of the status quo, but it did not summon people to try to change the structures of power that emanated those patterns in the first place. To historians interested in and sympathetic to collective efforts to change the structures of power, the folk ethic may seem to contain no "politics."

Organized efforts of the poor to change the regional structures of power did take place in the New South, and they have received significant historical attention. Especially in the upheaval and turbulence of the 1930s, impoverished southerners mobilized to change regional power dynamics. Tenants and sharecroppers organized as the Sharecroppers Union and the Southern Tenant Farmers Union. Textile workers organized strikes with the aid of the Communist Party of the USA and the Congress of Industrial Organizations (CIO). Coal miners joined the United Mine Workers and became labor militants.[57] These varied labor uprisings met with violent repression and cultural ridicule that justified that repression. Diverse in scope, constituency, and goals, they achieved some modest short-term gains, but none of them succeeded in changing the regional structures of power. For millions, poverty and its confinements remained cold, hard facts of life.

The folk ethic did not imagine a collective attempt to transform the regional structures of power, but it did articulate a clear critique of the basis of economic power in the New South. It was a moral critique, one that challenged cultural valuations—not a critique that manifested itself in organized, visible mobilization. But as a critique of the cultural pillars undergirding economic power in the emergent market capitalism of the region, it definitely contained politics. G. W. Blevins's song hints at this critique: Who and what did Blevins choose to embody the way of death that he cautioned against? The rich man who never noticed the poor beggar Lazarus at his gate. Focused on his own accumulation of wealth, the rich man was indeed a respectable figure—a sharp contrast to dirty, sore-infested Lazarus, lying on the ground. And yet it is Lazarus, not the rich man, who goes on to heavenly rest in the bosom of Abraham. The rich man's blissful callousness is condemned, as religious valuations overturn the hierarchy of social status.

A number of songs about Lazarus circulated throughout the New South. Documented in western North Carolina around 1915, in east Tennessee in 1916 and 1937, in the Virginia Blue Ridge in 1924, in southwest Virginia in 1940, and in eastern Kentucky in the 1930s was a "Ballad of Lazarus," based loosely on an older English folksong.[58] It told of how Lazarus

> Was begging humbly for the crumbs
> That fell from his rich table
> But not a crumb would he bestow
> Or pity his condition

Like the cows who huddled around the infant Jesus and kept him warm when there was "no room at the inn," in this ballad dogs cared for the suffering Lazarus:

> The dogs took pity and licked his sores
> More ready to defend him
> Poor Lazarus died at the rich man's gate
> To heaven he ascended
> He rested in the bosom of Abraham
> Where all his troubles ended
> The rich man died and was buried too
> But o his awful station[59]

The dogs display neighborliness while the rich man, insulated by his own wealth, displays callous disregard for the poor man at his very gate. In judgment after death, it is the rich man's callousness, not his wealth, that is weighed in the balance of ultimate worth and found sorely lacking.

In the Ozarks, Arlie Freeman (one of the documented singers of "Conversation with Death") was singing an expanded variation on this ballad:

> The rich man he lived high, he thought he'd never need
> Then came a man named Lazarus, who he refused to feed
> Now Lazarus he was begging while lying at the gate
> But the rich man who had scorned him, he later met his fate . . .

Dear people, all take warning before it is too late
Remember the wicked rich man who met his awful fate
So now this is my warning to the young and old today
Except you live for Jesus, at the judgment you shall pay[60]

Living for Jesus was not pious feeling—it was care for the neighbors in one's midst. The self-absorbed rich man, condemned for his cold disregard, stood as a stark warning.

In "Po' Lazarus," a song heard in the mid-1920s in the Georgia Piedmont and in the 1930s in Virginia, South Carolina, Georgia, Mississippi, and Alabama (as performed by Vera Hall), the biblical Lazarus became a sharecropper. This Lazarus, though, directly challenged the economic structure and was deemed a "bad man" and an outlaw:

Oh, bad man Lazarus done broke in the commissary window
He been paid off, Lord, Lord, he been paid off
High sheriff told the deputy, "go out and bring me Lazarus
Bring him dead or alive, Lord, Lord, bring him dead or alive"

Lazarus was hunted down and punished with egregious violence:

Oh, they found poor Lazarus way out between two mountains
And they blowed him down, Lord, Lord, and they blowed him down
Old Lazarus told the deputy he had never been arrested
By no one man, Lord, Lord, by no one man
They shot poor Lazarus, shot him with a great big number
Number 45, Lord, Lord, number 45
And they taken poor Lazarus and they laid him on the commissary
    counter
And they walked away, Lord, Lord, and they walked away[61]

The concluding image is vivid: the regional power structure reckons Lazarus's worth as something that can be quantified at the commissary counter, something that can be calculated in dollars—like goods sold at the commissary or wages paid out to laborers. But the song imagines a different valuation. Poor Lazarus was brutally crushed by a system built on exploitation and the devaluation of human life. His modest challenge to this system meets with violence of an extraordinary degree. There is a radical imbalance between laborers and the system that accumulates wealth from their labors.

Valorization of Lazarus was a way of subverting the dominant valuations of the New South. The poor beggar was the hero, and seen from his point of view, the system of accumulation was revealed to be wicked and unjust. Such subversive revaluations were especially vivid in two distinct but related songs about the *Titanic*, "When That Great Ship Went Down" and "God Moves on the Water." Heard from a blind preacher traveling by train through New Orleans in 1912, in northwest Alabama circa 1915, in western North Carolina and the Piedmont in 1920, in east Tennessee in 1929, and in eastern Kentucky in 1937, and commercially recorded by West Virginia–based hillbilly singer Ernest Stoneman in 1925 and the North Carolina–based race performers William and Versey Smith in 1927, "When That Great Ship Went Down" was a vivid modern lament:[62]

> On a Monday morning
> Just about nine o'clock
> The Titanic
> Begin to reel and rock
> People a-kickin' and cryin'
> Guess I'm goin' to die
>
> Wasn't that sad when that great ship went down
> Sad when that great ship went down . . .
> Husband and wife, children lost their life
> Wasn't that sad when that great ship went down
>
> When that ship left England
> Makin' for that shore
> The rich paid their fares
> Would not ride with the poor
> Couldn't get boats a-lowered
> Fightin' at the door
>
> People on that ship
> Long way from home
> There's prayin' all around me
> They know they got to go
> Death came a-ridin' by
> They know they got to die

The mighty *Titanic*, emblem of modern power, is tossed on the waves like a little boat. Both the swallowing sea and the sinking ship manifest the stark, triumphant power of death, which drags everyone down. The haughtiness of the rich at the point of embarking is played out in the frantic fight for lifeboats—even as it only serves to ensure their grim demise.

"God Moves on the Water" was a staple in the oeuvre of Blind Willie Johnson.[63] He crafted other topical songs—"When the War Was On" offered a critical view of American mobilization for World War I, and "Jesus Is Coming Soon" evoked the mass suffering of the 1918 influenza epidemic—but "God Moves on the Water" was especially powerful:

> Year of nineteen hundred and twelve
> April, the fourteenth day
> Great Titanic struck an iceberg
> People had to run and pray
> God moves, God moves
> God moves
> And the people had to run and pray
>
> The guards who had been watching
> Asleep for they were tired
> When they heard the great excitement
> Many gunshots were fired
> God moves

Like folk preachers, Johnson's words paint a vivid, dramatic scene. The listener is quickly transported to the setting, made to feel the varied reactions of different people in a moment of unexpected catastrophe:

> Captain Smith gave orders
> "Women and children first"
> Many of the lifeboats piled right up
> Many lives were crushed . . .
>
> Women had to leave their loved ones
> See for their safety
> When they heard their loved ones' doom
> Hearts did almost break . . .
>
> A. G. Smith, mighty man
> Built a boat that he couldn't understand . . .
> God moves, God moves, God moves
> And the people had to run and pray

One variation on Johnson's song had this pointed stanza:

> Well, that Jacob Nash was a millionaire
> Lord, had plenty of money to spare

> When the great Titanic was sinkin' down
> Well, he could not pay his fare[64]

The *Titanic* was an unmistakable symbol of modern wealth, of a triumphal confidence rooted in the power of modern technology. Yet the colossal event of its sinking revealed such confidence to have a tragically thin basis. The hubris of wealth and technology was brought low, and the disaster revealed just how fragile human beings really were. In their essence, everyone was a vulnerable, finite mortal; here again was death, the great leveler. This was not vindictive resentment but God's judgment on modern mammonism. Only in this fateful crisis moment were the wealthy shocked out of their blithe security; only then did they display the charity and compassion of neighborliness. But for many, by that point it was too late.

The Lazarus and *Titanic* songs, documented in different corners of the region, suggest that Populism, with its vision of "man over money" and a "cooperative commonwealth," was not completely defeated after the 1890s.[65] Rather, it lived on in the lives of the New South poor. The ethic of neighborliness did not involve the Populists' experiments with cooperative buying and selling, or their vision of government buttressing the interests of small producers with subtreasuries and greenbacks; it was not seeking structural change in the political economy. More so than Populism, it was generated in lives of poverty that knew disenfranchisement and diminished political horizons. The circumscribed world it came from could not credibly imagine wholesale transformation. But neighborliness very definitely called for the self-giving of help to neighbors in the throes of poverty, in such critical areas as food sharing and health care. It imagined individual good as subservient to the good of the local community. It taught empathy for fellow sufferers, for others stuck in the hard world of New South poverty. It understood that without a vision of loving community, the forces of violence, deception, and despair could pull impoverished people into irreversible cycles of destruction.

Like Populism, the ethic of neighborliness was a challenge and rebuke to the acquisitive individualism of New South capitalism. While the dominant evangelical culture articulated an ethic of respectability that sanctioned habits conducive to capitalist accumulation, folk Christians nurtured a different vision, in which the need of neighbor always beckoned and called for compassionate giving of the self. The ethic of respectability fortified a hierarchical culture in which the poor could be dismissed because of their transparent moral failure, but the ethic of neighborliness taught an empathetic compassion in which (metaphysically) homeless "strangers" helped one another in a world without sure supports. Perhaps because it was a rebuke and challenge to the dominant ethic, perhaps because the hierarchical culture dismissed the poor as degenerate, or perhaps for both reasons, representatives of the dominant religion could not see the ethic of neighborliness. Instead, they were left imagining and insisting that folk Christians had no ethic.

Ultimately, the ethic of neighborliness was part of a larger mentality that departed in a critical way from the visions of Populism and the New South's dominant evangelical culture, both of which participated in an optimistic American millennialism: Populism with its hope for a dramatic new day in the national political economy, a restoration of government to its democratic wellsprings; and New South evangelicalism in its model of the attainability of individual moral uprightness, with the "bad" being pushed triumphantly to the social margins. Neighborliness, by contrast, was an ethic for a fragile world, a social fabric whose sinews were always threatening to unravel. It showed a way that impoverished people could sustain one another in the face of forces that threatened to destroy their lives—both from within and from without. It imagined compassion and self-giving charity to counter and prevent a fatal slide into destructive chaos—a chaos that was always present, lurking as a real and dangerous possibility. There was no triumph, no plateau of social or moral victory. Put differently, the devil lay always in wait, undermining, attacking, seeking to snatch souls into irretrievable abandonment.

# The Unraveling of the Folk Christian World

Beginning around 1940, the confined world of the New South began to come undone. This was a generational process; it did not happen overnight. Some places experienced rapid, dizzying change, while other places—such as Appalachia, the Ozarks, and stretches of the old Black Belt—displayed older patterns well into the 1960s. Flannery O'Connor's Hazel Motes, the protagonist of *Wise Blood* (1952), has essentially no home to return to after his four years in the military. The village of his upbringing has dried up due to an exodus from the land, so he goes instead to the expanding town of Taukinham, a new world of movie theaters, soda fountains, and shiny automobiles. But Mason Tarwater and his nephew Francis Marion, the protagonists of *The Violent Bear It Away* (1960), still live in a rough cabin in a clearing in the woods, raising corn to eat and to distill. From this clearing, called Powderhead, they venture forth to prophesy to "the city." Robert Coles encountered repeated instances of incremental change in his fieldwork for *Migrants, Sharecroppers, Mountaineers* (1971): "I would hear about it: the gradual collapse of yet another small farm; the gradual mechanization of a plantation in this or that parish of Louisiana or county of Mississippi . . . the choice various sharecropper or tenant farmers made—such as 'try Florida, try harvesting the crops over there.'"[1]

In an uneven process in the period 1940–70, the cumulative effects of New Deal policy and the World War II experience were fundamentally transforming the region. New agricultural programs fostered a dramatic shift from labor-intensive to capital-intensive agriculture. Agriculture became mechanized, farms were consolidated into increasingly larger units, and the countryside witnessed a massive depopulation. Established industries were initially unable to absorb this huge labor surplus, as the new minimum wage requirement incentivized them to invest in labor-saving technology. With the nation's massive mobilization for war, good-paying jobs in the North and West opened up, and millions of southerners left the region altogether in the crux of this new push and pull. At the same time, regional elites began an aggressive new campaign to lure national industries to establish manufacturing in the South, attracting them with a combined package of lower wages, weak unions, loose environmental regulations, and generous government subsidies.

The clout of Southern elites within the Democratic Party likewise enabled them to steer federal largesse into the region, both directly and indirectly, in the form of new entities like NASA, the investment bank Stephens Inc., and the Centers for Disease Control.[2]

With all of these transformations, the New South poor were dispersed in a variety of directions. Richard Wright evocatively captured the changing countryside: "There come, with a tread as of doom, more and more of the thundering tractors and cotton-picking machines that more and more render our labor useless. . . . Black and white alike now go to the pea, celery, orange, grapefruit, cabbage, and lemon crops. . . . Our dog-trot, dog-run, shotgun, and gingerbread shacks fill with ghosts and tumble down from rot."[3] The exodus out of the region was largely a poor people's movement. In new contexts like Detroit, Seattle, and Bakersfield, Southern migrants established new lives as industrial workers. Other impoverished southerners moved to new places inside the region—to the quickly expanding cities, where jobs in traditional industries, recently recruited industries, and the defense state offered new opportunities. Still other impoverished southerners saw little change. Even as the region was surely changing, many who had lived the bulk of their lives in New South poverty died also in poverty—Willie Johnson at age forty-eight, in Beaumont in 1945, where he was buried in an unmarked grave in a city cemetery; Vera Hall at age sixty-one, in Livingston in 1964, where she was buried in an unmarked grave in the Morning Star Baptist Church cemetery; Lloyd Chandler at age eighty-one, in Asheville in 1978, with his burial back in Madison County, in a secluded cemetery in a small hilltop clearing in the woods, in his home community of Sodom.

But the broad regional trend was clear: beginning around 1940, per capita income in the South began a decisive upward trajectory toward the national average.[4] The "Nation's No. 1 economic problem" was being incorporated into the postwar "consumers' republic," and by the late 1960s, looking closely at population growth and economic development, Kevin Phillips could proclaim that something new was being born. This "Sun Belt" stretched from South Carolina to Southern California, and it was characterized by population boom, economic growth, and a broad middle class.[5]

These tectonic economic and demographic shifts reshaped the religious landscape. Only fairly recently, though, have historians and religion scholars sought to understand these complicated religious transformations. Bethany Moreton's *To Serve God and Wal-Mart* argues that through its embodiment in a multinational corporation, an ideology of Christian free enterprise took shape in the Ozarks and became a defining feature of the postindustrial service economy. Darren Dochuk's *From Bible Belt to Sunbelt* seeks to show how migrants from the fading New South found, in Southern California, soil ripe for a fusion of Southern religion and conservative politics that emerged as an ascendant force in late twentieth-century U.S. politics. Elizabeth Fones-Wolf and Ken Fones-Wolf's *Struggle for the Soul of the Postwar South* argues that the CIO's Operation Dixie could not ultimately convince a majority of working-class evangelicals that unionization was a righteous cause, while Alison Collis Greene's *No Depression in Heaven* shows that with the New Deal state's taking the mantle of social services from the church, the Great Depression marked the beginning of a major religious and political realignment.[6]

The folk Christianity of the New South poor was also being dramatically transformed. A focused glimpse of its changing status comes through clearly in sociologist Morton Rubin's field study of Wilcox County, Alabama, in the late 1940s. A Black Belt county historically known for cotton production, large plantations, and tenant farmers, by the time of Rubin's study it was undergoing major change. Large landowners were switching from cotton to cattle raising, requiring significantly less labor, and Rubin wondered what the effect would be of the "enforced mass exodus of Negro and white tenants from the old cotton country." At the same time, a new mind-set was in evidence. "Hell and the Devil are gradually giving way to more lofty ethical sentiments," he noted optimistically, and "the teachers utilize the schools and the churches to teach the younger generation Protestant Christian values"— presumably, the middle-class ethic of respectability. "Young people with their educated ways demand a preacher who is more than a country farmhand who got a 'calling' one day and began to 'feel a lightness and a oneness with God.'" And it seemed that the basis for religious belonging was changing too: "People do not now join the church as in the old days because they have 'experienced religion.' The Sunday School indoctrinates the children."[7]

The white Branchley family succinctly embodied tension between the fading older world and the emergent new one. They were poor in background, but in moving to Camden, the county seat, they came to find modest prosperity. They bought and remodeled an "old plantation-style house," and Mr. Branchley made a good living as an auto mechanic, also picking up a variety of odd jobs. The family seemed to be enjoying new opportunities in the postwar "consumers' republic." Religiously, though, their identity lay in the world they had left behind. They did not join any of the churches in Camden, saying that there was "too much emphasis on dress and form." Instead, they went back into the countryside for church, to what Rubin called a "sect" but to what may have simply been a grassroots folk church, like the one organized by the Tingles. Mrs. Branchley candidly told Rubin that "this group has 'real religion' since they concern themselves with teaching about God rather than with 'show.'" Rubin noted that the Branchleys' income, house, and work ethic should have made them middle class, but their "aloof[ness] from community affairs"—like town churches—marked them still as poor. In the eyes of the town's middle class, the Branchleys were a weird mix of two classes, "honest folks who'll never get ahead."[8]

The story of the Branchleys suggests that sustaining a folk Christianity generated in poverty now involved an active struggle of competing identities in the face of social isolation, ridicule, and incentive to simply do what was convenient (join one of the churches in town). It also suggests that once-poor southerners could not simply enjoy the material feast of the consumers' republic as a unilateral gain. Even as they benefited from it, some harbored feelings that the religious ethos that sanctioned it was too preoccupied with "dress and show."

More gradually but arguably more powerfully, the rapid electrification of the South and the region's expanding purchasing power undermined the folk techniques that had been the sinews of folk Christianity. Folk revivalist John Cohen captured this succinctly in his 1960s film *The End of an Old Song.* Cohen, it will be remembered, had found his way to sixty-nine-year-old Lloyd Chandler's cabin porch, where Chandler recorded "Conversation with Death" for the first time, a half century after he had composed it. Cohen's film focused on Lloyd's cousin Dillard, who himself performed "Conversation" for the film. Dillard lived, like Lloyd, in a rough, unelectrified, spartanly furnished cabin of unpainted wood. And yet the film followed Dillard into town, where he enjoyed the sociability of a beer joint, with its food cooked to order and new popular music on the shiny jukebox. The juxtaposition was clear: a new culture of mass-produced consumer goods—a national pop culture—was reaching even remote parts of the region, while the older, orally disseminated, localized culture—a folk culture—was fading away as it was being supplanted, ceasing to be passed on to the rising generation.[9]

Folk Christianity became, increasingly, the preserve of the elderly. Older people whose lives had been defined by New South poverty and its confinements sustained folk beliefs and practices in the face of a changing social world. Vera Hall was still telling her Christmas narrative in 1959, when Alan Lomax first recorded it. People like Bessie Jones in the late 1950s and Dock Boggs in the early 1960s were singing variations of "Conversation with Death" that they had learned decades earlier. Into the 1970s, older people in the Appalachians and on the Sea Islands could still narrate their conversion in the form in which they had some fifty years earlier. Instances of grave decoration with personal objects could still be glimpsed in remote places in the 1970s, and aging itinerant evangelists could still be heard singing "God Moves on the Water" and "Jesus Make Up My Dying Bed" on the streets of Sun Belt cities. But in all of this, folk Christianity was changing from a creative grassroots culture, perpetuated by oral and imitative techniques, to something more ossified, documented for posterity by folklorists and folk revivalists. It was ceasing to be a living tradition.

In this transforming South, some children of folk Christians found a new home in the Holiness and Pentecostal movement. This movement was not new to the region, but before 1940 it had only made limited inroads, and those among the middle class. After 1940, it expanded significantly among once-impoverished southerners.[10] A critical factor in its appeal was its rigid moral code, an unambiguous guide as the once-poor faced an expanded arena of consumption. "The newer Holiness church," Jim Garland noted of the Kentucky coal areas, "demanded that its members live without sin, just like Jesus Christ: no dancing, no parties, no snuff, no smoking, no cussing."[11] From the Black Belt, Alan Lomax wrote that "the urban Holiness cults are notably more Puritan than the older Baptist church.... Holiness singing is more tense than the older spiritual style."[12] In the Appalachian foothills of Alabama, Herman Nixon noted "big Holyroller meetings," how after a Methodist meeting house burned down, "a large Holyroller center arose three miles away."[13]

And others, born into the culture of folk Christianity, were finding it to resonate less and less in the face of the emergent new world. For some, the delights of expanded consumption were sufficient. "As our children grow older," Richard Wright evoked the thoughts of aging poor blacks, "they leave us to fulfill the sense of happiness that sleeps in their hearts. Unlike us, they have been influenced by the movies, magazines, and glimpses of town life."[14] For others, the emergent world meant a profoundly disorienting culture shock. Seeking out the children of the three white tenant families that James Agee and Walker Evans had documented in 1936, Dale Maharidge and Michael Williamson found, in the 1980s, that while some had flourished as members of the expanded middle class, others displayed the pathos of disorientation in personal dissipation, continued dire poverty, and suicide.[15]

Complicating all of this was the fact that "the poor" were simply ceasing to exist as a distinct class. Certainly there were impoverished people living in the region even as the Sun Belt's arrival was proclaimed. But the dominant ethos of the postwar consumers' republic taught a wide swath of the population to see itself as "middle class," defined most basically by what it could buy: a house, an automobile, and new appliances. In this consumerist model, workers at a textile mill or one of the newer chemical plants could afford the trappings of middle-class status and find fortification for that status if (unlike the Branchleys) they joined a middle-class church and appropriated its ideals.

Federal programs and Southern state recruitment efforts were also disrupting a once-large class of poor blacks and poor whites. Federal initiatives like the GI Bill and FHA loans disproportionately underwrote the advancement of whites, and the emblematic figure at the heart of the consumers' republic was the white patriarch.[16] In the expanding industrial economy, "most new jobs were reserved for whites"; as a result, the racial composition of the region was changing dramatically. Whereas in 1940, almost 80 percent of the nation's African American population lived in the South, by 1970, the percentage had dropped to barely one-half.[17] "The poor" documented in the 1938 *Report on Economic Conditions of the South*—that large group of blacks and whites who together were the nation's largest single group of poor people— were ceasing to exist as a distinct class.

THIS BOOK OFFERS one window into the complicated interwoven dynamics of religion, class, and race in the American South. Race originated in the late seventeenth century as a radical innovation, a way to quash incipient class-based alliances between English indentured servants and African slaves. Bacon's Rebellion displayed the subversive power such alliances could have, and in reaction, the colonial gentry used the law to craft a new hierarchy of "white" and "black" as signifiers of inherent difference—that between "free" and "slave." Religion—Anglican Christianity—was a critical part of this newly imagined hierarchy of race.[18] English colonists of all classes learned to see themselves as white, free, and Christian, in contrast to black, slave, and heathen. Wide, substantive differences in the social structure were patched over, and class tensions were diffused with identities grounded in race and religion.

So potent was this construction that it shaped social life for almost two centuries. In the late eighteenth century, Baptists and Methodists opened the door to a challenge to this order. Their insistence on small exclusivist communities and the interiority of genuine faith led them to striking instances of interracial community, and their critique of the ethos of the gentry pushed them to valorize traits associated with the common folk. In brief moments in the early evangelical movement, it could seem as if religion might be the unifying force in an interracial movement of the lower classes. But such moments were fleeting, and by the early nineteenth century, Baptist and Methodist leaders were actively seeking to dampen leveling, egalitarian impulses and instances. By the 1840s, they were uniting with Episcopal, Presbyterian, and Catholic leaders in the crafting of elaborate theological defenses of slavery. The colonial fusion of religion and race was thus fortified and deepened.

But this became untenable in the wake of the Civil War. Emancipation destroyed the hierarchy of slave and free, and as evangelicals regrouped and sought to point the way forward into a New South, their message of respectability and domesticity was distinctly class based. It was the ethos around which an emergent middle class could coalesce. Yet what materialized as the New South took shape was not a social order built on a new, religiously informed class hierarchy; rather, it was a social order that minimized class differences under the canopy of a resurgent racism. The aggressive architects of Jim Crow sought to craft a new hierarchy of segregation, of a white supremacy that circumscribed the lives of an "inferior," less "civilized" race while buttressing the power of a "superior," "civilized" race. In this new order, as in the older colonial and antebellum order, whites of all classes could enjoy the privileges of whiteness, and the new order could likewise diffuse potential class tensions among whites with the powerful symbolic appeal of racial solidarity. In Ulrich Phillips's famous formulation, whites could rally around "a common resolve indomitably maintained—that [the South] shall be and remain a white man's country."[19]

So powerful was this new order that religious life fell into place on either side of its color line. Despite the ascendant evangelical culture of the New South encompassing both whites and blacks, its ideals of respectability and domesticity took on sharply divergent social meanings. In modeling these ideals, whites were fortifying the new racial hierarchy and imbuing it with a sacred aura, becoming "archdefenders of the status quo" in Martin Luther King's phrase. At the same time, in also modeling these ideals, blacks were presenting an embodied rebuttal to the messages of white supremacy, and "the Negro church" became a crucial space of resistance.[20] Coalescing in the late nineteenth century, these divergent religious configurations were on vivid display two generations later, when, in the decades of the New South's unmaking, the civil rights movement challenged and ultimately toppled segregation.

Indeed, so powerful are images from the civil rights era—oppositional, racially divergent religious forms in a class-blurring hierarchy of Jim Crow—that it can seem as if it has always been so. But race, class, and religion need to be rigorously historicized. They are historical phenomena, and they change shape over time and coalesce in different configurations. This book has argued for one specific configuration in a specific time. It has sought to show—beneath the order of Jim Crow, beneath the well-known Bible Belt—a hidden world of unfamiliar dynamics. It has sought to excavate a submerged folk Christianity, and it has sought to trace out the people and places of this grassroots religious culture. It has argued that in a historically contingent moment—the New South—religion became a space of interracial exchange among the poor. It has thus tried to offer an alternative voice to the established historiographical wisdom about religion, class, and race in the post-Reconstruction, pre–civil rights South.

For over a century, different observers of the region have ruminated on the possibility of a class-based alliance of poor blacks and poor whites and the barriers to it. In the 1890s, as he worked to build the People's Party in the South, Tom Watson sought to articulate the common ground shared by black and white tenants. "Their every material interest is identical," he argued, and "the moment this becomes a conviction, mere selfishness, the mere desire to better their conditions . . . will drive these two men together, just as their mutually inflamed prejudices now drive them apart."[21] Racism was a chimera that artificially divided the poor, the "keystone of the arch of financial despotism" that ensnared both white and black. A generation later, in a critical essay on Georgia as the "Invisible Empire State," W. E. B. Du Bois similarly argued that "the method" for maintaining a submerged class of dependable laborers was "deliberately to encourage race hatred." But his essay moved to an unexpectedly hopeful conclusion. Riding through the Georgia mountains on a segregated train, looking out at malnourished, impoverished whites, Du Bois thought he saw glimpses of a new social order: "I look out of the window, and somehow it seems to me that here in the Jim Crow car and there in the mountain cabin lies the future of Georgia—in the intelligence and union of these laborers, white and black, on this soil wet with their blood and tears."[22]

In our own time, there are striking echoes of the ruminations of Watson and Du Bois. Speaking at the 2016 Democratic National Convention, Sen. Elizabeth Warren sought to highlight the common economic interest of whites and blacks, and she gave a thumbnail sketch of history to explain the barrier to seeing it: "'Divide and Conquer' is an old story in America. Dr. Martin Luther King knew it. After his march from Selma to Montgomery, he spoke of how segregation was created to keep people divided. Instead of higher wages for workers, Dr. King described how poor whites in the South were fed Jim Crow, which told a poor white worker that, 'No matter how bad off he was, at least he was a white man, better than the black man.' Racial hatred was part of keeping the powerful on top."[23]

In her seminal essay "Ideology and Race in American History," Barbara Fields argued not only that race was a manufactured idea, which, like anything else in history, originated at some point and has changed over time, but that race, like all ideologies, was manufactured to fortify the power of some over others. It wasn't some irrational, primal force; rather, it served an agenda. It did something for those who believed in it. There was (and is) both a purpose and a logic to it.

Near the end of the essay, she speculated on missed opportunities in the Reconstruction/late nineteenth-century South. She argued that an alliance of white yeomen and black freedmen could have been the basis for a radical reshaping of the South. Had this alliance materialized, the racialized structures of power in the early twentieth-century South would have looked very different—the door could have been opened to a South *after* race. But, Fields argued, the absence of any significant land redistribution hamstrung the possibility of such an alliance. The lack of material commonalities—smallholding white yeomen versus landless black tenants and sharecroppers—prevented the two groups from coming together and seeing common interests over and against the planters. In the end, with no material basis, an interracial class alliance couldn't emerge. Racialist ideology pervaded the different classes of whites. It took different shapes and meanings based on different class position, but it also fostered a remarkable solidarity, nowhere more visible than in the spectacle of "Solid South" politics.[24]

More recently, labor historian Brian Kelly ruminated on Phillips, Fields, and the strange world of the New South in his essay "Labor, Race, and the Search for a Central Theme in the History of the Jim Crow South." In the Fields model, he argued that the new racism of the New South served an important purpose for the region's planters and industrialists. In the arena of capitalist competition to which they were newcomers, it helped them maintain the core of their competitiveness: "an abundant supply of cheap labor." Systematic and violent suppression of the rights of black citizens was basic to maintaining such a labor supply. But the new white supremacy served this purpose in another way too: for the elite, disturbed by the Populist revolt, it sought to foster racial solidarity and "exorcise the frightening specter of looming class conflict among whites." Just as race had done in its beginnings—on the heels of Bacon's Rebellion in the late seventeenth century—so too would it do in the late nineteenth century: separate black and white laborers with different legal rights, diffuse class tension among whites, and make a collective rebellion of black and white laborers unimaginable.

Kelly went on to argue for a very different trajectory than Fields. Whereas she saw the lost possibility of a door that never really opened during Reconstruction, Kelly argued that despite the "ubiquitous influence of white supremacy," the early twentieth-century South "gave rise to a resilient tradition of working class interracialism that emerged under even the most unfavorable circumstances." In different Southern settings, where black and white workers found themselves in roughly common material contexts, they could imagine shared goals. Sometimes those goals materialized into the very thing that the region's elite feared: an open revolt of the laborers. On the docks of New Orleans, in the timber camps of East Texas, in the Alabama coalfields, in the tobacco warehouses of North Carolina, in the new cotton frontier of the Missouri bootheel, at least for a time, white and black could see themselves as part of a "southern working class."[25]

Perhaps ironically, the New South furnished the material basis for such an interracial alliance by fostering a modern poverty of landlessness and low wages that touched millions of whites and blacks. Put differently, the New South's extractive economy did what the politics of Reconstruction failed to do: it provided a material basis for cooperation. Indeed, from the demise of Populism to World War II, millions of whites and blacks in the South arguably came closer in the material conditions of their lives than at any time since the years before Bacon's Rebellion. Paradoxically, of course, this was also the era of Jim Crow. But labor history reveals that race was only one variable—certainly a very powerful one—but not *the* central theme. White and black workers could and did come together in labor activism, in an activism grounded in a roughly shared class position.

These conceptualizations are important, and yet they rest on a Marxist frame: material conditions can generate interracial solidarity—or the chimera of race can create a "false consciousness" that deviates from material reality. Marx's materialist philosophy looms in the background here. Material conditions are the base, and culture is the mere superstructure. This book has imagined, instead, the spiritual element in human life. Spirit is not a thing but a capacity—the anxiety one feels in the face of one's own mortality, the imagination through which one creatively envisions the world, the power by which one triumphs over socioeconomic circumstances. In the vision of this book, spirit is just as real and historically powerful as matter, though matter is hardly unimportant. Indeed, religion scholars have paid too little attention to matter, often analyzing religious life in a way that leaves it disembodied and floating above social existence. On the other hand, historians have paid too little attention to spirit, reducing religion to social morality or proto-politics, or pigeonholing it into a discrete compartment of life with little causative effect.

In seeking to weigh both matter and spirit, *Hard, Hard Religion* has argued that close analysis of religion reveals an extended instance of class-based interracial dynamics. Coalescing as a creative New South development, folk Christianity was a fragile but genuine space in which poor blacks and poor whites (the "southern working class" of labor historians) could express commonalities in their lives. Though this certainly had a powerful material element—visible in worn and disease-racked bodies, in tattered clothes, in unpainted shacks and cabins—this book has departed from the Marxist idea of material base and cultural superstructure. Rather, it has sought to show how in creative fusion with material conditions, religious culture became the basis for an interracial, class-based sense of solidarity.

This folk Christianity was not trying to change the world—at least not in the ways that historians typically see as activism, or "politics." In their folk Christianity, though, poor blacks and poor whites creatively used an array of cultural material to probe the depths of mortality, of personal transformation, of manifesting the sacred, of living as a neighbor. Through indirect techniques such as song, story, lore, proverb, and material display, with vivid symbol and rich metaphor, they explored such modern phenomena as the value of a single small life, alienation and genuine identity, glimpsing the sacred in a disenchanted world, and fighting chaos and a nihilistic spiral of violence. At the most basic level, their folk Christianity was their fervent attempt to live *in* this world—not in some compensatory other world. They sought liberation to live fully in *this* life, within the powerful structures that confined and circumscribed it. In material lack, they displayed great inner strength, spiritual creativity, and a complex interiority. Their hard, hard religion called them to persistent struggle: to assert the worth of every individual life, the basic goodness of the world, God's close and tangible presence, and the subversive example of non-retaliatory, self-giving Jesus.

One of folk Christianity's practitioners—the farm laborer who coined the evocative phrase "hard, hard religion"—succinctly expressed the seeming limitation of its vision and the this-worldly struggle at its core, even as his self-deprecating modesty concealed the richness of the culture from which he spoke. "The snake came, and Adam and Eve couldn't stay away from that snake; it got to them, that's what happened, it just got to them. Every day there's a snake in our lives; every day, I tell you. . . . There's nothing so bad on the outside, that it don't have its equal on the inside," he said plaintively. "I'm just a bad soul, trying to get as good as possible, before I'm called."[26]

# Notes

## Introduction

A special thank you to Sarah Craddock and Jamil Drake for their helpful critiques of this chapter.

1. Gruber, *Benton and the American South*, 49–53.

2. McDannell, *Picturing Faith*, 79, 84, 111.

3. O'Connor, *Wise Blood*, 16.

4. O'Connor, *Mystery and Manners*, 131; "God-Intoxicated Hillbillies," 118–19.

5. O'Connor, *Mystery and Manners*, 207.

6. Americana, *American Mercury*, 171.

7. Hall, *Lived Religion in America*; Orsi, *Madonna of 115th Street*; Primiano, "Vernacular Religion"; Maffly-Kipp, Schmidt, and Valeri, *Practicing Protestants*; Ammerman, *Everyday Religion*; McGuire, *Lived Religion*; Sullivan, *Living Faith*.

8. Donald Mathews, "Christianizing the South: Sketching a Synthesis," in Stout and Hart, *New Perspectives*, 108.

9. Charles Reagan Wilson, "William Faulkner and the Southern Religious Culture" and "Digging Up Bones: Death in Country Music," in Wilson, *Judgment and Grace*, 62, 68, 97; Harvey, *Freedom's Coming*, 114–20, 123–26; Harvey, *Moses, Jesus, and the Trickster*, 123–25. Newer scholarship has explored grassroots religious creativity in specific subregions: Richard Callahan in the eastern Kentucky coal areas (*Work and Faith in the Kentucky Coalfields*), Jarod Roll in the Missouri bootheel (*Spirit of Rebellion*), and Alison Greene in the delta (*No Depression in Heaven*). This book is interested in a religious milieu of broad *regional* scope.

10. Carlton and Coclanis, *Confronting Southern Poverty*, 42.

11. Gwynn and Blotner, *Faulkner in the University*, 86.

12. Raboteau, *Fire in the Bones*, 188. For classic statements of this scholarship, see Mays and Nicholson, *Negro's Church*; Hill, *Southern Churches in Crisis*; Hill et al., *Religion and the Solid South*; Lincoln, *Black Experience in Religion*; Frazier, *Negro Church in America*; Donald Mathews, "Lynching Is Part of the Religion of Our People," in Schweiger and Mathews, *Religion in the American South*; William Montgomery, "Semi-Involuntary: African-American Religion," in Wilson and Silk, *Religion and Public Life in the South*. For exceptions—works that analyze both white and black Southern Christianity—see Harvey, *Redeeming the South*; Harvey, *Freedom's Coming*; Stephens, *Fire Spreads*; Roll, *Spirit of Rebellion*; Gellman and Roll, *Gospel of the Working Class*; Greene, *No Depression in Heaven*.

13. Hale, *Making Whiteness*, 21–22. See also Jones, *Dispossessed*, 103: "Martha Brown's vision of a world of color-blind souls united in religious faith would find no place in the

Jim Crow Southern countryside." For leading works in this historiography, see Gilmore, *Gender and Jim Crow*; Litwack, *Trouble in Mind*; Dailey, Gilmore, and Simon, *Jumpin' Jim Crow*; Kantrowitz, *Ben Tillman*; Brundage, *Southern Past*; Ritterhouse, *Growing Up Jim Crow*.

14. Du Bois, *Souls of Black Folk*, 135.

15. Richard Wright, *Twelve Million Black Voices*, 46.

16. Harvey, *Freedom's Coming*, 111.

17. Coles, *Flannery O'Connor's South*, xxxi.

18. Ayers, *Promise of the New South*.

19. McCloud, *Divine Hierarchies*; Cobb, "Beyond Planters and Industrialists."

20. Eley and Nield, *Future of Class in History*, 186.

21. Sean McCloud, "The Ghost of Marx and the Stench of Deprivation," in McCloud and Mirola, *Religion and Class in America*; Troeltsch, *Social Teaching*, 331–43; Niebuhr, *Social Sources*, 31; David Harrell, "The Evolution of Plain-Folk Religion in the South, 1835–1920," in Hill, *Varieties of Southern Religious Experience*, 36; David Harrell, "The South: Seedbed of Sectarianism," in Harrell, *Varieties of Southern Evangelicalism*, 54; Flynt, "Religion for the Blues," 38.

22. O'Connor, *Mystery and Manners*, 203.

23. Lindahl, *American Folktales*, 440–42.

24. Ibid., 442.

25. Vera Hall, "No Room at the Inn," T920R05-06, T920R08-09, T921R01-03, Southern U.S. 1959 and 1960, Alan Lomax Archive. I have combined excerpts from two versions of Hall's "No Room at the Inn" story. They were recorded in the same October 1959 session.

26. Ibid.

27. Thurman, *Jesus and the Disinherited*, 28.

28. Certainly there were folk religious elements in the New South that did not fall under the canopy of Christianity. Folklorists in the New South era and contemporary historians have documented the power and presence of non-Christian religious beliefs and practices in the early twentieth-century South. These were of African and European origin, and while some became Christianized in the nineteenth and early twentieth centuries, others resisted Christianization and continued to embody non-Christian meanings. Paul Harvey argues that the figure of the Trickster embodies this folk religious world: "Morally ambiguous," a "figure of grey," the Trickster represents beliefs and practices at odds with Christianity. Such beliefs and practices were real parts of the early twentieth-century South, but they fall outside the scope of this book. This book is interested in the primary religious expression of the poor of the New South, a distinct, hidden Christianity beneath the well-known, much-documented Christianities of the Bible Belt. See Harvey, *Moses, Jesus, and the Trickster*, 26–36.

29. Goff, *Close Harmony*; Charles Reagan Wilson, "Church Fans," in Wilson, *Judgment and Grace*, 84–93; Giggie, *After Redemption*, 59–95; MacLean, *Behind the Mask*; Ayers, *Promise of the New South*, 160–86.

30. Lomax, *Adventures*, 232; Halli, *Alabama Songbook*, 216; Rev. Gary Davis, "I am the True Vine," Brunswick 17875/*Goodbye, Babylon* CD 4:21; White, *American Negro Folk-Songs*, 101–2.

31. Coles, *Migrants, Sharecroppers, Mountaineers*; Jones, *Dispossessed*, 104–66; Wray, *Not Quite White*, 96–132.

32. Yoder, "Towards a Definition of Folk Religion," 3. In Yoder's more extensive categorization, the folk religion being explored here involves (1) survivals of earlier religious phenomena—though creatively employed and given new meanings in a new context; (2) syncretism—of European American and African American traditions; (3) fringe phenomena, the unpermitted, the unsanctioned—religious expression at odds with dominant religion; and (4) the local coloration that common people give to official religion—the fact that the characters here were overwhelmingly Baptist and Methodist and drew on material in these religious forms. More broadly, folklorist John Burrison offers a helpful definition of folk *culture*: "a community-shared resource of accumulated knowledge . . . learned informally, preserved in memory and practice, and passed on through speech and body action to others in any group whose members have a common bond" (Burrison, *Roots of a Region*, 19). See also Titon, "Stance, Role, and Identity"; Titon, *Powerhouse for God*, 144–49.

33. Kelley, "Notes on Deconstructing 'the Folk'"; Whisnant, *All That Is Native and Fine*; Filene, *Romancing the Folk*.

34. Coles, *Migrants, Sharecroppers, Mountaineers*, 16, 19.

35. Coles, *O'Connor's South*, 60–61.

## Chapter One

1. Crews, *Childhood*, 42–44.

2. Carlton and Coclanis, *Confronting Southern Poverty*, 47, 54–55, 78; Cohen, *Consumers' Republic*.

3. Carlton and Coclanis, *Confronting Southern Poverty*, 62, 63, 59, 61.

4. Ibid., 63.

5. Ted Ownby, "Three Agrarianisms and the Idea of a South without Poverty," in Godden and Crawford, *Reading Southern Poverty*.

6. Ibid., 69.

7. Moody, *Coming of Age*, 3–10.

8. Carlton and Coclanis, *Confronting Southern Poverty*, 73, 70.

9. Grady, *New South*, 255–57.

10. Woodward, *Origins of the New South*; Eller, *Miners, Millhands, and Mountaineers*; Hahn, *Roots of Southern Populism*; Daniel, *Breaking the Land*; Gavin Wright, *Old South, New South*; Jacquelyn Hall et al., *Like a Family*; Ayers, *Promise of the New South*; Woodward, *Origins*, 120; Wright, *Old South, New South*, 22 for railroad statistics.

11. Du Bois, *Souls of Black Folk*, 43–48.

12. Haygood, *New South*, 9, 11–12.

13. Washington, *Frustrated Fellowship*, 197.

14. Gerth and Mills, *From Max Weber*, 304–5.

15. Peacock and Tyson, *Pilgrims of Paradox*, xvii–xix; Schweiger, "Max Weber in Mount Airy, Or, Revivals and Social Theory in the Early South," in Schweiger and Mathews, *Religion in the American South*, 31.

16. Federal Writers' Project, *North Carolina*, 394.

17. Isaac, *Transformation of Virginia*; Winner, *Cheerful and Comfortable Faith*.

18. Faust, *Creation of Confederate Nationalism*; McCurry, *Masters of Small Worlds*; Heyrman, *Southern Cross*; Schweiger, *Gospel Working Up*; Irons, *Origins of Proslavery Christianity*.

19. Raboteau, *Slave Religion*; Sobel, *Trabelin' On*; Creel, *Peculiar People*; Frey and Wood, *Come Shouting to Zion*; Fountain, *Slavery, Civil War, and Salvation*.

20. Harvey, *Redeeming the South*; Harvey, *Freedom's Coming*.

21. Ownby, *Subduing Satan*; Higginbotham, *Righteous Discontent*; Montgomery, *Under Their Own Vine*; Harvey, *Redeeming the South*; Harvey, *Freedom's Coming*; Giggie, *After Redemption*.

22. Harvey, *Freedom's Coming*; Giggie, *After Redemption*.

23. Du Bois, *Souls of Black Folk*, 57.

24. Ownby, *Subduing Satan*; Higginbotham, *Righteous Discontent*; Harvey, *Redeeming the South*; Giggie, *After Redemption*.

25. U.S. Bureau of the Census, *Religious Bodies: 1890*, 38–43; U.S. Bureau of the Census, *Religious Bodies: 1926*, 142–268. I assumed even population growth per year from 1920 to 1930 to calculate the 1926 population. By "adult," I mean members over the age of thirteen. With their emphasis on conversion, Baptists and Methodists did not consider infants and young children to be members; age twelve or thirteen often marked the age at which children officially became members.

26. On the ideological ties between respectability and the middle class, see Skeggs, *Class, Self, Culture*.

27. Sparks, *Religion in Mississippi*, 186.

28. Du Bois, *Souls of Black Folk*, 49–52.

29. Agee and Evans, *Let Us Now Praise Famous Men*, 118–19.

30. Warman, *Corn and Capitalism*, 151–73.

31. Alan Lomax, *Rainbow Sign*.

32. Davis, Gardner, and Gardner, *Deep South*, 59–73, 228–34; Dollard, *Caste and Class*, 76, 85–86, 93–95; Pope, *Millhands and Preachers*, 49–69. Frank Owsley's venerable term "plain folk"—suggesting a broad group of modest, middling people—simply fails to capture the class dynamics of the New South. In his 1989 *Plain Folk in the New South*, I. A. Newby brought the category into the historiography of the New South; and more recently, Darren Dochuk (*From Bible Belt to Sunbelt*, 2011) and Fred Smith (*Trouble in Goshen*, 2014) have employed the category and connected it to religious life. Dochuk and Smith are both analyzing a late 1930s–early 1940s South in transition, with new opportunities opening up (industrial jobs in Southern California; agricultural resettlement communities in the Delta)—and, with those new opportunities, some

class fluidity. I think "the poor" more accurately evokes the circumscription and pathos of the New South before these transformations.

33. Agee and Evans, *Let Us Now Praise Famous Men*, 79–80.

34. Rubin, *Plantation County*, 53, 105.

35. Dollard, *Caste and Class*, 85–88; see also Leonard Doob, "Poor Whites: A Frustrated Class," in Dollard, *Caste and Class*, 447, 455.

36. Percy, *Lanterns on the Levee*, 20, 22–23.

37. Ayers, *Promise of the New South*, 24, 71, 115, 163, 201. Both local geography and kin networks could work against this class distancing. A small merchant (seemingly "middle class") in a remote area might identify more with his poor neighbors, while a young tenant family (the son or daughter of a local teacher) could identify with the middle class.

38. Kousser, *Shaping of Southern Politics*.

39. *Lynchburg Story*; White, "Horror of Forced Sterilization."

40. Dollard, *Caste and Class*, 220–49; Agee and Evans, *Cotton Tenants*, 175–76; Pope, *Millhands and Preachers*, 70–95; Ardery, *Welcome the Traveler*, 26; Southern Rural Life Council, *Church and Rural Community Living*, 21; Richardson, *Dark Glory*, 37, 47; Raper, *Preface to Peasantry*, 351, 361.

41. Mary Livermore, "Mission Work Among Backward People," *Our Home Field*, October 1911; Woodson, *Rural Negro*, 137, 174; Bruce Crawford, "The Coal Miner," in Couch, *Culture in the South*, 367; Caldwell, *Bunglers*, 29, 34; Mays and Nicholson, *Negro's Church*, 10; Rubin, *Plantation County*, 141; L. G. Wilson, "Church and Landless Men," 7.

42. Faduma, "Defects of the Negro Church," 6–7; *Our Home Field*, January 1909 and October 1911; Livermore, "Mission Work"; Caldwell, *Bunglers*, 25; Woodson, *Rural Negro*, 160; Southern Rural Life Council, *Church and Rural Community Living*, 21.

43. L. G. Wilson, "Church and Landless Men"; Ormond, *Country Church in North Carolina*, 338; Richardson, *Dark Glory*, 49.

44. U.S. Bureau of the Census, *Religious Bodies: 1926*, 142–268. This is an approximate figure for non-members of religious institutions. I assumed even population growth from 1920 to 1930 to calculate an over-thirteen regional population of 21,684,353. Precise statistics for religious members over the age of thirteen do not exist, but I have taken the Southern state average of 10 percent members below the age of thirteen as a guide, to arrive at a total over-thirteen religious membership of 13,023,762.

45. Harrell, *White Sects and Black Men*; David Harrell, "Religious Pluralism: Catholics, Jews, Sectarians," in Charles Reagan Wilson, *Religion in the South*; Harrell, "Evolution of Plain-Folk Religion," in Hill, *Varieties*; Harrell, "The South," in Harrell, *Varieties*; Hill, *One Name but Several Faces*; Dorgan, *Old Regular Baptists*; Brasher, *Sanctified South*; Butler, *Women in the Church of God in Christ*; Stephens, *Fire Spreads*; Guthman, *Strangers Below*.

46. McCauley, *Appalachian Mountain Religion*; Jones, *Faith and Meaning*; Callahan, *Work and Faith*; Samuel Hill, "The Peripheral South: Florida and Appalachia," in Wilson and Silk, *Religion and Public Life*.

47. Dunbar, *Against the Grain*; Roll, *Spirit of Rebellion*; Gellman and Roll, *Gospel of the Working Class*.

48. L. G. Wilson, "The Church and Landless Men"; Dollard, *Caste and Class*; Pope, *Millhands and Preachers*, 70; Southern Rural Life Council, *Church and Rural Community Living*, 21, 137; Rubin, *Plantation County*, 46; Ardery, *Welcome the Traveler Home*, 26. Such distancing was the dominant practice. Some industrialists took a paternalistic approach to their workers, especially in mill villages and coal towns. They sponsored churches and "wholesome" recreation for their workers, seeking to lift them up to the standard of respectability. Such paternalism imagined that the poor could be transformed rather than dismissed and denigrated, and was thus a softer version of the region's class hierarchy.

49. *Southern Baptist Convention Handbook, 1923*.

50. Agee and Evans, *Cotton Tenants*, 182–88.

51. Masters, *Country Church in the South*, 98.

52. Sparks, *Religion in Mississippi*, 186.

53. Dollard, *Caste and Class*, 230.

54. Mays and Nicholson, *Negro's Church*, 247 (my emphasis).

55. "Revival Sermon," AFS 4920B, AFC; Alan Lomax, *Rainbow Sign*, 115; Alexander, "Religion in a Rural Community," 242; Jackson, *White and Negro Spirituals*, 220–21.

## Chapter Two

1. Sandburg, *American Songbag*, 447 [Columbia, SC]; Halli, *Alabama Songbook*, 241 [Mobile, AL]; Randolph, *Ozark Folksongs*, 38 [Little Rock, AR]. The race performer Joshua White recorded it in 1933 (Banner 32918), and the hillbilly group the Carolina Tar Heels recorded it in 1929 (Victor V40053).

2. Work, *American Negro Songs*, 113.

3. Lomax and Lomax, *Our Singing Country*, 46 [Paintsville, KY]; Scarborough, *On the Trail*, 260–61 [TX]; White, *American Negro Folk Songs*, 65 [Creedmoor, NC]; Grissom, *Negro Sings a New Heaven*, 10; Brewster et al., *Frank C. Brown* 3:598–99. The popular race performer J. M. Gates recorded it in 1926 (Columbia 14145-D), and the popular hillbilly group the Carter Family recorded it in 1935 (Okeh 03112).

4. Courlander, *Negro Folk Music*, 70 [AL or MS].

5. Lomax and Lomax, *Our Singing Country*, 30 [Livingston, AL].

6. Perrow, "Songs and Rhymes from the South," 154–55 [eastern NC].

7. McIlhenny, *Befo' de War Spirituals*, 73–74; Work, *American Negro Songs*, 107.

8. Johnson's chorus line—"Jesus gonna make up my dying bed"—was heard in southern Louisiana (the New Orleans vicinity) before 1925 (Kennedy, *Mellows*, 114–15), and a variation on Johnson's song (five stanzas with several similar lines but without the chorus line) was heard in 1924–25 somewhere in the Carolinas, Tennessee, or Georgia (Odum and Johnson, *Negro Workaday Songs*, 197–98). It's possible that the chorus line was a floating lyric that Johnson worked into his own composition, or that "Dyin-Bed Maker" was a preexisting song that Johnson modi-

fied with his own stanzas. It is also possible that the entire song as he recorded it is not Johnson's composition but a preexisting song that he picked up and popular- ized. But Zora Neale Hurston's characterization of the song as recent, its notable spread after the mid-1920s, the thematic coherence of its four stanzas, and the high number of pressings for Johnson's recording of it lend plausibility to the claim that he was the composer.

9. Blind Willie Johnson, "Jesus Make Up My Dying Bed," Columbia 14276/*Complete Blind Willie Johnson*.

10. Odum and Johnson, *Negro Workaday Songs*, 197–98 [unspecified location in NC, SC, TN, or GA]; Work, *American Negro Songs*, 112; Halli, *Alabama Songbook*, 237–38 [Livingston, AL; Montgomery, AL]; Courlander, *Negro Folk Music from Alabama*, 49 [AL or MS].

11. Hurston, *Folklore*, 869–70. Based on existing documentation, 15,400 copies of Blind Willie Johnson's record were pressed (9,400 initially, then a second pressing of 6,000)—though there may have been third and fourth pressings (author correspon- dence with David Freeman, December 3, 2016). If every copy of the first two pressings sold, this would be well above the average of four thousand sales for commercially re- corded religious songs (Charles Wolfe, liner notes to *Goodbye, Babylon*, vi). Even then, the song clearly had life in an oral culture whose reach was much more extensive than that of commercial records.

12. Lindahl, "Thrills and Miracles," 133–71. I am deeply indebted to Lindahl's exten- sive research—fieldwork in Madison County, North Carolina, in the early 2000s, with some thirty people who knew Lloyd Chandler. I also owe a great debt to Todd Harvey of the Library of Congress's Archive of Folk Culture for telling me about Lloyd Chan- dler and "Conversation with Death" in the first place.

13. Lindahl, "Thrills and Miracles," 136; Chandler, "Why I Believe," 129.

14. Lindahl, "Thrills and Miracles," 139; Chandler, "Why I Believe," 131.

15. Lindahl, "Thrills and Miracles," 135–36; Chandler, "Why I Believe," 130.

16. Lindahl, "Thrills and Miracles," 152; Chandler, "Why I Believe," 131–32.

17. I am again deeply indebted to the work of a team of folklorists—especially Todd Harvey and Jan Sohayda—who searched for all variations and instances of the song. Their collective work appears as table 2 accompanying Lindahl's article, and Lindahl's analysis of these findings (148–60) has been essential.

18. "Oh Lord Spare Me," as sung by Hobel Day to Jean Thomas, box 16, folder 3, Jean Thomas Collection.

19. "What Is This That I Can See," as sung by Clarence Waring to Jean Thomas, box 16 folder 3, Jean Thomas Collection.

20. Chandler, "Conversation with Death," 128–29; Homer Davidson, "Oh, Death," box 3 folder 8, Burton-Manning Collection.

21. Crabtree, "Songs and Ballads," 134–35.

22. Sara Martin, "Conversation with Death," Bascom Lamar Lunsford Collection; Stegemeier, *Dance of Death in Folksong*, 170–71.

23. Rand McNally, *1936 Road Atlas*, 8–9; Rand McNally, *Handy Railroad Atlas*, 19.

24. Vera Hall, "Awful Death," AFS 2682 A2, John and Ruby Lomax 1939 Southern States Trip, AFC.

25. "Oh Death," box 5 K-12 #76, Ruby Pickens Tartt Collection.

26. "Oh Death Is Awful," ibid. A fourth Sumter County version was sung by Brant Bolden for John Lomax in 1937 (AFS 1312 A1). Almost all of its lines appear either in Vera Hall's version (from 1939) or in the two anonymous transcribed versions (c. 1940). I have not included it in the text because the three other versions are more extensive, even though they were documented a few years later.

27. Middle Georgia Singers, "Death Is an Awful Thing," AFS 7049 A1, AFC.

28. "Oh! Death," Winston Wilkinson, Manuscript Folk Music; also Downes and Siegmeister, *Treasury of American Song*, 263–64.

29. Laura Hunsucker, "Oh Death," 72/00829, Hamilton and Adams MSS.

30. Polly Johnson, "Oh! Death," 70/00552, Hamilton and Adams MSS.

31. "Oh Death," box 1, folder 7, Jean Thomas Collection; Thomas, *Ballad Makin'*, 200–202. As she wrote about this version in her 1939 *Ballad Makin' in the Mountains of Kentucky*, Jean Thomas recalled hearing this song when she was a child, in a small church of her kinfolk in the Kentucky mountains. Thomas was born in 1881, so this would date the song much earlier than Chandler's 1916 vision—and would challenge the claim that Chandler composed the song. However, the version that Thomas quotes shares only two lines with Chandler's song. It's probable, then, that fragments of Chandler's song were grafted onto another song (thus explaining the very different stanzas), and that this other song predates Chandler's. This older song would be the source of the "spare me over" refrain—which, as already noted, was interwoven with parts of Chandler's song at an early date. This explanation would fit the basic argument of this chapter: that a whole catalog of death songs were being crafted and circulated in the late nineteenth–early twentieth-century South, and that Chandler's "Conversation" is the pinnacle of the genre.

32. Thomas, *Ballad Makin'*, 200–202.

33. Randolph, *Ozark Folksongs*, 98–99.

34. Anderson Johnson, "Death in the Morning," Glory 15057-1/*Goodbye, Babylon* CD 3:24.

35. Bessie Jones, "O Death," T922R03, Southern U.S. 1959 and 1960, Alan Lomax Archive.

36. Vera Hall, "Death Have Mercy," T921R20-02, Southern U.S. 1959 and 1960, Alan Lomax Archive.

37. Barks, *Death and a Lady*, 25–26.

38. Lindahl, "Thrills and Miracles," 165–66.

39. Ibid., 171.

40. With the exception of Anderson Johnson's recording (which was on the short-lived Glory label and was simply an extension of his vocation as a preacher), I have limited this analysis of the song's spread to its noncommercial documentations. Overlapping with the above chronology, the song was commercially recorded by professional performers, though in fewer instances. The popular hillbilly singer Vernon

Dalhart recorded it in 1928 (Columbia 15585-D), the Anglin Brothers in 1938 (Vocalion 04579), and Charlie Monroe's Boys in 1939 (Bluebird B-8092). (It was also known to the Carter Family by 1938.) These records reached the poor—they were not isolated from an incipient popular culture spread through mass production—and yet in every instance noted in this chapter, singers/bearers of the song describe hearing it from another person, not a record. This speaks to the power of an oral culture, one for which (at this stage) recorded music was simply a supplement. It's also worth noting that aside from Dalhart, these professional performers were all from the broad area of the song's early spread—north Alabama (the Anglin Brothers), southwest Virginia (the Carter Family), Kentucky (Charlie Monroe's Boys). Finally, though Dalhart was one of the most popular early hillbilly performers, his recording of "Conversation with Death" (released in 1930) sold only a meager 1,172 copies (author correspondence with David Freeman, December 3, 2016). Average sales for a hillbilly record were around 15,600, with the highest selling over 300,000 copies. See Wolfe, "Columbia Records and Old-Time Music," 124.

This analysis is also limited solely to the words of the song. For singers, hearers, and carriers of the song, it was of course not solely words but words linked to a tune. Unfortunately, in most of the documentation, only the words were recorded, not the tunes. I have therefore limited comparative analysis to the words because they are the (necessarily) common element in all the documentation, even as I realize that this reduces the original feel of the oral culture. Where tunes *were* documented, though, they parallel the textual comparisons in uncanny ways. The Floyd County, Kentucky (Winston Wilkinson Manuscript), and eastern Kentucky (Jean Thomas Collection) melodies are very similar to Chandler's—which makes sense given their geographic proximity to Chandler—but the rhythms of all three have notable differences. Bessie Jones's and Vera Hall's two melodies are likewise similar to each other, just as their texts are. The music of Anderson Johnson's song—the only one in a major key, with ensemble voices—is the most distinguishable, matching the notable distinction of his words. At the same time, a pentatonic scale unites *all* the tunes, fortifying the claim that they are all variations and borrowings of the same core song. A special thank-you to Chelsea Hodge for the tune analysis.

41. These sketches are based on five censuses (1900, 1910, 1920, 1930, and 1940) and hints of biographical information in notes accompanying the varied song collections.

42. *National Baptist Hymnal*; *Baptist Hymn and Praise Book*; *Methodist Hymnal*; *Gospel Pearls*; *Cokesbury Hymnal*; *Modern Hymnal*.

43. For a recent analysis, see Gertsman, *Dance of Death*.

44. Gertsman, *Dance of Death*; Stegemeier, *Dance of Death*.

45. Stegemeier, *Dance of Death*, 170–72.

46. Barks, *Death and a Lady*, 5–7.

47. Stegemeier, *Dance of Death*, 41.

48. Lindahl, "Thrills and Miracles," 151; "Cecil Sharp's Appalachian Diaries," August 29, 1916; Sharp, *English Folk Songs*, 102–3. Sharp traveled from Marshall to White Rock, where a "Floyd" or "Lloyd" Chandler sang "Matty Grove." From Allegheny,

north of White Rock, he collected a "Floyd" Chandler singing "Young Hunting." Sharp noted that "Floyd" was only fifteen, while Lloyd would have been twenty at the time. A Floyd Chandler did live in Madison County and would have been fifteen in 1916, but he lived in the eastern part of the county, not the northern area where Sharp traveled. In his travels to White Rock and Allegheny, Sharp was just across a mountain ridge from Lloyd's family's home in Sodom. The evidence of connection is therefore possible but not definite.

49. For these songs in denominational hymnals, see *National Baptist Hymnal*; *Baptist Hymn and Praise Book*; *Methodist Hymnal*; *Gospel Pearls*; *Cokesbury Hymnal*; *Modern Hymnal*. It's worth noting that a majority of the composers of these songs were Northern, and that the Southern composers were writing in this idiom at a slightly later date.

50. C. W. Ray, "Death Is Only a Dream" (1892). For late antebellum evangelical culture that was beginning to display these themes, see Sparks, "Southern Way of Death."

51. Aries, *Hour of Our Death*, 610–11. See also Douglas, "Heaven Our Home"; Charles Reagan Wilson, "Southern Funeral Director."

52. Ginger Stickney, "Godly Riches: The Nineteenth Century Roots of the Modern Prosperity Gospel," in McCloud and Mirola, *Religion and Class*, 159–74.


## Chapter Three

1. Florence Cheek, "A Vision in a Tobacco Barn," *Children of the Heav'nly King*, 38, Blue Ridge Parkway Folklife Project Collection.

2. Clifton Johnson, *God Struck Me Dead*, 150–52.

3. Hurston, *Folklore, Memoirs*, 848–49.

4. Sutton, "In the Good Old Way," 98–99.

5. Hurston, *Folklore, Memoirs*, 758.

6. R. P. Smith, *Experiences in Mountain Mission Work*, 67.

7. Cooley, *School Acres*, 151–52.

8. Nathaniel Colley, "An Exploratory Study of the Customs, Attitudes, and Folkways of the People in the Community of Gee's Bend," Gee's Bend Collection.

9. Woodson, *Rural Negro*, 163–64.

10. For early examples, see Raboteau, *Slave Religion*, 266–71; Sobel, *Trabelin' On*, 108–22.

11. Campbell, *Southern Highlander and His Homeland*, 180.

12. Terry and Sims, *They Live on the Land*, 10.

13. Lindahl, "Thrills and Miracles."

14. *Children of the Heav'nly King*, 6–7.

15. Raboteau, *Fire in the Bones*, 193.

16. Ong, *Orality and Literacy*, 24; see also Rosenberg, *Can These Bones Live?*

17. Hurston, *Dust Tracks on a Road*, 198.

18. Hurston, *Folklore, Memoirs*, 848.

19. Rankin, *Sacred Space*, 19–20.

20. Mullen, *Listening to Old Voices*, 186–87.

21. Lindahl, "Thrills and Miracles"; *Children of the Heavn'ly King*; Hurston, "Conversions and Visions"; Bruce Grindal, "The Religious Interpretation of Experience in a Rural Black Community," in Hall and Stack, *Holding On*, 93; Peacock and Tyson, *Pilgrims of Paradox*, 130–40; Alan Lomax, *Rainbow Sign*; Head, "Granny Reed"; Brett Sutton, "Language, Vision, Myth: The Primitive Baptist Experience of Grace," in Hall and Stack, *Holding On*. Of the tellers of these narratives, the names of twenty-four were documented: Samuel Adams (white, Letcher County, KY), James Benton (white, Patrick County, VA), G. W. Blevins (white, Wise County, VA), Tom Bronner (black, Bolivar County, MS), Leonard Bryan (black, Alleghany County, NC), Edgar Cassell (white, Meadows of Dan, VA), Lloyd Chandler (white, Madison County, NC), Florence Cheek (white, Wilkes County, NC), Thomas Claytor (black, Roanoke, VA), Walter Evans (white, Alleghany County, NC), ? Fields (black, McLennan County, TX), Rachel Franklin (black, Bolivar/Sunflower County, MS), Quincy Higgins (white, Alleghany County, NC), Eddie House (black, Mississippi Delta), Ernest Huffman (black, FL/AL/LA Gulf Coast), Jessie Jefferson (black, FL/AL/LA Gulf Coast), Rosie Reed (white, Macon County, NC), John Reynolds (white, Roanoke, VA), Floyd Roe (black, LA/OK/TX), Susanna Springer (black, likely New Orleans, LA), Henry Truvilion (black, east TX), Elihu Trusty (white, Paintsville, KY), Lavere Walker (white, Franklin County, FL), Richard Young (white, Franklin County, VA).

22. Lindahl, "Thrills and Miracles"; Peacock and Tyson, *Pilgrims of Paradox*; Titon, "Son House," 4–5; Rankin, *Sacred Space*; Titon and George, "Testimonies," 71; Roosevelt Fields, 3, Baylor Institute for Oral History; Sutton, "Language, Vision, Myth"; *Children of the Heav'nly King*; Hurston, "Conversions and Visions"; Clifton Johnson, *God Struck Me Dead*, 169; Elihu Trusty, "Monologue on His Visions," AFS 1398A2-B1, Alan and Elizabeth Lomax KY Collection, AFC.

23. Lindahl, "Thrills and Miracles"; Colley, "Exploratory Study"; *Children of the Heav'nly King*.

24. Samuel Adams, AFS 2793B1-2794B, H. Halpert 1939 Southern States Recordings, AFC; Hurston, "Conversions and Visions"; Sutton, "Language, Vision, Myth"; Eidse, *Voices of the Apalachicola*.

25. Hurston, "Conversions and Visions"; *Children of the Heav'nly King*; Alan Lomax, *Rainbow Sign*.

26. James Benton, Reel 180/2 FT 768 and Thomas Claytor, Reel 181/1 FT 769, Sutton and Hartman Collection; Clifton Johnson, *God Struck Me Dead*, 20–21.

27. Lindahl, "Thrills and Miracles"; Sutton, "In the Good Old Way"; Colley, "Exploratory Study"; Head, "Granny Reed"; Grindal, "Religious Interpretation"; Clifton Johnson, *God Struck Me Dead*, 59.

28. Samuel Adams, AFS 27931-2794B; Rankin, *Sacred Space*; *Children of the Heav'nly King*; Peacock and Tyson, *Pilgrims of Paradox*; Alan Lomax, *Rainbow Sign*; G. W. Blevins, AFS 2766A-2767A, H. Halpert 1939 Southern States Recordings, AFC.

29. Samuel Adams, AFS 2793B1-2794B; Lindahl, "Thrills and Miracles"; Hurston, "Conversions and Visions"; *Children of the Heav'nly King*; Peacock and Tyson, *Pilgrims of Paradox*; G. W. Blevins, AFS 2766A-2767A.

30. Hurston, "Conversions and Visions"; Eidse, *Voices of the Apalachicola*; Colley, "Exploratory Study."

31. Rankin, *Sacred Space*; *Children of the Heavn'ly King*; Alan Lomax, *Rainbow Sign*; Elihu Trusty, AFS 1398A2-B1; Henry Truvillion, "Monologue on His Call to Preach," AFS 3983A, AFC; Thomas Claytor, Reel 181/1 FT 769 and John Reynolds, Reel 182/1 FT 7??, Sutton and Hartman Collection.

32. *Children of the Heav'nly King*; Head, "Granny Reed"; Titon and George, "Testimonies"; Peacock and Tyson, *Pilgrims of Paradox*; Clifton Johnson, *God Struck Me Dead*, 100.

33. Sutton, "In the Good Old Way"; Grindal, "Religious Interpretation"; Sutton, "Language, Vision, Myth"; Hurston, "Conversions and Visions"; G. W. Blevins, AFS 2763A-B; Clifton Johnson, *God Struck Me Dead*, 17; *Children of the Heav'nly King*; Johnson, *God Struck Me Dead*, 59, 67, 91.

34. Lindahl, "Thrills and Miracles," 141.

35. This account closely follows and is very much indebted to the extensive fieldwork of James Peacock and Ruel Tyson. Peacock and Tyson, *Pilgrims of Paradox*, 133–39.

36. Hindmarsh, *Evangelical Conversion Narrative*, 1.

37. Sobel, *Trabelin' On*, 15; Turner, *Ritual Process*, 4; Frey and Wood, *Come Shouting to Zion*, 13; Albert Raboteau, introduction to Clifton Johnson, *God Struck Me Dead*, xxii–xxiii.

38. Creel, *Peculiar People*, 286.

39. Raboteau, *Canaan Land*, 79; Harvey, *Freedom's Coming*, 115.

40. *Our Home Field*, November 1917; Lee Scarborough, *Tears of Jesus*; Ownby, *Subduing Satan*, 154–55.

41. H. L. Gilmour, "The Haven of Rest"; Will Thompson, "Softly and Tenderly." For the recurring presence of these songs, see *National Baptist Hymnal*; *Baptist Hymn and Praise Book*; *Methodist Hymnal*; *Gospel Pearls*; *Cokesbury Hymnal*; *Modern Hymnal*; *Revival Gems*.

42. Ownby, *Subduing Satan*; Giggie, *After Redemption*; see also Sizer, *Gospel Hymns and Social Religion*.

43. Allen, Ware, and Garrison, *Slave Songs*, 14.

44. Turner, *Ritual Process*, 96, 4, 167.

45. Woodson, *Rural Negro*, 156–57; Ray, *Country Preacher*, 14; Charles Greaves, "The Country Pastor," *Our Home Field*, September 1912; D. H. Howerton, *Our Home Field*, August 1921; W. H. Holloway, "A Black Belt County, Georgia," in Du Bois, *Negro Church*, 61; Mays and Nicholson, *Negro's Church*.

46. Elizabeth Carpenter, "Granny," *Our Home Field*, November 1913; Richardson, *Dark Glory*, 91, 125.

47. Heyrman, *Southern Cross*; Schweiger, *Gospel Working Up*; Harvey, *Redeeming the South*.

48. Harvey, *Redeeming the South*, 145; Poteat, *Reverend John Doe*; Mays and Nicholson, *Negro's Church*, 50.

49. Pope, *Millhands and Preachers*, 93.

50. R. P. Smith, *Experiences in Mountain Mission Work*, 90; Felton, *These My Brethren*, 56–57.

51. Sherwin Sizemore, AFS 1958A-1960A, AFC.

52. *Atlanta Constitution*, September 27, 1914, quoted in Kester, *Revolt among the Sharecroppers*, 24.


## Chapter Four

1. Ingersoll, "Decoration of Negro Graves," 68–69.

2. Bolton, "Decoration of Graves," 214; Davis, "Negro Folk-Lore," 248.

3. Showers, "A Weddin' and a Buryin'," 481.

4. Brannon, "Central Alabama Negro Superstitions."

5. Puckett, *Folk Beliefs*, 104–6; Parsons, *Folk-Lore*, 214; Guy Johnson, *Folk Culture*, 172.

6. Jones, *For the Ancestors*, 76.

7. Brewster et al., *Frank C. Brown* 1:259–60.

8. Parrish, *Slave Songs*, 31; Georgia Writers, *Drums and Shadows*, 127, 136.

9. Killion and Waller, *Treasury of Georgia Folklore*, 210.

10. Stetson Kennedy, *Palmetto Country*, 168–69.

11. Bass, "Little Man," 395.

12. Saxon, *Gumbo Ya-Ya*, 319.

13. Boatright and Day, *Backwoods to Border*, 129–31.

14. Agee and Evans, *Let Us Now Praise*, 437–38.

15. Peterkin and Ulmann, *Roll, Jordan, Roll*, 216, 219.

16. Cate and Wightman, *Early Days of Coastal Georgia*, 207.

17. Combes, "Ethnography," 53, 60; Vlach, *Afro-American Tradition*, 143–44.

18. Jeane, "Traditional Upland South Cemetery," 41.

19. Pitchford, "Material Culture," 284–85.

20. Vlach, *Afro-American Tradition*, 139 [quoting Combes, "Ethnography," 52].

21. Faulkner, *Go Down, Moses*, 131–32. Thanks to Vlach, *Afro-American Tradition*, for noting this Faulkner passage.

22. Bolton, "Decoration," 214. In *Slave Religion* (p. 84), Albert Raboteau juxtaposed this engraving (from the April 1891 issue of *Century*) with a Doris Ulmann photograph from Ulmann and Julia Peterkin's *Roll, Jordan, Roll* (p. 217) as an example of African influence on slave religion. The similarities are uncanny and sure proof of the power of African burial tradition. The influence documented in these sources, however, belongs not to the era of slavery but rather to the New South—the grave in question is of a man who was born in 1878 and died in 1926.

23. Georgia Writers' Project, *Drums and Shadows*, 231.

24. Vlach, *Afro-American Tradition*, 142.

25. Frey and Wood, *Come Shouting*, 22–25.

26. Brewster et al., *Frank C. Brown* 1:259.

27. Faulkner, *Go Down, Moses*, 132.

28. Bolton, "Decoration," 214; Showers, "A Weddin' and a Buryin'," 481; Stetson Kennedy, *Palmetto Country*, 168; Brewster et al., *Frank C. Brown* 1:260.

29. Boatright and Day, *Backwoods to Border*, 129.

30. Faulkner, *Go Down, Moses*, 131.

31. Peterkin and Ulmann, *Roll, Jordan, Roll*, 219.

32. Brannon, "Central Alabama Negro Superstitions."

33. Jeane, "Traditional Upland South Cemetery," 38.

34. Showers, "A Weddin' and a Buryin'," 481; Brannon, "Central Alabama Negro Superstitions"; Agee, *Let Us Now*, 435; Cate and Wightman, *Early Days*, 213; Parsons, *Folk-Lore*, 214; Saxon, *Gumbo Ya-Ya*, 318.

35. Combes, "Ethnography," 54–56.

36. Boatright and Day, *Backwoods to Border*, 129.

37. Aries, *Hour of Our Death*, 531–33.

38. Parsons, "Folk-Lore," 393.

39. Brewster et al., *Frank C. Brown* 1:239–40.

40. "Praying Cattle," 72/01699-52, Hamilton and Adams MSS.

41. Puckett, "Religious Folk-Beliefs," 15, 17.

42. Bass, "Little Man," 391.

43. Roberts, "Louisiana Superstitions," 148; Randolph, "Folk-Beliefs," 93.

44. Randolph, *Ozark Superstitions*, 77–78.

45. Hand, *Frank C. Brown*, 201.

46. Hunt, *Popular Romances*, 389 [also quoting Brand, *Observations*, 243–44].

47. Parsons, "Folk-Lore," 393.

48. Brewster et al., *Frank C. Brown* 1:240.

49. "Christmas Superstitions," 72/00504, Hamilton and Adams MSS.

50. Randolph, *Ozark Superstitions*, 77.

51. Peterkin and Ulmann, *Roll, Jordan, Roll*, 250–51.

52. Randolph, *Ozark Superstitions*, 77–78.

53. Puckett, "Religious Folk-Beliefs," 17.

54. Roberts, "Louisiana Superstitions," 191.

55. Thomas, *Blue Ridge Country*, 160.

56. Randolph, *Ozark Superstitions*, 77.

57. "Christmas Superstitions," 70/00843, Hamilton and Adams MSS.

58. Elizabeth Carpenter, "The Old Man of the Mountains," *Our Home Field*, May 1914.

59. Snyder, "A Plantation Revival Service," 172.

60. Richardson, *Dark Glory*, 91–92.

61. Rosenberg, *Can These Bones Live?*

62. Faulk, "Quickened by De Spurit," 34.

63. George Dinsmore, "Sermon at Laurel Grove Primitive Baptist Church," AFS 2769A-B2, H. Halpert 1939 Southern States Recordings, AFC.

64. Faulk, "Quickened by De Spurit," 10–11.

65. Ibid., 70.

66. Pipes, *Say Amen Brother*, 40–41.

67. Sin-Killer Griffin, "Church Service, Easter," AFS 187A, John Lomax Southern States Collection, AFC.

68. Raper, *Preface to Peasantry*, 368.

69. Charles Johnson, *Shadow of the Plantation*, 159.

70. Faulk, "Quickened by De Spurit," 55–56.

71. Bennett, "Revival Sermon," 260.

72. Dollard, *Caste and Class*, 227.

73. O'Connor, *Mystery and Manners*, 207; Coles, *Flannery O'Connor's South*, 64.

74. Glass, *Strangers in Zion*.

75. Marsden, *Fundamentalism and American Culture*.

76. Cooley, *School Acres*, 135.

77. Dorothy Scarborough, *On the Trail*, 14–16.

78. "An Annual Primitive Baptist Sacrament Meeting," 72/00373-00375, Hamilton and Adams MSS.

79. Seales, "An Old Love for New Things."

80. Rankin, *Sacred Space*, 19.

81. Dollard, *Caste and Class*, 239.

82. Hall and Stack, *Holding On*, 93.

83. Clifton Johnson, *God Struck Me Dead*, 20.

84. "Hung by the Lord," 72/0637, Hamilton and Adams MSS; Pope, *Millhands and Preachers*, 87.

85. Harvey, *Redeeming the South*, 78, 109; Harvey, *Freedom's Coming*, 115, 119.

*Chapter Five*

1. Corcoran, "Blind Willie Johnson"; Michael Hall, "The Soul of a Man"; Samuel Charters, liner notes to *Complete Blind Willie Johnson*. Oral interviews in the 1950s and 1970s with people who knew Johnson offer conflicting testimony, and they also conflict with written documentation from Johnson's own time. (For example, was his father George, Willie Sr., or Dock? Was he born in Independence (Washington County) or Pendleton (Bell County)? Was he blinded by his stepmother (at age seven or thirteen?) or by a solar eclipse?) I have tried to weigh the conflicting evidence and claim what I think is most probable.

2. Charles Johnson, *Shadow of the Plantation*, 144.

3. Crews, *A Childhood*, 12.

4. Marcus, *Invisible Republic*, 160.

5. Ibid., 165.

6. Dock Boggs, "Country Blues," Brunswick 131A, available on *Dock Boggs*.

7. Lewis, *Children of Sanchez*, xii, xxiv.

8. Faduma, "Defects," 7–8, 10; Eldridge Hatcher, "The Country Church as a Transforming Power in the Life of Individuals, Community, State and Nation," *Our Home Field*, May 1918; Woodson, *Rural Negro*, 46; L. G. Wilson, "Church and Landless Men," 3, 7; John D. White, "The Backward People of the South," John D. White, "The Backward People of the South," *Our Home Field*, May 1909; Kester, *Revolt among the Sharecroppers*, 24.

9. Thurman, *Jesus and the Disinherited*, 54.

10. Coles, *Migrants*, 594–95.

11. Ibid., 589.

12. All songs (originally recorded 1927–30) are on *The Complete Blind Willie Johnson*.

13. Gunning, "Christ Was a Wayworn Traveler," on *Girl of Constant Sorrow*.

14. Tilman Cadle, "My Savior First of All," AFS 2018A, AFC.

15. Findlay Donaldson, "Look at Him Dying" and "He Shed His Blood for Me," AFS 1986A-B, AFC.

16. Findlay Donaldson, AFS 1979A-1983A, AFC.

17. G. W. Blevins, "Blevins's Christian Song," AFS 2766A-2767A, H. Halpert 1939 Southern States Recordings, AFC.

18. Aries, *Hour of Our Death*, 613.

19. Lears, *No Place of Grace*, 45–46.

20. Heyrman, *Southern Cross*, 28.

21. Ownby, *Subduing Satan*.

22. Lillian Smith, *Killers of the Dream*, 85.

23. Russell, *Mephistopheles*, 286–95.

24. O'Connor, *Mystery and Manners*, 41, 209.

25. Odum, *Religious Folk-Songs*, 23.

26. Carpenter, "Old Man," *Our Home Field*, May 1914.

27. Faulk, "Ten Negro Sermons," 10, 14.

28. Findlay Donaldson, AFS 1979A-1983A, AFC.

29. Lindahl, "Thrills and Miracles," 140.

30. Colley, "Exploratory Study," 13; Richard Wright, *12 Million Black Voices*, 69–72.

31. Alexander, "Religion in a Rural Community," 242.

32. Alan Lomax, *Rainbow Sign*, 181.

33. Coles, *Flannery O'Connor's South*, 97.

34. Grindal, "Religious Interpretation of Experience," in Hall and Stack, *Holding On*, 96–97.

35. Mullen, *Listening to Old Voices*, 48–49. Though he did not publish their stories or anecdotes, anthropologist Charles Hudson found pervasive belief in the devil among working-class white southerners in his 1961 fieldwork in North Carolina. See Charles Hudson, "The Structure of a Fundamentalist Christian Belief-System," in Hill et al., *Religion and the Solid South*, 122–42.

36. Woodson, *Rural Negro*, 159–60.

37. Alexander, "Religion in a Rural Community," 248.

38. Jent, *Challenge of the Country Church*, 109.

39. Felton, *These My Brethren*.

40. D. H. Howerton, *Our Home Field*, August 1921.

41. Raper, *Preface to Peasantry*, 368.

42. Erskine Caldwell, *Deep South*.

43. Southern Rural Life Council, *Church and Rural Community Living*, 21.

44. William Gardiner Ellis, 45; Edith McKee, 10; Roosevelt Fields, 5; Carl Neal, 47, 51; Baylor Institute for Oral History.

45. The phrase is Dolly Parton's.

46. Raboteau, *Fire in the Bones*, 193.

47. Crabtree, "Ballads and Songs."

48. Agee and Evans, *Cotton Tenants*, 199.

49. Agee and Evans, *Let Us Now*, 36.

50. Alan Lomax, *Rainbow Sign*, 115.

51. Peacock and Tyson, *Pilgrims of Paradox*, 139.

52. Alan Lomax, *Rainbow Sign*, 174.

53. G. W. Blevins, "Monologue on His Conversion," AFS 2766A-2767A, H. Halpert 1939 Southern States Recordings, AFC.

54. Marcus, *Invisible Republic*, 186.

55. Alexander, "Religion in a Rural Community," 243.

56. Richardson, *Dark Glory*, 175.

57. Grubbs, *Cry from the Cotton*; Rosengarten, *All God's Dangers*; Green, *Grassroots Socialism*; Kelley, *Hammer and Hoe*; Arnesen, *Waterfront Workers of New Orleans*; Kelly, *Race, Class, and Power*; Fannin, *Labor's Promised Land*; Roll, *Spirit of Rebellion*; Gellman and Roll, *Gospel of the Working Class*.

58. Brewster et al., *Frank C. Brown* 2:210–11; Sharp, *English Folk-Songs* 2:29–30; Kirkland and Kirkland, "Popular Ballads," 66–67; Davis, ed. *Traditional Ballads*, 14; "Lazarus and the Rich Man," Hamilton and Adams MSS; Child, *Ballads* 2:11.

59. Mary Magdalene Garland ("Aunt Molly Jackson"), "The Ballad of Lazarus," AFS 2583A-B, Alan Lomax Recordings of Aunt Molly Jackson, AFC.

60. Randolph, *Ozark Folksongs*, 96–97.

61. Odum and Johnson, *Negro Workaday Songs*, 49–55; AFS 750 A3, AFC [State Farm, VA]; AFS 730 B1 [State Penitentiary, Richmond, VA]; AFS 267A, John Lomax Southern States Collection, AFC [Reid Farm, Boykin, SC]; AFS 252 B1, John Lomax Southern States Collection, AFC [Bellwood Prison Camp, Atlanta, GA]; AFS 261 A1-B2, John Lomax Southern States Collection, AFC [State Prison Farm, Milledgeville, GA]; AFS 132 A1, AFC [Livingston, AL]; AFS 735A, AFC [Parchman, MS].

62. Perkins, "Negro Spirituals from the Far South," 223; White, *American Negro Folk-Songs*, 347–48; Brewster et al., *Frank C. Brown* 2:666–67; Henry, "More Songs from the Southern Highlands," 111–12; Walter Caldwell, AFS 1023 A1, AFC; Ernest Stoneman, "The Titanic," Okeh 40288; William and Versey Smith, "When That Great Ship Went Down," Paramount 12505B. In an interview in the May 23, 1967, issue of the *New York*

*Clipper,* Ernest Stoneman recalled originally learning the song around 1914 as a written poem (Horstman, *Sing Your Heart Out,* 91–93). The *Clipper* was published on Saturdays, but on May 18 and 25 in 1912. I have been unable to locate the poem in the *Clipper* in the pertinent months. Further confusing matters, "The Sinking of the Titanic" (essentially the same lyrics as Stoneman's) was copyrighted in September 1927 by a Robert Brown, with Peer International. The New Orleans race singer Richard "Rabbit" Brown recorded "Sinking of the Titanic" in March 1927, for Ralph Peer on Victor (Victor 35840)—yet the lyrics differ in many ways from the copyrighted version. The origins of the song, with the signature chorus line "when that great ship went down," are therefore unclear. What *is* clear is the song's notable presence in an oral culture in disparate areas of the South in the 1910s, 1920s, and 1930s.

63. "God Moves on the Water," Columbia 14520-D. It's worth noting that with the onset of the Depression, when record companies were pressing fewer copies, Columbia pressed 5,830 copies of "God Moves" when it was released in 1930—well above the typical number of pressings that year. Folklorist Dorothy Scarborough heard a slightly longer version of "God Moves" in the years before she published it in 1919, and the Trinity College (now Duke University) janitor was singing a variation circa 1920 (Scarborough, *From a Southern Porch,* 305–7; Brewster et al., *Frank C. Brown* 2:667–68). Scarborough was from Waco, Texas, in Johnson's home base in the Blackland Prairie, but in *From a Southern Porch,* the song is said to come from Savannah. Trinity College was even farther away, in Durham, North Carolina. Clearly the song spread quickly, either from central Texas to the east coast or the other way around. It's likely that Johnson learned it from the Robertson County, Texas-based Madkin Butler, a blind preacher and singer who was a mentor to him and who may have originally composed the song (Corcoran, "Blind Willie Johnson").

64. Lightnin' Washington and group of Negro convicts, "God Moves on the Water," AFS 188 B2, John Lomax Southern States Collection, AFC [Darrington State Farm, TX].

65. Palmer, *"Man over Money"*; Goodwyn, *Populist Moment.*


## Conclusion

1. Coles, *Migrants,* 32–33.

2. Cobb, *Selling of the South*; Gavin Wright, *Old South, New South*; Kirby, *Rural Worlds Lost*; Schulman, *From Cotton Belt to Sun Belt.*

3. Richard Wright, *Twelve Million Black Voices,* 79.

4. Gavin Wright, "Economic Revolution," 173.

5. Kevin Phillips, *Emerging Republican Majority.*

6. Moreton, *To Serve God and Wal-Mart*; Dochuk, *From Bible Belt to Sunbelt*; Fones-Wolf and Fones-Wolf, *Struggle for the Soul*; Greene, *No Depression in Heaven.*

7. Rubin, *Plantation County,* 21, 127, 141–42, 144.

8. Ibid., 120.

9. John Cohen, *End of an Old Song.*

10. Stephens, *Fire Spreads*, 230–32.

11. Ardery, *Welcome the Traveler*, 86.

12. Alan Lomax, *Rainbow Sign*, 17.

13. Nixon, *Possum Trot*, 55, 67.

14. Richard Wright, *Twelve Million Black Voices*, 75.

15. Maharidge and Williamson, *And Their Children After Them*.

16. Katznelson, *When Affirmative Action Was White*; Lizabeth Cohen, *Consumers' Republic*.

17. Gavin Wright, *Old South, New South*, 255–56.

18. Jennings, *Christian Imagination*; Goetz, *Baptism of Early Virginia*.

19. Ulrich Phillips, "Central Theme," 31.

20. King, "Letter from Birmingham Jail," in *Why We Can't Wait*, 96.

21. Thomas E. Watson, "The Negro Question in the South" *Arena* 6 (October 1892), in Dailey, *Age of Jim Crow*, 43.

22. W. E. B. Du Bois, "Georgia: Invisible Empire State," *Nation* 120 (January 21, 1925), in Dailey, *Age of Jim Crow*, 142–43, 148.

23. Drabold, "Read Elizabeth Warren's Anti-Trump Speech."

24. Barbara Fields, "Ideology and Race in American History," in Kousser and McPherson, *Region, Race, and Reconstruction*.

25. Kelly, "Labor, Race, and the Search," 60, 62, 67.

26. Coles, *Flannery O'Connor's South*, 60–61.

# Bibliography

*Archival Collections*

Chapel Hill, NC
  University of North Carolina, Wilson Library, Southern Folklife Collection
    Brett Sutton and Peter Hartman Collection
Charlottesville, VA
  University of Virginia, Albert and Shirley Small Special Collections Library
    Winston Wilkinson, Manuscript Folk Music, Accession #128
Johnson City, TN
  East Tennessee State University, Archives of Appalachia
    Burton-Manning Collection
Livingston, AL
  University of West Alabama, Julia Tutwiler Library
    Ruby Pickens Tartt Collection
Louisville, KY
  University of Louisville, Dwight Anderson Memorial Music Library
    Jean Thomas Collection
Mars Hill, NC
  Mars Hill University, Southern Appalachian Archives, Liston B. Ramsey Center for
  Regional Studies
    Bascom Lamar Lunsford Collection
New York, NY
  Hunter College, Association for Cultural Equity
    Alan Lomax Archive
Philadelphia, PA
  University of Pennsylvania, Penn Museum Archives
    Hamilton and Adams MSS, MacEdward Leach Collection
Waco, TX
  Baylor University, Institute for Oral History
    William Gardiner Ellis, interview by Lois E. Myers on January 27, 2000
    Roosevelt Fields, interview by Lois E. Myers on May 14, 1999
    Edith McKee, interview by Glenn Jonas on June 21, 1990
    Carl Neal, interview by Lois E. Myers on February 4, 1993
Washington, DC
  Library of Congress, Archive of Folk Culture, American Folklife Center (AFC)
    Alan and Elizabeth Lomax Kentucky Collection (AFC 1937/001)

Alan Lomax Recordings of Aunt Molly Jackson (AFC 1939/012)
Blue Ridge Parkway Folklife Project Collection (AFC 1982/009)
Gee's Bend Collection (AFC 1941/018)
Herbert Halpert 1939 Southern States Recording Expedition (AFC 1939/005)
John A. Lomax Southern States Collection, 1933–1937 (AFC 1935/002)
John and Ruby Lomax 1939 Southern States Recording Trip (AFC 1939/001)

*Books, Articles, Essays, and Other Sources*

Agee, James, and Walker Evans. *Cotton Tenants: Three Families.* Brooklyn: Melville House, 2013.

———. *Let Us Now Praise Famous Men.* 1941. Reprint, Boston: Houghton Mifflin, 1988.

Alexander, Frank. "Religion in a Rural Community of the South." *American Sociological Review* 5 (1941): 241–51.

Allen, William Francis, Charles Pickard Ware, and Lucy McKim Garrison, eds. *Slave Songs of the United States.* 1867. Reprint, New York: Dover, 1995.

Americana, *American Mercury*, October 1924, 171–74.

Ammerman, Nancy, ed. *Everyday Religion: Observing Modern Religious Lives.* Oxford: Oxford University Press, 2007.

Ardery, Julia, ed. *Welcome the Traveler Home: Jim Garland's Story of the Kentucky Mountains.* Lexington: University of Kentucky Press, 1983.

Aries, Philippe. *The Hour of Our Death.* New York: Vintage, 1982.

Arnesen, Eric. *Waterfront Workers of New Orleans: Race, Class, and Politics, 1863–1923.* Urbana: University of Illinois Press, 1994.

Ayers, Edward. *The Promise of the New South: Life After Reconstruction.* New York: Oxford University Press, 1992.

*The Baptist Hymn and Praise Book.* Nashville: Baptist Sunday School Board, 1904.

Barks, Susan K. *Death and a Lady: Echoes of a Mortal Conversation in English and American Folk Song.* Chapel Hill: University of North Carolina Press, 1966.

Bass, Ruth. "The Little Man." In *Mother Wit from the Laughing Barrel: Readings in the Interpretation of Afro-American Folklore*, edited by Alan Dundes, 388–96. Englewood Cliffs, NJ: Prentice-Hall, 1972.

Bennett, John. "A Revival Sermon at Little St. John's." *Atlantic Monthly*, August 1906, 256–68.

Boatwright, Mody, and Donald Day, eds. *Backwoods to Border.* Texas Folk-Lore Society Publications 28. Austin: Texas Folk-lore Society, 1943.

Bolton, H. Carrington. "Decoration of Graves of Negroes in South Carolina." *Journal of American Folklore* 4 (1891): 214.

Brannon, Peter. "Central Alabama Negro Superstitions." *Birmingham News*, January 18, 1925.

Brasher, J. Lawrence. *The Sanctified South: John Lakin Brasher and the Holiness Movement.* Urbana: University of Illinois Press, 1994.

Brewster, Paul, Archer Taylor, Bartlett Whiting, George Wilson, and Stith Thompson. *The Frank C. Brown Collection of North Carolina Folklore*. 6 vols. Durham, NC: Duke University Press, 1952.

Brundage, W. Fitzhugh. *The Southern Past: A Clash of Race and Memory*. Cambridge, MA: Harvard University Press, 2005.

Burrison, John. *Roots of a Region: Southern Folk Culture*. Jackson: University Press of Mississippi, 2007.

Butler, Anthea. *Women in the Church of God in Christ: Making a Sanctified World*. Chapel Hill: University of North Carolina Press, 2007.

Caldwell, Erskine. *Deep South: Memory and Observation*. Athens: University of Georgia Press, 1980.

Caldwell, Ira. *The Bunglers*. New Haven, CT: Galton, 1930.

Callahan, Richard. *Work and Faith in the Kentucky Coalfields: Subject to Dust*. Bloomington: Indiana University Press, 2009.

Campbell, John C. *The Southern Highlander and His Homeland*. New York: Russell Sage Foundation, 1921.

Carlton, David, and Peter Coclanis, eds. *Confronting Southern Poverty in the Great Depression: "The Report on Economic Conditions of the South."* Boston: Bedford/ St. Martin's, 1996.

Carpenter, Elizabeth. "Granny." *Our Home Field*. November 1913.

———. "The Old Man of the Mountains." *Our Home Field*. May 1914.

Cate, Margaret, and Orrin Wightman. *Early Days of Coastal Georgia*. St. Simons Island, GA: Fort Frederica Association, 1955.

"Cecil Sharp's Appalachian Diaries: 1915–1918." Vaughn Williams Memorial Library, March 10, 2015. https://www.vwml.org/vwml-projects/vwml-cecil-sharp-diaries.

Chandler, Barbara. "Why I Believe That Lloyd Chandler Wrote 'Conversation with Death,' also Known as 'O Death.'" *Journal of Folklore Research* 41, no. 2/3 (May– December 2004): 127–32.

Chandler, Lloyd. "Conversation with Death." *Journal of Folklore Research* 41, no. 2/3 (May–December 2004): 125–26.

Child, Francis James, ed. *The English and Scottish Popular Ballads*. 2 vols. 1885. Reprint, New York: Dover, 1965.

Clements, William. "Conversion and Communitas." *Western Folklore* 35 (1976): 35–45.

Cobb, James C. "Beyond Planters and Industrialists: A New Perspective on the New South." *Journal of Southern History* 54, no. 1 (February 1988): 45–68.

———. *The Selling of the South: The Southern Crusade for Industrial Development, 1936–1980*. Baton Rouge: Louisiana State University Press, 1982.

Cohen, John. *The End of an Old Song. That High Lonesome Sound*. DVD. Shanachie 1404, 2002.

Cohen, Lizabeth. *A Consumers' Republic: The Politics of Mass Consumption in Postwar America*. New York: Knopf, 2003.

*The Cokesbury Hymnal*. Nashville: Cokesbury Press, 1923.

Coles, Robert. *Flannery O'Connor's South*. Athens: University of Georgia Press, 1993.

———. *Migrants, Sharecroppers, Mountaineers.* Boston: Little, Brown, 1971.

Combes, John D. "Ethnography, Archaeology, and Burial Practice among Coastal South Carolina Blacks." Conference on Historic Sites Archaeology Papers 7 (1972): 52–61.

*The Complete Blind Willie Johnson.* Columbia C2K 52835, 1993.

Cooley, Rossa. *School Acres: An Adventure in Rural Education.* New Haven, CT: Yale University Press, 1930.

Corcoran, Michael. "Blind Willie Johnson: Revelations in the Dark." January 8, 2016. http://www.michaelcorcoran.net/archives/3826.

Couch, W. T., ed. *Culture in the South.* Chapel Hill: University of North Carolina Press, 1934.

Courlander, Harold. *Negro Folk Music from Alabama.* New York: Oak, 1963.

———. *Negro Folk Music USA.* New York: Columbia University Press, 1963.

Crabtree, Lillian. "Songs and Ballads Sung in Overton County, Tennessee." MA thesis, Peabody College for Teachers, 1936.

Creel, Margaret Washington. *A Peculiar People: Slave Religion and Community-Culture among the Gullahs.* New York: New York University Press, 1988.

Crews, Harry. *A Childhood: The Biography of a Place.* 1978; Athens: University of Georgia Press, 1995.

Dailey, Jane, ed. *The Age of Jim Crow.* New York: W.W. Norton, 2009.

Dailey, Jane, Glenda Gilmore, and Bryant Simon, eds. *Jumpin' Jim Crow: Southern Politics from Civil War to Civil Rights.* Princeton, NJ: Princeton University Press, 2000.

Daniel, Pete. *Breaking the Land: The Transformation of Cotton, Tobacco, and Rice Cultures since 1880.* Urbana: University of Illinois Press, 1985.

Davis, Allison, Burleigh Gardner, and Mary Gardner. *Deep South: A Study of Social Class and Color Caste in a Southern City.* Chicago: University of Chicago Press, 1941.

Davis, Arthur, ed. *Traditional Ballads of Virginia.* Cambridge, MA: Harvard University Press, 1929.

Davis, Henry. "Negro Folk-Lore in South Carolina." *Journal of American Folklore* 27, no. 105 (July–September 1914): 241–54.

Dochuk, Darren. *From Bible Belt to Sunbelt: Plain-Folk Religion, Grassroots Politics, and the Rise of Evangelical Conservatism.* New York: W.W. Norton, 2011.

*Dock Boggs—His Twelve Original Recordings.* Smithsonian Folkways FWRBF 654, 2004.

Dollard, John. *Caste and Class in a Southern Town.* New York: Doubleday, 1937.

Dorgan, Howard. *Old Regular Baptists of Central Appalachia: Brothers and Sisters in Hope.* Knoxville: University of Tennessee Press, 1989.

Douglas, Ann. "Heaven Our Home: Consolation Literature in the Northern United States, 1830–1860." *American Quarterly* 26, no. 5 (December 1974): 496–515.

Downes, Olin, and Elie Siegmeister. *A Treasury of American Song.* New York: Knopf, 1943.

Drabold, Will. "Read Elizabeth Warren's Anti-Trump Speech at the Democratic Convention." *Time*, July 25, 2016. http://time.com/4421731/democratic -convention-elizabeth-warren-transcript-speech/.

Du Bois, W. E. B., ed. *The Negro Church*. 1903. Reprint, Walnut Creek, CA: Altamira, 2003.

———. *The Souls of Black Folk*. 1903. Reprint, New York: Bantam, 1989.

Dunbar, Anthony. *Against the Grain: Southern Radicals and Prophets, 1929–1959*. Charlottesville: University Press of Virginia, 1981.

Eidse, Faith. *Voices of the Apalachicola*. Gainesville: University of Florida Press, 2006.

Eley, Geoff, and Keith Nield. *The Future of Class in History: What's Left of the Social?* Ann Arbor: University of Michigan Press, 2007.

Eller, Ronald. *Miners, Millhands, and Mountaineers: Industrialization of the Appalachian South 1880–1930*. Knoxville: University of Tennessee Press, 1982.

Faduma, Orishatukeh. "The Defects of the Negro Church." In *The American Negro Academy Occasional Papers*, edited by Ernest Kaiser, 1–22. 1904. Reprint, New York: Arno, 1969.

Fannin, Mark. *Labor's Promised Land: Radical Visions of Gender, Race, and Religion in the South*. Knoxville: University of Tennessee Press, 2003.

Faulk, John Henry. "Quickened by De Spurit: Ten Negro Sermons." MA thesis, University of Texas, 1941.

Faulkner, William. *Go Down, Moses*. 1942. Reprint, New York: Vintage, 1990.

Faust, Drew. *The Creation of Confederate Nationalism: Ideology and Identity in the Civil War South*. Baton Rouge: Louisiana State University Press, 1988.

Federal Writers' Project. *North Carolina: A Guide to the Old North State*. Chapel Hill: University of North Carolina Press, 1939.

Felton, Ralph. *These My Brethren: A Study of 570 Negro Churches and 1542 Negro Homes in the Rural South*. Madison, NJ: Drew Theological Seminary, 1950.

Filene, Benjamin. *Romancing the Folk: Public Memory and American Roots Music*. Chapel Hill: University of North Carolina Press, 2000.

Flynt, Wayne. *Dixie's Forgotten People: The South's Poor Whites*. Bloomington: Indiana University Press, 1979.

———. "Religion for the Blues: Evangelicalism, Poor Whites, and the Great Depression." *Journal of Southern History* 71, no. 1 (February 2005): 3–38.

Fones-Wolf, Elizabeth, and Ken Fones-Wolf. *Struggle for the Soul of the Postwar South: White Evangelical Protestants and Operation Dixie*. Urbana: University of Illinois Press, 2015.

Fountain, Daniel. *Slavery, Civil War, and Salvation: African American Slaves and Christianity, 1830–1870*. Baton Rouge: Louisiana State University Press, 2010.

Frazier, E. Franklin. *The Negro Church in America*. New York: Schocken, 1964.

Frey, Sylvia, and Betty Wood. *Come Shouting to Zion: African American Protestantism in the American South and British Caribbean to 1830*. Chapel Hill: University of North Carolina Press, 1998.

Gellman, Eric, and Jarod Roll. *Gospel of the Working Class: Labor's Southern Prophets in New Deal America.* Urbana: University of Illinois Press, 2011.

Georgia Writers' Project. *Drums and Shadows: Survival Stories among the Georgia Coastal Negroes.* Athens: University of Georgia Press, 1940.

Gerth, H. H., and C. Wright Mills, eds. *From Max Weber: Essays in Sociology.* New York: Oxford University Press, 1958.

Gertsman, Elina. *The Dance of Death in the Middle Ages: Image, Text, Performance.* Turnhout, Belgium: Brepols, 2010.

Giggie, John. *After Redemption: Jim Crow and the Transformation of African American Religion in the Delta, 1875–1915.* New York: Oxford University Press, 2008.

Gilmore, Glenda. *Gender and Jim Crow: Women and the Politics of White Supremacy in North Carolina, 1896–1920.* Chapel Hill: University of North Carolina Press, 1996.

Glass, William. *Strangers in Zion: Fundamentalists in the South, 1900–1950.* Macon, GA: Mercer University Press, 2001.

Godden, Richard, and Martin Crawford. *Reading Southern Poverty between the Wars, 1918–1939.* Athens: University of Georgia Press, 2006.

"God-Intoxicated Hillbillies." *Time,* February 29, 1960, 118–19.

Goetz, Rebecca. *The Baptism of Early Virginia: How Christianity Created Race.* Baltimore: Johns Hopkins University Press, 2012.

Goff, James R. *Close Harmony: A History of Southern Gospel.* Chapel Hill: University of North Carolina Press, 2002.

*Goodbye, Babylon.* Dust-to-Digital, October 2003, 6 compact discs.

Goodwyn, Lawrence. *The Populist Moment: A Short History of the Agrarian Revolt in America.* New York: Oxford University Press, 1978.

*Gospel Pearls.* Nashville: National Baptist Sunday School Publishing Board, 1921.

Grady, Henry. *The New South.* New York: Robert Bonner's Sons, 1889.

Greaves, Charles. "The Country Pastor." *Our Home Field.* September 1912.

Green, James R. *Grassroots Socialism: Radical Movements in the Southwest, 1895–1943.* Baton Rouge: Louisiana State University Press, 1978.

Greene, Alison Collis. *No Depression in Heaven: The Great Depression, the New Deal, and the Transformation of Religion in the Delta.* Oxford: Oxford University Press, 2015.

Grissom, Mary Allen. *The Negro Sings a New Heaven.* Chapel Hill: University of North Carolina Press, 1930.

Grubbs, Donald. *Cry from the Cotton: The Southern Tenant Farmers' Union and the New Deal.* Chapel Hill: University of North Carolina Press, 1971.

Gruber, J. Richard. *Thomas Hart Benton and the American South.* Augusta, GA: Morris Museum, 1998.

Gunning, Sarah Ogan. *Girl of Constant Sorrow.* Folk-Legacy CD-26, 2006. Originally released in 1965.

Guthman, Joshua. *Strangers Below: Primitive Baptists and American Culture.* Chapel Hill: University of North Carolina Press, 2015.

Gwynn, Frederick, and Joseph Blotner, eds. *Faulkner in the University: Class Conferences at the University of Virginia, 1957–1958.* Charlottesville: University of Virginia Press, 1959.

Hahn, Steven. *The Roots of Southern Populism: Yeoman Farmers and the Transformation of the Georgia Upcountry, 1850–1890.* New York: Oxford University Press, 1983.

Hale, Grace. *Making Whiteness: The Culture of Segregation in the South, 1890–1940.* New York: Vintage, 1998.

Hall, David, ed. *Lived Religion in America: Towards a History of Practice.* Princeton, NJ: Princeton University Press, 1997.

Hall, Jacquelyn, James Leloudis, Robert Korstad, Mary Murphy, Lu Ann Jones, and Christopher Daly. *Like a Family: The Making of a Southern Cotton Mill World.* Chapel Hill: University of North Carolina Press, 1987.

Hall, Michael. "The Soul of a Man: Who Was Blind Willie Johnson?" *Texas Monthly,* December 2010.

Hall, Robert, and Carol Stack, eds. *Holding On to the Land and the Lord.* Athens: University of Georgia Press, 1982.

Halli, Robert, ed. *An Alabama Songbook: Ballads, Folksongs, and Spirituals.* Tuscaloosa: University of Alabama Press, 2004.

Hand, Wayland, ed. *The Frank C. Brown Collection of North Carolina Folklore.* Vol. 7. Durham, NC: Duke University Press, 1964.

Harrell, David, ed. *Varieties of Southern Evangelicalism.* Macon, GA: Mercer University Press, 1981.

———. *White Sects and Black Men in the Recent South.* Nashville: Vanderbilt University Press, 1971.

Harvey, Paul. *Freedom's Coming: Religious Culture and the Shaping of the South from the Civil War to the Civil Rights Movement.* Chapel Hill: University of North Carolina Press, 2005.

———. *Moses, Jesus, and the Trickster in the Evangelical South.* Athens: University of Georgia Press, 2011.

———. *Redeeming the South: Religious Cultures and Racial Identities among Southern Baptists, 1865–1925.* Chapel Hill: University of North Carolina Press, 1997.

Hatcher, Eldridge. "The Country Church as a Transforming Power in the Life of Individuals, Community, State, and Nation." *Our Home Field.* May 1918.

Haygood, Atticus. *The New South: Gratitude, Hope, Amendment.* Oxford, GA, 1880.

Head, Keith. "Granny Reed: A Testimony." *Southern Exposure* 4, no. 3 (1976): 33–37.

Henry, Mellinger E. "More Songs from the Southern Highlands." *Journal of American Folklore* 44, no. 171 (January–March 1931): 61–115.

Heyrman, Christine. *Southern Cross: The Beginnings of the Bible Belt.* Chapel Hill: University of North Carolina Press, 1997.

Higginbotham, Evelyn Brooks. *Righteous Discontent: The Women's Movement in the Black Baptist Church.* Cambridge, MA: Harvard University Press, 1993.

Hill, Samuel. *One Name but Several Faces: Variety in Popular Christian Denominations in Southern History.* Athens: University of Georgia Press, 1996.

———. *Southern Churches in Crisis*. Boston: Beacon, 1966.

———, ed. *Varieties of Southern Religious Experience*. Baton Rouge: Louisiana State University Press, 1988.

Hill, Samuel, Edgar Thompson, Anne Firor Scott, Charles Hudson, and Edwin Gaustad. *Religion and the Solid South*. Nashville: Abingdon, 1972.

Hindmarsh, D. Bruce. *The Evangelical Conversion Narrative*. Oxford: Oxford University Press, 2005.

Horstman, Dorothy. *Sing Your Heart Out, Country Boy*. Nashville: Country Music Foundation, 1996.

Hunt, Robert. *Popular Romances of the West of England*. New York: Benjamin Blom, 1916.

Hurston, Zora Neale. *Dust Tracks on a Road: An Autobiography*. 1942. Reprint, New York: Harper Perennial, 1991.

———. *Folklore, Memoirs, and Other Writings*. New York: Library of America, 1995.

Ingersoll, Ernest. "Decoration of Negro Graves." *Journal of American Folklore* 5 (1892): 68–69.

Irons, Charles. *The Origins of Proslavery Christianity: White and Black Evangelicals in Colonial and Antebellum Virginia*. Chapel Hill: University of North Carolina Press, 2008.

Isaac, Rhys. *The Transformation of Virginia 1740–1790*. Chapel Hill: University of North Carolina Press, 1982.

Jackson, George. *White and Negro Spirituals: Their Life Span and Kinship*. New York: J. J. Augustin, 1943.

Jeane, Donald. "The Traditional Upland South Cemetery." *Landscape* 18, no. 2 (Spring–Summer 1969): 139–42.

Jennings, Willie James. *The Christian Imagination: Theology and the Origins of Race*. New Haven, CT: Yale University, 2010.

Jent, J. W. *The Challenge of the Country Church*. Nashville: Sunday School Board, 1924.

Johnson, Alonzo, and Paul Jersild, eds. *"Ain't Gonna Lay My 'Ligion Down:" African American Religion in the South*. Columbia: University of South Carolina Press, 1996.

Johnson, Charles. *Shadow of the Plantation*. Chicago: University of Chicago Press, 1934.

Johnson, Clifton, ed. *God Struck Me Dead: Voices of Ex-Slaves*. 1969. Reprint, Eugene: Wipf & Stock, 2010.

Johnson, Guy. *Folk Culture on St. Helena Island, South Carolina*. Chapel Hill: University of North Carolina Press, 1930.

Jones, Bessie. *For the Ancestors: Autobiographical Memories*. Athens: University of Georgia Press, 1989.

Jones, Jacqueline. *The Dispossessed: America's Underclasses from the Civil War to the Present*. New York: Basic, 1992.

Jones, Loyal. *Faith and Meaning in the Southern Uplands*. Urbana: University of Illinois Press, 1999.

Joyner, Charles. *Down by the Riverside: A South Carolina Slave Community*. Urbana: University of Illinois Press, 1984.

———. *Shared Traditions: Southern History and Folk Culture*. Urbana: University of Illinois Press, 1999.

Kantrowitz, Stephen. *Ben Tillman and the Reconstruction of White Supremacy*. Chapel Hill: University of North Carolina Press, 2000.

Katznelson, Ira. *When Affirmative Action Was White: An Untold History of Racial Inequality in Twentieth-Century America*. New York: W.W. Norton, 2005.

Kelley, Robin. *Hammer and Hoe: Alabama Communists during the Great Depression*. Chapel Hill: University of North Carolina Press, 1990.

———. "Notes on Deconstructing 'the Folk.'" *American Historical Review* 97, no. 5 (December 1992): 1400–1408.

Kelly, Brian. "Labor, Race, and the Search for a Central Theme in the History of the Jim Crow South." *Irish Journal of American Studies* 10 (December 2001): 55–73.

———. *Race, Class, and Power in the Alabama Coalfields, 1908–1921*. Urbana: University of Illinois Press, 2001.

Kennedy, R. Emmet. *Mellows: A Chronicle of Unknown Singers*. New York: A. and C. Boni, 1925.

Kennedy, Stetson. *Palmetto Country*. New York: Duell, Sloan & Pearce, 1942.

Kester, Howard. *Revolt among the Sharecroppers*. New York: Covici, Friede, 1936.

Killion, Ronald, and Charles Waller. *A Treasury of Georgia Folklore*. Atlanta: Cherokee, 1972.

King, Martin Luther. *Why We Can't Wait*. New York: Harper and Row, 1964.

Kirby, Jack Temple. *Rural Worlds Lost: The American South, 1920–1960*. Baton Rouge: Louisiana State University Press, 1987.

Kirkland, Edwin, and Mary Kirkland. "Popular Ballads Recorded in Knoxville, Tenn." *Southern Folklore Quarterly* 2 (1938): 65–80.

Kousser, J. Morgan. *The Shaping of Southern Politics: Suffrage Restriction and the Establishment of the One-Party South, 1880–1910*. New Haven, CT: Yale University Press, 1974.

Kousser, J. Morgan, and James McPherson, eds. *Region, Race, and Reconstruction: Essays in Honor of C. Vann Woodward*. New York: Oxford University Press, 1982.

Lears, Jackson. *No Place of Grace*. Chicago: University of Chicago Press, 1994.

Lewis, Oscar. *The Children of Sanchez: Autobiography of a Mexican Family*. New York: Random House, 1961.

Lincoln, C. Eric, ed. *The Black Experience in Religion*. Garden City, NY: Anchor, 1974.

Lindahl, Carl, ed. *American Folktales from the Collections of the Library of Congress*. Vol. 2. Armonk, NY: M.E. Sharpe, 2004.

———. "Thrills and Miracles: Legends of Lloyd Chandler." *Journal of Folklore Research* 41, no. 2/3 (May–December 2004): 133–71.

Litwack, Leon. *Trouble in Mind: Black Southerners in the Age of Jim Crow*. New York: Knopf, 1998.

Livermore, Mary. "Mission Work Among Backward People." *Our Home Field.* October 1911.

Lomax, Alan. *The Rainbow Sign: A Southern Documentary.* New York: Duell, Sloan, and Pearce, 1959.

Lomax, John. *Adventures of a Ballad Hunter.* New York: Macmillan, 1947.

Lomax, John, and Alan Lomax. *Our Singing Country.* New York: Macmillan, 1941.

*The Lynchburg Story: Eugenic Sterilization in America.* New York: Filmmakers Library, 1993.

MacLean, Nancy. *Behind the Mask of Chivalry: The Making of the Second Ku Klux Klan.* Oxford: Oxford University, 1994.

Maffly-Kipp, Laurie, Leigh Eric Schmidt, and Mark Valeri, eds. *Practicing Protestants: Histories of Christian Life in America, 1630–1965.* Baltimore: Johns Hopkins University Press, 2006.

Maharidge, Dale, and Michael Williamson. *And Their Children After Them.* New York: Random House, 1989.

Marcus, Greil. *Invisible Republic: Bob Dylan's Basement Tapes.* New York: Henry Holt, 1997.

Marsden, George. *Fundamentalism and American Culture.* Oxford: Oxford University Press, 1980.

Masters, Victor. *The Country Church in the South.* Atlanta: Home Mission Board, 1916.

Mays, Benjamin, and Joseph Nicholson. *The Negro's Church.* 1933. Reprint, New York: Arno, 1969.

McCauley, Deborah. *Appalachian Mountain Religion: A History.* Urbana: University of Illinois Press, 1995.

McCloud, Sean. *Divine Hierarchies: Class in American Religion and Religious Studies.* Chapel Hill: University of North Carolina Press, 2007.

McCloud, Sean, and William Mirola, eds. *Religion and Class in America: Culture, History, and Politics.* Leiden, Netherlands: Brill, 2009.

McCurry, Stephanie. *Masters of Small Worlds: Yeoman Households, Gender Relations, and the Political Culture of the Antebellum South Carolina Low Country.* New York: Oxford University Press, 1995.

McDannell, Colleen. *Picturing Faith: Photography and the Great Depression.* New Haven, CT: Yale University Press, 2004.

McGuire, Meredith. *Lived Religion: Faith and Practice in Everyday Life.* Oxford: Oxford University Press, 2008.

McIlhenny, Edward. *Befo de War Spirituals.* Boston: Christopher, 1933.

*The Methodist Hymnal.* Cincinnati: Eaton and Mains, 1905.

*The Modern Hymnal.* Nashville: Baptist Sunday School Board, 1926.

Montgomery, William. *Under Their Own Vine and Fig Tree: The African-American Church in the South, 1865–1900.* Baton Rouge: Louisiana State University Press, 1993.

Moody, Anne. *Coming of Age in Mississippi.* 1968. Reprint, New York: Bantam Dell, 2004.

Moreton, Bethany. *To Serve God and Wal-Mart: The Making of Christian Free Enterprise*. Cambridge, MA: Harvard University Press, 2009.

Mullen, Patrick. *Listening to Old Voices: Folklore, Life Stories, and the Elderly*. Urbana: University of Illinois Press, 1992.

———. "Ritual and Sacred Narratives in the Blue Ridge Mountains." *Papers in Comparative Studies* 2 (1982–83): 17–38.

*The National Baptist Hymnal*. Nashville: National Baptist Publishing Board, 1904.

Newby, I. A. *Plain Folk in the New South: Social Change and Cultural Persistence, 1880–1915*. Baton Rouge: Louisiana State University Press, 1989.

Niebuhr, H. Richard. *The Social Sources of Denominationalism*. New York: Henry Holt, 1929.

Nixon, Herman Clarence. *Possum Trot: Rural Community, South*. Norman: University of Oklahoma Press, 1941.

O'Connor, Flannery. *Mystery and Manners*. New York: Farrar, Straus and Giroux, 1969.

———. *The Violent Bear It Away*. New York: Farrar, Straus and Giroux, 1960.

———. *Wise Blood*. 1952. Reprint, New York: Farrar, Straus and Giroux, 1962.

Odum, Howard. *Religious Folk-Songs of the Southern Negroes*. PhD diss., Clark University, 1909.

Odum, Howard, and Guy Johnson. *Negro Workaday Songs*. Chapel Hill: University of North Carolina Press, 1926.

Ong, Walter. *Orality and Literacy: The Technologizing of the Word*. London: Routledge, 1982.

Ormond, Jesse. *The Country Church in North Carolina*. Durham, NC: Duke University Press, 1931.

Orsi, Robert. *The Madonna of 115th Street: Faith and Community in Italian Harlem*. New Haven, CT: Yale University Press, 1985.

Ownby, Ted. *Subduing Satan: Religion, Recreation, and Manhood in the Rural South, 1865–1920*. Chapel Hill: University of North Carolina Press, 1990.

Palmer, Bruce. *"Man over Money:" The Southern Populist Critique of American Capitalism*. Chapel Hill: University of North Carolina Press, 1980.

Parrish, Lydia. *Slave Songs of the Georgia Sea Islands*. New York: Creative Age, 1942.

Parsons, Elsie Clews. "Folk-Lore of the Cherokee of Robeson County, North Carolina." *Journal of American Folklore* 32, no. 125 (July–September 1919): 384–93.

———. *Folk-Lore of the Sea Islands, South Carolina*. Cambridge, MA: American Folk Lore Society, 1923.

Peacock, James L., and Ruel Tyson Jr. *Pilgrims of Paradox: Calvinism and Experience among the Primitive Baptists of the Blue Ridge*. Washington, DC: Smithsonian, 1989.

Percy, William Alexander. *Lanterns on the Levee*. 1941. Reprint, Baton Rouge: Louisiana State University Press, 1991.

Perkins, A. E. "Negro Spirituals from the Far South." *Journal of American Folklore* 35, no. 137 (July–September 1922): 223–49.

Perrow, E. C. "Songs and Rhymes from the South." *Journal of American Folklore* 26, no. 100 (April–June 1913): 123–73.

Peterkin, Julia, and Doris Ulmann. *Roll, Jordan, Roll*. New York: Robert Ballou, 1933.

Phillips, Kevin. *The Emerging Republican Majority*. New Rochelle: Arlington House, 1969.

Phillips, Ulrich. "The Central Theme of Southern History." *American Historical Review* 34, no. 1 (October 1928): 30–43.

Pipes, William. *Say Amen, Brother! Old-Time Negro Preaching: A Study in American Frustration*. New York: William-Frederick, 1951.

Pitchford, Anita. "The Material Culture of the Traditional East Texas Graveyard." *Southern Folklore Quarterly* 43 (1979): 277–90.

Pope, Liston. *Millhands and Preachers: A Study of Gastonia*. New Haven, CT: Yale University Press, 1942.

Poteat, Edwin. *Reverend John Doe, D.D.: A Study of the Place of the Minister in the Modern World*. New York: Harper and Brothers, 1935.

Primiano, Leonard. "Vernacular Religion and the Search for Method in Religious Folklife." *Western Folklore* 54, no. 1 (January 1995): 37–56.

Puckett, Newbell. *Folk Beliefs of the Southern Negro*. Chapel Hill: University of North Carolina Press, 1926.

———. "Religious Folk-Beliefs of Whites and Negroes." *Journal of Negro History* 16, no. 1 (January 1931): 9–35.

Raboteau, Albert. *Canaan Land: A Religious History of African Americans*. New York: Oxford University Press, 1999.

———. *A Fire in the Bones: Reflections on African-American Religious History*. Boston: Beacon, 1995.

———. *Slave Religion: The "Invisible Institution" in the Antebellum South*. New York: Oxford University Press, 1978.

Rand McNally. *Handy Railroad Atlas*. Rand McNally: Chicago, 1944.

———. *1936 Road Atlas*. Rand McNally: Chicago, 1936.

Randolph, Vance. "Folk-Beliefs in the Ozark Mountains." *Journal of American Folklore* 40, no. 155 (January–March 1927): 78–93.

———. *Ozark Folksongs*. Vol. 4, *Religious Songs and Other Items*. Columbia: State Historical Society of Missouri, 1946–1950.

———. *Ozark Superstitions*. New York: Columbia University Press, 1947.

Rankin, Tom. *Sacred Space: Photographs from the Mississippi Delta*. Jackson: University Press of Mississippi, 1993.

Raper, Arthur. *Preface to Peasantry: A Tale of Two Black Belt Counties*. Chapel Hill: University of North Carolina Press, 1936.

Ray, Jefferson. *The Country Preacher*. Nashville: Sunday School Board, 1925.

Richardson, Harry. *Dark Glory: A Picture of the Church among Negroes of the Rural South*. New York: Friendship, 1947.

Ritterhouse, Jennifer. *Growing Up Jim Crow: How Black and White Southern Children Learned Race*. Chapel Hill: University of North Carolina Press, 2006.

Roberts, Hilda. "Louisiana Superstitions." *Journal of American Folklore* 40, no. 156 (April–June 1927): 144–208.

Roll, Jarod. *Spirit of Rebellion: Labor and Religion in the New Cotton South*. Urbana: University of Illinois Press, 2010.

Rosenberg, Bruce. *Can These Bones Live? The Art of the American Folk Preacher*. Urbana: University of Illinois Press, 1988.

Rosengarten, Theodore. *All God's Dangers: The Life of Nate Shaw*. New York: Knopf, 1974.

Rubin, Morton. *Plantation County*. Chapel Hill: University of North Carolina Press, 1951.

Russell, Jeffrey Burton. *Mephistopheles: The Devil in the Modern World*. Ithaca, NY: Cornell University Press, 1986.

Sandburg, Carl. *The American Songbag*. New York: Harcourt, Brace, 1927.

Saxon, Lyle, Edward Dreyer, and Robert Tallant, eds. *Gumbo Ya-Ya: A Collection of Louisiana Folk Tales*. New York: Bonanza, 1945.

Scarborough, Dorothy. *From a Southern Porch*. New York: G.P. Putnam's Sons, 1919.

———. *On the Trail of Negro Folk-Songs*. Cambridge, MA: Harvard University Press, 1925.

Scarborough, Lee. *The Tears of Jesus: Sermons to Aid Soul-Winners*. New York: George H. Doran, 1922.

Schulman, Bruce. *From Cotton Belt to Sunbelt: Federal Policy, Economic Development, and the Transformation of the South, 1938–1980*. New York: Oxford University Press, 1991.

Schweiger, Beth Barton. *The Gospel Working Up: Progress and the Pulpit in 19th Century Virginia*. New York: Oxford University Press, 2000.

Schweiger, Beth Barton, and Donald Mathews, eds. *Religion in the American South: Protestants and Others in History and Culture*. Chapel Hill: University of North Carolina Press, 2004.

Seales, Chad. "An Old Love for New Things: Southern Baptists and the Modern Technology of Indoor Baptisteries." *Journal of Southern Religion* 13 (2011). http://jsreligion.org/issues/vol13/seales.html.

Sharp, Cecil, and Maud Karpeles. *English Folk Songs from the Southern Appalachians*. 2 vols. London: Oxford University, 1932.

Showers, Susan. "A Weddin' and a Buryin' in the Black Belt." *New England Magazine* 18 (June 1898): 478–83.

Sizer, Sandra. *Gospel Hymns and Social Religion: The Rhetoric of Nineteenth-Century Revivalism*. Philadelphia: Temple University Press, 1978.

Skeggs, Beverly. *Class, Self, Culture*. New York: Routledge, 2004.

Smith, Fred C. *Trouble in Goshen: Plain Folk, Roosevelt, Jesus, and Marx in the Great Depression South*. Jackson: University Press of Mississippi, 2014.

Smith, Lillian. *Killers of the Dream*. New York: W.W. Norton, 1949.

Smith, R. P. *Experiences in Mountain Mission Work*. Richmond, VA: Presbyterian Committee of Publication, 1931.

Snyder, Howard. "A Plantation Revival Service." *Yale Review* 10, no. 1 (October 1920): 169–79.

Sobel, Mechal. *Trabelin' On: The Slave Journey to an Afro-Baptist Faith*. Westport, CT: Greenwood, 1979.

*Southern Baptist Convention Handbook, 1923*. Nashville: Sunday School Board, 1923.

Southern Rural Life Council. *The Church and Rural Community Living in the South*. Nashville: SRLC, 1947.

Sparks, Randy. *Religion in Mississippi*. Jackson: University Press of Mississippi, 2001.

———. "The Southern Way of Death: The Meaning of Death in Antebellum White Evangelical Culture." *Southern Quarterly* 44, no. 1 (Fall 2006): 32–50.

Stegemeier, Henri. *The Dance of Death in Folksong*. Chicago: University of Chicago Press, 1939.

Stephens, Randall. *The Fire Spreads: Holiness and Pentecostalism in the American South*. Cambridge, MA: Harvard University Press, 2008.

Stout, Harry, and Daryl Hart, eds. *New Perspectives in American Religious History*. New York: Oxford University Press, 1997.

Sullivan, Susan. *Living Faith: Everyday Religion and Mothers in Poverty*. Chicago: University of Chicago Press, 2011.

Sutton, Brett. "In the Good Old Way: Primitive Baptist Traditions." *Southern Exposure* 5, no. 2 (1977): 97–104.

Terry, Paul, and Verner Sims. *They Live on the Land: Life in an Open-Country Southern Community*. 1940. Reprint, Tuscaloosa: University of Alabama Press, 1993.

Thomas, Jean. *Ballad Makin' in the Mountains of Kentucky*. New York: Henry Holt and Company, 1939.

———. *Blue Ridge Country*. New York: Duell, Sloan and Pearce, 1942.

Thurman, Howard. *Jesus and the Disinherited*. New York: Abingdon-Cokesbury, 1949.

Titon, Jeff Todd. *Powerhouse for God: Speech, Chant, and Song in an Appalachian Baptist Church*. Austin: University of Texas Press, 1988.

———. "Son House: Two Narratives." *Alcheringa: Ethnopoetics* 2, no. 1 (1976): 2–6.

———. "Stance, Role, and Identity in Fieldwork among Folk Baptists and Pentecostals." *American Music* 3, no. 1 (Spring 1985): 16–24.

Titon, Jeff Todd, and Ken George. "Testimonies." *Alcheringa: Ethnopoetics* 4, no. 1 (1978): 69–83.

Troeltsch, Ernst. *The Social Teaching of the Christian Churches*. Translated by Olive Wyon. New York: Macmillan, 1931.

Turner, Victor. *The Ritual Process: Structure and Anti-Structure*. Chicago: University of Chicago Press, 1969.

U.S. Bureau of the Census. *Twelfth Census of the United States, 1900*. Washington, DC: National Archives and Records Administration, 1900.

———. *Thirteenth Census of the United States, 1910*. Washington, DC: National Archives and Records Administration, 1910.

———. *Fourteenth Census of the United States, 1920*. Washington, DC: National Archives and Records Administration, 1920.

————. *Fifteenth Census of the United States, 1930.* Washington, DC: National Archives and Records Administration, 1930.

————. *Sixteenth Census of the United States, 1940.* Washington, DC: National Archives and Records Administration, 1940.

————. *Religious Bodies: 1890.* Washington, DC: U.S. Government Printing Office, 1890.

————. *Religious Bodies: 1926, Volumes 1 and 2.* Washington, DC: U.S. Government Printing Office, 1930.

Vlach, John Michael. *The Afro-American Tradition in Decorative Arts.* Athens: University of Georgia Press, 1990.

Warman, Arturo. *Corn and Capitalism: How a Botanical Bastard Grew to Global Dominance.* Chapel Hill: University of North Carolina Press, 2003.

Washington, James. *Frustrated Fellowship: The Black Baptist Quest for Social Power.* Macon: Mercer University Press, 1986.

Weber, Max. *The Protestant Ethic and the Spirit of Capitalism.* London: Unwin, 1985.

Whisnant, David. *All That Is Native and Fine: The Politics of Culture in an American Region.* Chapel Hill: University of North Carolina Press, 1983.

White, Gayle. "The Horror of Forced Sterilization." *Atlanta Journal-Constitution,* February 4, 2007.

White, John. D. "The Backward People of the South." *Our Home Field.* May 1909.

White, Newman. *American Negro Folk-Songs.* 1928. Reprint, Hatboro: Folklore Associates, 1965.

Wilson, Charles Reagan. *Judgment and Grace in Dixie: Southern Faiths from Faulkner to Elvis.* Athens: University of Georgia Press, 1995.

————, ed. *Religion in the South.* Jackson: University Press of Mississippi, 1995.

————. "The Southern Funeral Director: Managing Death in the New South." *Georgia Historical Quarterly* 62, no. 1 (Spring 1983): 49–69.

Wilson, Charles Reagan, and Mark Silk, eds. *Religion and Public Life in the South: In the Evangelical Mode.* Walnut Creek, CA: Altamira, 2005.

Wilson, L. G. "The Church and Landless Men." *University of North Carolina Extension Bulletin* 1, no. 11 (September 1922): 3–26.

Winner, Lauren. *A Cheerful and Comfortable Faith: Anglican Religious Practice in the Elite Households of 18th Century Virginia.* New Haven, CT: Yale University Press, 2010.

Winslow, Ola. *American Broadside Verse.* New Haven, CT: Yale University Press, 1930.

Wolfe, Charles. "Columbia Records and Old-Time Music." *John Edwards Memorial Foundation Quarterly* 14, no. 51 (Autumn 1978): 118–25.

Wood, Ralph. *Flannery O'Connor and the Christ-Haunted South.* Grand Rapids, MI: William B. Eerdmans, 2004.

Woodson, Carter. *The Rural Negro.* Washington, DC: Association for the Study of Negro Life and History, 1930.

Woodward, C. Vann. *Origins of the New South, 1877–1917.* Baton Rouge: Louisiana State University Press, 1951.

Work, John W. *American Negro Songs.* New York: Howell, Soskin, 1940.

Wray, Matt. *Not Quite White: White Trash and the Boundaries of Whiteness.* Durham, NC: Duke University Press, 2006.

Wright, Gavin. "The Economic Revolution in the American South." *Journal of Economic Perspectives* 1, no. 1 (Summer 1987): 161–78.

———. *Old South, New South: Transformations of the Southern Economy since the Civil War.* New York: Basic, 1986.

Wright, Richard. *Twelve Million Black Voices: A Folk History of the Negro in the United States.* New York: Viking, 1941.

Yoder, Don. "Toward a Definition of Folk Religion." *Western Folklore* 33, no. 1 (January 1974): 2–15.

# Index

*Page numbers in italics refer to photographs*

CPSIA information can be obtained
at www.ICGtesting.com
Printed in the USA
LVHW09s2033190918
590676LV00004B/259/P